O9-BUA-275

The Semiotics of Culture and Language

Open Linguistics Series

The Open Linguistics Series, to which this two-volume work makes a highly significant contribution, is 'open' in two senses. First, it provides an open forum for works associated with any school of linguistics or with none. Linguistics has recently emerged from a period in which many (but never all) of the most lively minds in the subject seemed to assume that transformational generative grammar—or at least something fairly closely derived from it—would provide the main theoretical framework for linguistics for the forseeable future. In Kuhn's terms, linguistics appeared to some to have reached the 'paradigm' stage. Reality today is very different. More and more scholars are examining approaches to language that were formerly scorned for not accepting as central the particular set of concerns highlighted in the Chomskyan approach—such as Halliday's systemic-functional theory, Lamb's stratificational-relational model and Pike's tagmemics—while others are developing new or partly new theories. The series is open to all approaches, then, including work in the generativist-formalist tradition.

The second sense in which the series is 'open' is that it encourages works that open out 'core' linguistics in various ways: to encompass discourse and the description of natural texts; to explore the relationships between linguistics and its neighbouring disciplines such as semiotics, psychology, sociology, philosophy, artificial intelligence, and cultural and literary studies; and to apply it in fields such as education and language pathology.

This book is 'open' in many of these ways. Some of the papers present the recent thinking of active contributors to systemic-functional and stratificational-relational linguistics, but above all the book constitutes an 'opening out' of linguistics into the broad, interdisciplinary area of 'semiotics'. It thus makes an important contribution to this increasingly significant discipline.

Open Linguistics Series Editor
Robin P. Fawcett, The Polytechnic of Wales

Modal Expressions in English, Michael R. Perkins
Text and Tagmeme, Kenneth L. Pike and Evelyn G. Pike
The Semiotics of Language and Culture, 2 vols., eds: Robin P. Fawcett, M. A. K. Halliday, Sydney M. Lamb and Adam Makkai
Into the Mother Tongue: A Case Study in Early Language Development, Clare Painter

The Semiotics of Culture and Language

Volume 2
Language and other Semiotic Systems of Culture

Edited by
Robin P. Fawcett
M. A. K. Halliday
Sydney M. Lamb
Adam Makkai

Frances Pinter (Publishers)
London and Dover N.H.

First published in Great Britain in 1984 by
Frances Pinter (Publishers) Limited
5 Dryden Street, London WC2E 9NW

Published in the United States of America in 1984 by
Frances Pinter (Publishers), 51 Washington Street,
Dover, New Hampshire

British Library Cataloguing in Publication Data
The semiotics of culture and language.—
(Open linguistics series)
Vol. 2
I. Semiotics
I. Fawcett, Robin P. II. Series
401'.9 P99
ISBN 0-86187-469-2

Library of Congress Cataloging in Publication Data
The semiotics of culture and language.
(Open linguistics series)
Bibliography: p.
Includes index.
Contents: v. 1. Language as social semiotic—
v. 2. Language and other semiotic systems of culture.
1. Semiotics. 2. Language and languages.
3. Language and culture. I. Fawcett, Robin P.
II. Series.
P99 S393 1984 401'.41 83-242230

Typeset by Joshua Associates, Oxford
Printed in Great Britain by SRP Ltd, Exeter

Contents

VOLUME 1 LANGUAGE AS SOCIAL SEMIOTIC

VOLUME 2 LANGUAGE AND OTHER SEMIOTIC SYSTEMS OF CULTURE

List of Figures

VOLUME 1 LANGUAGE AS SOCIAL SEMIOTIC

VOLUME 2 LANGUAGE AND OTHER SEMIOTIC SYSTEMS OF CULTURE

List of Tables

VOLUME 1 LANGUAGE AS SOCIAL SEMIOTIC

VOLUME 2 LANGUAGE AND OTHER SEMIOTIC SYSTEMS OF CULTURE

Foreword

Semiotics, which I take to be the study of sign systems and their use, is not a subject that has many practitioners who actually *call* themselves 'semioticians' (or 'semiologists' to use the term favoured in the mainland European tradition). On the other hand it could well be argued that the world is full of applied semioticians, in that semiotic issues are inherently involved whenever a language is taught and learned, whenever a linguist studies language in general or a language in particular, whenever a psychologist studies gaze or proxemic behaviour, and whenever a student of art or music or literature is at work. But this is a little different: the student of semiotics is also concerned with the *general* principles of signs and sign systems. And it is perhaps here that we can locate the reason why, so far, semiotics has not captured the imagination of all these unconscious practitioners. It could be, I suggest, that, at each stage of the development of knowledge and for each broad class of phenomena, there is a crucial level of generality that operates. An analogy from the English lexical system would be our preference for the relatively specific terms **car**, **lorry/truck**, **bicycle**, etc., instead of **vehicle**. In both cases a key factor is prominence of the sub-categories in the affairs of the social group concerned, and so in its culture. The fact is that there is intense interest in language in society at large—and now increasingly in other specific semiotic systems such as body language—but relatively little, so far, in the general principles of sign systems.

Yet semiotics, it could be argued, is crucial to an understanding of human nature—both social and psychological. For it is the sign systems that we use for interaction with other living beings that determine our potential for thought and social action. Central among these, of course, is language, but other codes that till now have been studied less from a semiotic perspective, such as music and architecture, perhaps have a more important place in our cognitive and social lives than our current cultural prejudices allow. As the Editors' 'Introduction' suggests, one of the main tasks for the second half of the 1980s and of the 1990s may well be to bring the essentially humanistic science of semiotics to bear on the question of the impact on society of the current technology-led revolution in information storage and communication. An awareness of the importance of general semiotic principles could be crucial to the right conduct of this revolution.

The implicit claim of the contributors to this important two-volume work is that linguistics has something very specific to give to semiotics, and that relational network models of language in particular, i.e. systemic and stratificational linguistics, have a fundamental contribution to make. Their claim to this role is a double one. First, they are theories that give a central place in their overall framework to the concept of 'culture' as well as to that of 'language'—as indeed does tagmemics. Second, they make use of a 'network' notation that emphasizes *relationships* rather than *entities*. It is a notation which is certainly equally applicable to modelling language-like semiotic systems, and which may well be equally applicable to modelling culture.

This is an important book, and its two volumes should make a significant impact, both on the burgeoning field of semiotics and on the work of that growing number of linguists who recognize the need for a wider perspective—i.e. the semiotic perspective—in their study of language.

The Polytechnic of Wales — Robin P. Fawcett
February 1984

Introduction

It was three centuries ago that the philosopher John Locke proposed that we should recognize, as one of the three major sub-divisions of science, *semiotic*, 'the business whereof is to consider the nature of signs, the mind makes use of for the understanding of things or conveying the knowledge to others'. The modern term *semiotics*, however, was introduced to the English language only in 1962. It was proposed for this role by the anthropologist Margaret Mead, at an important conference whose scope included the fields of cultural anthropology, education, linguistics, psychiatry, and psychology. The proceedings are reported in *Approaches to Semiotics* (Sebeok, Hayes and Bateson: 1964), and on pages 275-6 we can read how 'semiotics' triumphed over 'communication' as the label for the field that Mead, in words that interestingly complement those of Locke, described as 'patterned communication in all modalities'. Today, however, both labels are in regular use: there are steadily growing numbers of courses and departments of 'communication studies' and 'human communication', while 'semiotics' tends to connote work at a more advanced level.

The conceptual territory proposed for semiotic(s) by Locke, and later claimed for their subject by semioticians such as C. S. Peirce and Charles Morris and others, was truly on the grand scale. And yet, while there has been steady progress in recent years, the promise of Locke's original striking proposal has barely begun to be fulfilled. It may be pertinent to ask why this should be so and, further, to suggest some ways in which we might begin to change this situation. We shall return to this topic in the closing section of this introduction.

The process of change in semiotics has, however, already begun. This can be demonstrated most obviously in terms of the increasing numbers of courses, departments and research centres devoted to this field. But fundamental to this has been the fact that linguistics, anthropology, literary analysis and, perhaps to a lesser extent, social psychology, have begun a historical convergence in the discipline of semiotics. Originally a branch of pragmatist philosophy (*à la* William James and C. S. Peirce), semiotics has undergone considerable changes within this century. The growth of interest in semiotics is evidenced by the setting up, in 1976, of the Semiotic Society of

America, to parallel similar societies in Germany, Poland, Hungary and elsewhere. Earlier, the Association Internationale de Sémiotique had been established, and its journal, *Semiotica* (edited by T. A. Sebeok), has been appearing since 1969. In all these ways, then, we are witnessing the emergence of this vital new and broadly interdisciplinary field.

However, it is an odd but noteworthy feature of the field that many of its practitioners have been working in it without labelling their efforts as semiotics. There is thus a relatively 'official' field of semiotics, labelled as such and practised by recognized semioticians, and a relatively 'unofficial' variety, which includes those with interests in various individual semiotic systems. Among these are an ever-growing number of scholars who are interested in the semiotic exploration of language in relation to other cultural systems that have not been labelled as semiotics. The present work represents in part a statement by practitioners of the latter variety who would now like to claim explicitly that their work, too, qualifies as semiotics. In so doing they hope to bring some fresh thinking into this fertile field.

For the contributors to this book, an event of particular significance in the development of the semiotic dimension in their work was the Burg Wartenstein Symposium, sponsored by the Wenner-Gren Foundation for Anthropological Research, held in August 1975. All the contributors were present, and in many cases the papers included here constitute a later and more complex working of ideas first presented there in tentative form. In other cases the papers are completely, or almost completely, different. That symposium was originally planned by Charles Frake, M. A. K. Halliday, Martin Kay, Sydney Lamb and W. C. Watt, and their purpose for it—and so the topic addressed by many of these papers—was summarized in the following background statement, which was sent to all the participants.

It has often been proposed that structural patterns found in language might exist also in other cultural systems, and that analytical tools developed in linguistics might prove illuminating if applied in cultural anthropology; but up to now the nature of linguistic structure has been too poorly understood to enable this proposal to be convincingly demonstrated. Against this background, recent developments in linguistics show promise of providing valuable new techniques in cultural anthropology and new insights into the structure of culture. Thus, perhaps there is now some chance of finally fulfilling the promise of old, and perhaps a firm basis can be established for breaking down the fences that separate linguistics, anthropology, sociology, and psychology.

The basic aim of the symposium is to promote the integration of linguistics and cultural anthropology by exploring (1) the use of methods of formal linguistics (especially relational network analysis) for illuminating our understanding of culture, and (2) the use of cultural and social information for illuminating our understanding of the structure and functions of language.

More particularly, it may be profitable to view the social system as a system of information and, accordingly, to view social interaction as information processing. In keeping with this viewpoint, the relation between language and culture can be considered as a relation between two (possibly intertwined) semiotic systems, the linguistic and the cultural.

The symposium itself was co-organized by M. A. K. Halliday, Sydney Lamb and John Regan, and it was a highly interactive, often very insightful, occasionally frustrating, and always stimulating week. The thanks of all of us go to the Wenner-Gren Foundation for Anthropological Research, and particularly to Dr Lita Osmundsen, the Foundation's Director of Research, and to the staff at Burg Wartenstein.

It may be of value to indicate some of the ways in which the subsequent work of most of the contributors to that symposium has grown more overtly semiotic. M. A. K. Halliday, for example, published in 1978 his influential *Language as Social Semiotic*. The intertwined topics of language, social context and culture are never far from the centre of his writings, and the courses in the Linguistics Department of the University of Sydney reflect this orientation. So, indeed, do those of his wife Ruqaiya Hasan at Macquarie University. W. C. Watt's interest in semiotics in general and the Roman alphabet in particular has continued in a series of articles entitled 'What is the proper characterisation of the alphabet? I, II and III'. Robin Fawcett has since moved to the Polytechnic of Wales, Cardiff, where he teaches and researches on linguistics in the context of a BA(Hons) Communications Studies degree, in which semiotics plays a unifying role. This is one of half a dozen such courses that have been developed over the last few years in British polytechnics, and the work of Kress, Fiske and others is now leading to the development of similarly academic courses in Australia and the United States. Fawcett's recent *Cognitive Linguistics and Social Interaction* (1980) places language in a cognitive-social (and so cultural) framework that embraces other codes beside language, and in 1982 he gave the Invited Lecture to the Linguistic Association of Canada and the United States, 'Language as a semiological system: a re-interpretation of Saussure'. Michael O'Toole has moved to the Chair of Human Communication at Murdoch University, Perth, Australia, where there are now lively undergraduate courses that give semiotics a central place. Similarly, Sydney Lamb has moved to Rice University, where he has been prominent in the foundation of the new Department of Linguistics and Semiotics—the first in existence—together with the Doctoral Program in Linguistics and Semiotics. It was inaugurated by an important symposium 'Directions in linguistics and semiotics', in March 1983, and contributors included Lamb, Halliday and Preziosi from the Wenner-Gren Symposium, as well as many other well-known linguists and semioticians, including Conklin, Fillmore, Hockett, Longacre, Ross and Sebeok. The proceedings of that symposium have been published as Copeland (1984). The Rice tradition continued with a second symposium in February 1984, and the participants included, from this book, Fawcett, Halliday, Hasan and Lamb. We could give even more examples, but the above will illustrate how the semiotic dimension is becoming an increasingly strong force, both in the work of the contributors to this volume and in the academic world at large.

This work is arranged in three parts. Volume 1 contains Part I, and volume 2 Parts II and III. The title of Part I is 'Language as social semiotic'—a form of words taken from the title of the well-known book by M. A. K. Halliday mentioned above. Part I offers five perspectives on this topic, and the first, appropriately, is by Halliday himself.

The first part of Halliday's chapter provides an interesting perspective on recent work in linguistics, and so a perspective for the book as a whole. He shows us that linguistics has in recent decades been undergoing a period in which the view of language as code, which he terms the 'logical-philosophical', has for most linguists been divorced from the 'ethnographic-descriptive' view of language as behaviour, but he suggests, significantly, that this should be regarded simply as a temporary phase. Systemic functional linguistics, to the development of which he has been the pre-eminent contributor, can then be seen as a contribution to the search for a 'unified "code-and-behaviour" linguistics'—as indeed can stratificational-relational grammar. So far so good, but where does culture come in? Halliday's answer is that, just as the social context of linguistic *behaviour* is the 'context of situation', so the social context of the linguistic *code* is the 'context of culture' (to use Malinowski's terms). In order to relate the two, Halliday suggests, 'we need to represent the culture as . . . a network of information systems: that is, in semiotic terms.' And he continues: 'the central problem is to interpret language in a way which enables us to relate it to other semiotic processes.' Halliday then illustrates his own approach to this problem: he represents certain aspects of culture relating to the code for dialogue as 'behaviour potential' (using a simple system network) and then in turn relates these to their 'realisation' in networks at the 'semantic' and the 'lexico-grammatical' levels of language. He then comments on some short texts in the light of these proposals, and finally outlines the ontogeny of dialogue as it occurred in the case of a single child (Nigel). These closing sections thus serve as an exemplification of the relationship of culture to language, as Halliday sees it in relation to the dialogue of a child. The chapter also includes a brief addition to his proposals for modality.

John Regan's contribution traces the relationship between teacher and pupil as mirrored in and constructed by the discourse patterns of instruction. A long-time student of the Whorf hypothesis, Regan presents data suggesting that the discourse patterns employed by teachers in various countries—and these exhibit a surprising uniformity—exert a powerful influence on the child's conceptual system, quite apart from the content of the instructional material which is overtly being conveyed.

Yoshihiko Ikegami presents a wealth of evidence exploring the notion that all linguistic expressions of change and state are modelled after those of the most concrete types of change and state, i.e. motion and existence in location. Since this type of meaning ('transitivity' in Halliday's terms, 'cases' in Fillmore's) would, in a Whorfian view of language, be held to be closely bound up with the wider culture of the society using the language in question, the whole paper is, in a sense, concerned with language and culture. He concludes that, although there is clearly a set of common underlying patterns in the linguistic representation of change and state, and that these patterns can very closely be approximated to those for representing motion and location, the claim of universal priority of the localistic notions does not hold.

Jeffrey Ellis proposes a framework for exploring relationships among descriptive linguistics, historical linguistics, and socio-linguistics, with particular reference to the socio-cultural aspects of language contact. He draws extensively upon data of language use in Ghana, including problems of contact between English and native languages, and socio-cultural aspects of the use of English by the British, as opposed to natives who use English as a second language.

Ruqaiya Hasan develops the fascinating concept of semantic distance across languages, using data from English and Urdu, and argues that a culture has a characteristic semiotic style, whose crucial characteristics are reflected in all systems of communication, whether verbal or non-verbal. She concludes that semantic differences between languages cannot be properly studied without consideration of their socio-cultural settings, and moreover that the failure of most testers of the Whorfian hypothesis to properly include such considerations 'effectively bears Whorf out in his assertion that it is a characteristic of the SAE [Standard Average European] cultures to treat the abstract relational notion as a concrete object'. This emphasis on relations as distinct from entities is a concept that is taken up in other papers, most notably Lamb's.

Volume 2 contains both Part II and Part III. If the central object of study in semiotics is semiotic systems, Part II offers three stimulating approaches to fulfilling this task. It is a task that in traditional semiotics has received rather less attention than semioticians coming from a linguistics background might expect. This, then, is one of the ways in which 'semiotically aware' linguists may have something very specific to contribute to the general field of semiotics: the commitment to constructing working grammars that make clear predictions about what will and will not occur when a semiotic system is being employed. Each of the three contributors develops a treatment of a specific cultural system which appears to have structural analogies to language. In two of the cases the analogies are well-known and have received considerable study in the past: writing systems and narrative structures. The third, environmental structure, is less obviously a semiotic system, and is a relative newcomer in this family of related topics.

W. C. Watt frames his study of our system of capital letters within an examination of the case for an area of study to be called 'psycho-semiotics', on the model of 'psycho-linguistics'. He thus brings an explicitly cognitive approach to the study of semiotic systems—an approach taken up again later in the contributions of Lamb and Fawcett. Watt argues for the view that 'for human sign-systems "what people have in their heads" is not a peripheral enquiry: it is the *only* enquiry.' He discusses the nature of evidence and criteria in semiotics, and presents a specific semiotic study of structural patterns in the Roman alphabet. The semiotic system that he is discussing is thus not language itself, strictly speaking, though it is one that relates closely to, and is indeed parasitic on, language.

In a somewhat similar way, L. M. O'Toole's contribution concerns a semiotic system that is closely related to language, but is not the code of language itself, as this is usually conceived. His paper concerns a particular genre of *discourse*—as indeed do those of Halliday and Regan—but here the genre is written rather than oral. O'Toole presents and compares two contrasting models for the analysis and interpretation of fictional narrative: an analytic model that he has used for some time in the interpretation of Russian short stories, and a generative model proposed by the Russians Zholkovsky and Scheglov. He emphasizes, among other things, the patterns of relations between the social roles and functions of the dramatis personae and the linguistic devices used by the author in characterizing them, and he concludes with an evaluation of the two models.

The semiotic system that is the object of study in Donald Preziosi's contribution is, on the other hand, quite unrelated to language—except that it is another semiotic system. He draws on the concepts and notation of stratificational-relational grammar to describe the relations between human beings, their culture and the semiotic system that is realized in the spatial structures that we surround ourselves with. In so doing, he demonstrates the use of relational network analysis for the study of architectural form, and concludes that 'it remains a reasonable assumption . . . that common cognitive operations underlie' the deep semantic organizations of both language and architecture.

Before leaving Part II, it may be of interest to mention that, while Preziosi's paper illustrates the application of stratificational-relational grammar to a semiotic system that is very different from language, there are also examples of the application of a systemic approach to non-linguistic codes. One such is Terry Winograd's (1968/81) systemic study of (Western classical) music.

The question of the nature of the relationship between language and culture hovers in the background, as it were, of most of the contributions to Parts I and II. But the three extended papers in Part III stand out from the others in that all three are specifically addressed to this question. Each of the three offers a general scheme for the study of semiotics, each based upon a somewhat different approach from the other two.

Sydney Lamb explores the possibility of extending the relational network theory of stratificational grammar to a general relational semiotics. Lamb gives Saussure's concept of the 'sign' a relational network definition, and then uses it to explore the concept that the structure of a culture is a network of relations. He thus presents the hypothesis that 'the relation between language and culture can be considered as a relation between two (possibly intertwined) semiotic systems' in the strongest form to be encountered in this book. A notable feature of the paper is the breadth of the variety of examples given to support this view. In an approach such as Lamb's, in which the emphasis is on relationships rather than entities, the question arises of how the relational network relates out to non-semiotic phenomena; how the mental (since Lamb's is a cognitive model) relates out to the physical. There has long been an answer at the 'phonetic' end of the language—in principle, that is: phonologists and phoneticians are in practice still far from agreement about the nature of the phonetics-phonology interface. But at the other end of language matters are even more difficult; it might for some be arguable that 'concepts' are non-semiotic, but concepts are certainly not part of the physical world. Here Lamb comes up with a bold new proposal to justify his strong adherence to the concept that semiosis is purely relational.

In his ambitiously titled 'Prolegomena to an understanding of semiotics and culture', Ashok R. Kelkar draws more heavily on philosophy than do the other contributors, to present a 'cosmology', as one might term it, that is lengthy (despite being most economically written) and highly structured. Its scope is extraordinary, and Kelkar locates in his overall framework—and so relates to each other—many of the main concepts of semiotics and linguistics, as well as the worlds of **gnosis** (cognition, insight), **aesthesis** (appreciation, evaluation), **praxis** (work, play), **poesis** (production, creation) and **cathexis** (love, loyalty). One of the pleasures of reading it is the incorporation of an aspect of Indian expository discourse: at regular intervals there are **sutras** that recapitulate the preceding section.

In the final paper Robin P. Fawcett presents an overall cognitive model of *language* (together with the other codes and semiotic systems) and *culture* (together with other aspects of the 'knowledge of the universe'). As with Lamb, there is a strong emphasis on modelling semiotic systems as relationships. But here there is also an equal emphasis on the complementary concept that a semiotic system is a *procedure* or, in the computing metaphor, a *program* for behaving. This leads him, in contrast with Lamb, to make a prime distinction between semiotic systems and the 'knowledge' that we draw upon in choosing between options at the semantic stratum in such a system—while not venturing a committed position on the ways in which that knowledge is stored. Thus, Fawcett's model does not preclude the possibility that some knowledge at least is stored in the way proposed by Lamb. Fawcett's emphasis, however, is less on how cultural knowledge is *stored* than on how it is *used*, in relation to system networks. Fawcett, like Halliday, is a systemicist, and the prime characteristic of systemic linguistics is that it gives a central place to the concept of choice between alternative meanings in social contexts. This paper introduces some key systemic concepts, illustrating these with a fragment from the grammar of English. Fawcett then makes the proposal that the systemic mode of modelling language should be extended to other semiotic systems, and offers a taxonomy of such systems. He next distinguishes culture from other aspects of 'knowledge of the universe', and illustrates the working relationship between language and culture, together with other aspects of the social context, through a detailed example. The paper concludes with a number of brief comparisons between Fawcett's own approach and the contributions to this book of Halliday, Watt, Lamb, and Kelkar.

One notable name was missing from the first section of this introduction—that of Saussure. Yet he is often referred to—and with justification—as the father of modern linguistics and, with Peirce, of semiotics. It can be argued, however, that most linguists and most semioticians have not paid sufficient attention to his emphasis on the interdependence of the two. One highly relevant piece of advice (directed in this case to linguists) is as follows:

> If we are to discover the true nature of language, we must learn what it has in common with other semiological systems. [Saussure 1916/74: 17.]

Perhaps we can agree that a stereotypical sign system consists of choices between contrasting 'meanings' which are realized in contrasting 'forms'; and that, while many signs have only very simple internal syntax, language is well towards the complex end of the continuum between simple and complex syntax. This last fact is no doubt part of the reason why, over the past few decades, much of the work in linguistics has focused on problems in formal syntagmatic relations. Some linguists might argue that the relatively peripheral status given to paradigmatic as opposed to syntagmatic relations in standard transformational theory and its successors reflects the intrinsic nature of human language. But in that case one would like to be told why we tolerate all these complex contrasting structures, if it is not to realize complex contrasting meanings—and this brings us back to the missing statements on paradigmatic relations. It may therefore be useful to point out that most contributors to these volumes are distinguished by the fact that, in one way or another, they give equal weight to these paradigmatic relations of choice: to what might have been, but isn't, as well as to what is. In this they point a possible way forward for both their fellow linguists and for other semioticians.

We saw earlier how semiotic(s) has been defined by Locke and by Mead. It is instructive to see how it is defined in the new 1982 edition of *The Concise Oxford Dictionary* (COD). It is defined as a 'branch of linguistics concerned with signs and symbols'. This seems a somewhat odd definition in at least two ways. First, most modern scholars would surely recognize that semiotics must be concerned less with individual signs (or symbols) than with *sign systems*. A semiotic unit only has 'value', as Saussure emphasized, in terms of what we would today call its paradigmatic, syntagmatic and realizational relations with other semiotic units. And yet, although it has been fully explicit since Hjelmslev (1943/61) that the semiotician's task is to study not just signs but sign systems (i.e. grammars), introductory textbooks on semiotics still place excessive emphasis on the individual sign. Admittedly, it is an understandable tendency, since it is easier to comprehend a single instance of a sign than the abstract potential of a whole sign system, but if semiotics is to develop into a mature subject such issues must be faced. Perhaps the problem is that we lack sufficient grammars of semiotic systems other than language? If so, the next step is obvious: we need more grammars, and several contributors to this book discuss or illustrate ways of doing this.

It could also be argued that a major weakness in much of the current semiotics literature is that many semioticians seem to be simply unaware of developments in modern linguistics other than transformational generative grammar. Yet semioticians will certainly find useful many of the concepts of stratificational-relational grammar (Lamb 1966, 1970/73 and in this book, Lockwood 1972, Makkai and Lockwood 1973, and Preziosi's paper in this book). And semioticians of music and other semiotic systems are already putting to use concepts drawn from systemic theory (which is essentially complementary to, rather than a rival of, stratificational-relational grammar), such as the concept that the heart of the model consists of networks of choices between 'meaning' options, and the concept of functional components (Halliday, 1970, 1973, etc., Berry 1975, Fawcett 1980, Halliday and Martin 1981 and Halliday and Fawcett (to appear)).

The second and greater oddity in the COD's definition of semiotics lies in its assertion that semiotics is a branch of linguistics. This is, of course, a reversal of the true relationship; logically, since languages are just one class among myriads of classes of semiotic systems, linguistics is a branch of semiotics. Yet the COD definition contains a grain of truth, both because semioticians have traditionally drawn on linguistics for their basic concepts, and because there are incomparably more scholars whose central business is language than there are for all the rest of the sign systems put together.

The ideas we have been considering raise a number of issues for those who would at present call themselves either linguists or semioticians. The Society of Friends (Quakers) has a little booklet called *Advices and Queries*, and every now and then one will be read aloud in a meeting. Three 'queries' constructed on that model that linguists and semioticians might usefully put to themselves in the mid-1980s are these:

1 (to linguists) In view of the guiding principle proposed by Saussure that was cited above, have you set your study of language in the framework of the study of semiotic systems in general, so that, through realizing what language has in common with other semiological systems, you may distinguish its essential from its merely contingent characteristics, and so 'discover the true nature of language'?
2 (to semioticians) Have you relied too much on the early concepts in linguistics of Saussure, perhaps seasoned by Jakobson and supplemented by the initially attractive but now largely discarded Harris-Chomsky notion of the transformation, and have you consequently failed to draw adequately upon the relational network models of systemic and stratificational-relational grammar, as vital sources of linguistic concepts that may be relevant to the explication of other semiotic systems?
3 (to both) Given that at present linguists typically function as a separate, though numerically overwhelming, sub-group within the wider family of semioticians, and given that most of the fragmented scattering of other semioticians are left studying the various other sign systems as best they can, with academic attachments to departments where their work is often regarded as peripheral and eccentric rather than the crucial contribution to the study of man that it in fact is, has the time now come to press for the creation of more research centres and departments of Linguistics and Semiotics and/or of (Human) Communication (Studies)—as has already happened at, among others, Indiana University, USA, Rice University (Houston, USA), Murdoch University (Perth, Australia) and several polytechnics in Britain?

If the 1970s were the decade of 'social man', perhaps we should now, in this age of the explosion of information technology, begin to prepare for the 1990s to be the decade of 'semiotic man'. Indeed, it may well be that semiotics, with its strong humanistic tradition, has an important role to play in ensuring that we make the machines (and their programs) fit man, rather than man having to fit the machines.

Robin P. Fawcett
M. A. K. Halliday
Sydney M. Lamb
Adam Makkai

BIBLIOGRAPHY

Berry, M. (1975), *Introduction to Systemic Linguistics*, London, Batsford.

Copeland, J. E. (ed.) (1984), *New Directions in Linguistics and Semiotics*, Houston, Rice University Studies and Amsterdam, John Benjamins BV.

Fawcett, R. P. (1980), *Cognitive Linguistics and Social Interaction: Towards an Integrated Model of a Systemic Functional Grammar and the Other Components of a Communicating Mind*, Heidelberg, Julius Groos & Exeter University.

Fawcett, R. P. (1983), 'Language as a semiological system: a re-interpretation of Saussure', Invited Lecture to the Linguistics Association of Canada and the United States 1982, in Morreall (1983).

Garvin, P. (ed.) (1970), *Cognition: A Multiple View*, New York, Spartan.

Halliday, M. A. K. (1970), 'Language structure and language function', in Lyons (1970: 140-65).

Halliday, M. A. K. (1978), *Language as Social Semiotic*, London, Edward Arnold.

Halliday, M. A. K., and Fawcett, R. P. (eds) (to appear), *New Developments in Systemic Linguistics*, London, Batsford.

Halliday, M. A. K., and Martin, J. R. (eds) (1981), *Readings in Systemic Linguistics, 1956-1974*, London, Batsford.

Hjelmslev, L. (1943-61), *Prolegomena to a Theory of Language*, revised English edition, tr. Francis J. Whitfield, Madison, University of Wisconsin Press (original Danish version 1943.)

Lamb, S. M. (1966), *Outline of Stratificational Grammar*, Washington, D.C., Georgetown University Press.

Lamb, S. M. (1970-3), 'Linguistic and cognitive networks', in Garvin (1970) and in Makkai and Lockwood (1973).

Lockwood, D. G. (1972), *Introduction to Stratificational Linguistics*, New York, Harcourt, Brace and Jovanovich.

Lyons, J. (1970), *New Horizons in Linguistics*, Harmondsworth, Penguin.

Makkai, A., and Lockwood, D. G., (eds) (1973) *Readings in Stratificational Linguistics*, University; University of Alabama Press.

Morreall, J., (ed.) (1983), *The Ninth LACUS Formum 1982*, Columbia, Hornbeam Press.

Saussure, F. de (1916/74), *Course in General Linguistics*, English edition tr. W. Baskin, London, Fontana (original French version 1916).

Sebeok, T. A., *et al.*, (eds) (1964), *Approaches to Semiotics*, The Hague, Mouton.

Watt, W. C. (1975), 'What is the proper characterization of the alphabet? I: Desiderata' in *Visible Language*, 9, 293-327.

Watt, W. C. (1980), 'What is the proper characterisation of the alphabet? II: Composition' in *Ars Semiotica III*, 1, 13-46.

Watt, W. C. (1981), 'What is the proper characterisation of the alphabet? III: Appearance' in *Ars Semiotica IV*, 3, 269-313.

Winograd, T. (1968/81), 'Linguistics and the computer analysis of tonal harmony', *Journal of music theory*, 21, 1968 (2-49, 6-22, 42-3, 49-5) and in Halliday and Martin 1981.

Part II
Some semiotic systems other than language

6 As to psychosemiotics

W. C. Watt
University of California at Irvine, U.S.A.

6.1 INTRODUCTION

My purpose here[1] is to treat of the concept and term 'psychosemiotics'—to define it, to defend it, and finally to discard it.

6.2 TO DEFINE IT

By 'psychosemiotics' I mean roughly the intersection of psychology and semiotics proper. (I assume without further ado that such an intersection exists.) Psychosemiotics is to semiotics as psycholinguistics is to linguistics. It should cover all aspects of semiotic theory whose validation must ultimately appeal to psychological findings (whether experimental or observational), as well as all aspects of psychology inspired by or designed to test semiotic research. In particular, psychosemiotics should include: (1) psychological experimentation designed to gauge the extent to which people actually have in their heads the semiotic systems constructed to account for their semiotic behaviour; (2) developmental studies of how children master such semiotic systems, if they do; (3) the construction of semiotic theories to accommodate and explain psychological data bearing on how people learn and misremember semiotic systems, especially those other than language; (4) psychological explications of diachronic semiotics; and (5) 'comparative psychosemiotics', or 'zoosemiotics',[2] the close study of how creatures other than humans use signs, if they do; and so on. Some results of this sort of cross-pollination might be: (1) experimental confirmation of the psychological reality of one or more of the Peircean trichotomies (e.g., index/icon/symbol);[3] (2) longitudinal studies confirming that children master semiotic systems in some manner or sequence predicted by semiotic theory; (3) a detailed experiment-based account, sensitive to the diverse modalities involved, of people's systematic misrecollections of various semiotic systems, providing both a partial explanation of why those systems assume the shapes they do and also a 'window' into a hitherto cloudy abstract mental capacity; (4) a principled account of how semiotic systems change, to the extent that they change predictably; and (5) a specification of the differences between the Ameslan (ASL) mastered by apes and the Ameslan mastered by young deaf children.[4]

Psychosemiotics, then, is rather neatly bounded at either end by two other disciplines: i.e., by semiotics as usually thought of and by the future science of 'neurosemiotics', which will study how the cognitive realities demonstrated by psychosemiotics are physically realized in the brain, with implications for yet further disciplines (e.g., aphasiology and neurology).

Now, the discussion thus far has been couched in such terms as perhaps to suggest that psychosemiotics is only here achieving parturition: but this would be an egregious misconstrual. From its very inception modern semiotics—at least its Peircean half—has viewed itself as being allied with psychology, in some sense. Certainly this was Peirce's own attitude. Writing to Lady Welby in 1908 he said:

> I define a Sign as anything which is so determined by something else . . . and *so determines an effect upon a person* . . . that the latter is thereby mediately determined by the former. [Peirce 1977: 80 f.; italics mine.]

Even if Peirce had never said this, or if he had not meant what he said,[5] for the past twenty years or so it would have been reasonable to think of psychosemiotics as simply the fulfilment of the 'linguistic analogy': the notion, perilous but persistent, that to an appreciable extent some semiotic systems other than language are enough like language to profit from the comparison.[6] And indeed, though under other headings, there has long been what we can now recognize as 'psychosemiotic' research among psychologists and semioticians alike: among, for instance, psychologists delving into how people process visual symbols[7] and semiotic theorists exploring questions of animal communication.[8] The purpose of this paper could not be to invent psychosemiotics, then, but rather to affirm the existence of the field and to discuss its potential in terms of a few past and present successes and in terms of gaps yet unfilled. Since the field is relatively new and has virtually never been practised as a unified discipline, there is no lack of gaps: places where experimental findings could have been clarified by appeal to a semiotic study of differences among sign-functions; places where semiotic theory could have benefited from access to the results of psychological experimentation; and places where a unified attack might have proved fruitful.

Before proceeding further let me explicitly confirm what has been implied in the foregoing: namely, that the kind of psychological observations under consideration here vary in their degree of intrusiveness (or experimental rigour), and indeed in their degree of reliability; but this will be evident in what follows.

Below, in section 6.3, I will deal somewhat more deeply with the question of whether or not semiotics meshes naturally with psychological evidence of one sort or another; and I will discuss how the 'generalizations' which appear to underlie certain semiotic behaviours are well expressed as the 'rules' of a putative cognitive semiotic 'grammar'. One class of such generalizations will be looked at in a little detail. Next, in section 6.3.2.1, I will briefly take up the thorny question of 'parsimony' as a possible guide to psychosemiotic verisimilitude. Then in section 6.3.2.2 I will introduce the possibility that for a given semiotic system the various 'levels' of a formal semiotic description, or grammar, may correspond to (and in this limited sense 'explain') differing responses exhibited by people dealing with that system, where those competing responses take the form of competing results from experiments demanding different kinds of performance. And finally, in sections 6.3.3 and 6.4, I will sum up these diverse issues—admittedly only highlights, peaks of a continent that is still to rise—and draw conclusions from them.

6.3 TO DEFEND IT

6.3.1 Concentrating now on just the sign-systems used by humans, it would seem the merest truism to assert that for each such system what semiotics seeks to find is the analysis or 'grammar' that the human users of that system have put into their heads. How could it be otherwise? Properly viewed, surely, the Chomskyan revolution in linguistics is a revolution in the superordinate field of semiotics: and surely the most perdurable aspect of that revolution is the insight that the human users of a semiotic system hold in their heads a grammar, a set of rules which makes that use possible and which conditions that use. If this is so then for a given sign-system how could semiotic research accept as adequate any solution that did not bid fair to be homomorphic to the solution that the users of that system—unconsciously, of course—arrived at themselves? For human sign-systems 'what people have in their heads' is not a peripheral enquiry: it is the *only* enquiry.

Consider the alternative. Suppose that children learning the semiotic system called 'the alphabet'—say the upper case or capital

'English' or Roman alphabet—*did not* unconsciously form a grammar for those letters at all. In other words, suppose American schoolchildren learnt 'A' independently from 'B', 'B' independently from 'C', 'C' independently from 'D', and so on: just one pigeon-hole after another. How could this supposition be disputed? Look for yourself. If the children form no semiotic grammar for the letters —form none of the systematic generalizations that we represent as rules of grammar—then each letter must indeed be learnt and retained altogether independently. How one letter is learnt or retained or recalled or executed should not influence the uses of any other letter in the system because there *is* no system. On the other hand, if the children do form generalizations of rules then errors (and corrections) should 'spread', attacking sets of letters (those falling under the generalizations) in some systematic fashion. On observation, which pattern of behaviour is found in actuality? The latter. To take just the most common error, that of reversal (e.g., replacing 'D' with 'ᗡ'), children mostly proceed in a quite orderly fashion through these four states of learning:

1. They randomly reverse any letter at all.
2. Suddenly they get them all right except 'J', which now they consistently reverse to 'Ⴑ', and 'N' which they sometimes reverse, and either 'S' or 'Z', one of which they reverse.
3. They get all the letters consistently right except 'J'.
4. They get all the letters consistently right.

What could possibly account for this universal chain of events unless the children are generalizing features of groups of letters—attributes they have in common? How but by forming such groups, unconsciously, and by mistakenly assigning group-attributes to individual letters, could they perform as they do? Surely it is plain that the reason that 'J' is almost invariably the last letter to be consistently free of reversal, is that 'J' must be exposed to some generalization that each child unconsciously applies to all of the reversible letters (correctly for all the others, but incorrectly for 'J'). Nor is it hard to guess what this generalization is (see below). If this is so then any semiotic account of the alphabet that treated the twenty-six capital letters as a congeries of unrelated pictorial elements (the only alternative to accommodating generalizations)—any semiotic account that missed the children's apparent generalization governing reversibility—would clearly be less adequate, in any sense, than a semiotic account or grammar that did square with these facts. To take this part of the argument one step further, such a judgement need by no means be based just on a bias for psychological explanation: semiotic systems like the alphabet undergo historical change, and surely in semiotics as in linguistics historical change stands in the forefront of what is to be accounted for; then if historical change is conditioned by psychological factors a semiotic grammar kept in the dark about such factors must miss many explanations for historical change, and so be hopelessly inadequate just on the face of it. Yet who could doubt that historical changes to the alphabet are indeed conditioned by just such factors as turn up in children's mistakes: by misrecollection or over-generalization? Who could doubt, for instance, that a group of kindergarteners isolated on some 'Isle of the Flies' could be expected to change their alphabet, lacking any correction from society, so that 'J' would be *permanently* reversed to '⅃'? So that the epichoric variant of the English alphabet found on the Isle of the Flies would have undergone historical change? Would anyone be astounded to learn that the illiterate Greeks of about 800 BC, on first picking up the alphabet from the Phoenicians, made precisely the same error with the similar letter '↓', reversing it to '⇂'? For such was certainly the case.[9]

Picking up an earlier thread, let us clarify the nature of the children's generalization at Stage II.

Of the twenty-six English capital letters, eleven are symmetrical on the vertical axis, and so can be reversed with no observable effect: these are 'A', 'H', 'I', 'M', 'O', 'T', 'U', 'V', 'W', 'X', and 'Y'. Thus the set of letters over which significant 'reversal generalizations' can be formed contains but fifteen elements. Of these, fully ten 'face rightwards' in the sense that they consist either of a vertical stroke plus an augmentation to the right, or of another letter ('C', 'O') plus an augmentation, again to the right ('G', 'Q').[10] These ten letters are 'B', 'D', 'E', 'F', 'G', 'K', 'L', 'P', 'Q', and 'R'. In addition, if 'G' faces right then presumably 'C' itself does as well. This leaves only four letters: 'N', 'S', 'Z', and lastly 'J'. But these are precisely the letters that children have great trouble keeping unreversed, at Stage II. It would be silly to refrain from concluding that the generalization that children derive at Stage II is something like, 'if letters face either way, they face right', for deriving this generalization would account for exactly the salient facts in the matter: (1) the child typically gets all of the reversibles correctly orientated all at the same time, precisely as if obeying a generalization, with four exceptions; and (2) the four exceptions are exceptions to the generalization hypothesized.

In short, what ails 'J' is that it faces left. Children will inevitably get it wrong as soon as the hypothesized generalization is formed. What ails 'N' is less serious: it faces neither way, so that—since both 'N' and 'И' meet the generalizations, 'N' may be replaced by its reversal until it is realized to require special treatment as a one-member class. What ails the pair 'S/Z' is more serious and more curious: neither letter faces either way (or both face both ways), but on the other hand the two are very similar, 'Z' being but an angularization and reversal of 'S'.[11] So, while 'S' and 'Z' escape the 'letters face right' generalization, they may fall under the generalization, applying just to this two-member class, 'S and Z face the same way'. Alternatively, some children may form the broader generalization 'all reversible letters face the same way' instead of 'all reversible letters face right': notice that the broader generalization will serve the child well if he just remembers any one of the ten 'right-facing' letters (since then the rest can be induced from that one); but notice, too, that under this generalization either 'S' or 'Z' will surely be reversed.

It seems, then, that a generalization of some sort is formed by children learning the alphabet: even though they are obliged to learn but twenty-six forms, a task they could assuredly achieve by learning each form individually, they do not (ever) do this but instead, in at least the primitive sense under discussion just here, form the sort of generalizations which, so I claim, are in essence rules of semiotic grammar. Concluding this point, we note that the generalization 'letters face right' is equivalently expressed, as it affects the 'vexillary' letters 'B', 'D', 'E', 'F', 'K', 'L', 'P', and 'R'—as well as 'J', of course—as the rule:

$$\text{LETTER} \rightarrow [\text{VERTICAL-STROKE} + \text{AUGMENTATION}].$$

We are claiming, then, in effect, that people learning the alphabet—and presumably many other semiotic systems—do so by learning a semiotic grammar incorporating generalizations as rules and incorporating exceptions to those generalizations as exceptions to those rules. We might thus seem to run afoul of Chomsky's assertion (1975: 40-4) that the grammatical rules, of e.g. English, that people acquire when learning that language *cannot* just be equivalent to generalizations arrived at in the way we imagine 'letters face right' to have been: rather, those rules must at least in part be conditioned by a 'universal grammar' already in the learner's mind (in fact, from birth). Chomsky states as his 'surmise' that this universal grammar is a property of humans only: it is something that only we have evolved, then, given the 'enormous selectional advantage' offered by 'even minimal linguistic skills' (1975: 40)—an advantage with selectional force, of course, only if these skills are put to use in the real world. (Thus Chomsky rejects the notion that other primates, who can be taught such skills, possess a rudimentary universal grammar as their birthright, since they seem never to acquire these skills on their own or to use them in the wild). How these remarks, and the many others in like vein, apply elsewhere in semiotics is at present a question yet to be settled. But notice, in the meantime, that though 'even minimal literacy' must also offer an 'enormous selectional advantage'—since it furthers technological advances—no one could claim that the people who invented the alphabet (the Phoenicians) possessed a rudimentary universal semiotic grammar, at birth, in some sense that those who had to be taught the alphabet (the Greeks) did not.

Returning to the capital letters and the generalizations that children appear to form about them, we now ask: where else might those putative generalizations disclose themselves? Well, they might be expected to condition the learning of the *next* set of symbols to be mastered. Suppose this is the set of so-called Arabic numerals, comparable to but in fact quite different from the capital letters:

Table 6.1 A comparison of the capital letters and Arabic numerals

(a) Capital letters			
Reversible			Irreversible
Right-facing	Left-facing	Ambiguous	
B, D, E, F, G, K, L, P, Q, R; C	J	N, S, Z	A, H, I, M, O, T, U, V, W, X, Y

(b) Numerals			
Reversible			Irreversible
Right-facing	Left-facing	Ambiguous	
6	1, 2, 3, 4, 7, 9	5	0, 8

As we see, as respects reversibility or orientation the numerals are precisely the opposite of the capital letters: in brief, they are as left-facing as the capital letters are right-facing.[12] What will the child who has just learnt the capital letters, with the aid of the generalization 'letters face right', make of the numerals, which conform to that generalization not at all? In fact, what children do is to follow either of two strategies:

1 *The similarity strategy*. 'Numerals are letters too.' Result: the numerals are in effect converted into letters, with the consequence that initially—at 'Stage II'—*all* left-facing numerals are reversed so as to constitute right-facing or letter-like forms. Following this strategy, the child gets nearly all of the numerals (at least six out of ten) wrong: '8' and '0' he gets right, as irreversibles; '6' he gets right because it does face right like a letter; '5', which like 'N', 'S', and 'Z' seems to face either or neither way, he may get right or wrong.
2 *The antithesis strategy*. 'Numerals are the opposite of letters.' Result: the numerals are recognized as left-facing, hence the opposite of letters, and the new derived generalization to which this recognition is tantamount ('numerals face left') is applied to all the numerals. In consequence, the child gets nearly all of the numerals right, though of course he reverses '6' and gets it wrong; again, '0' and '8' will be right and '5' may or may not be.

These strategies are real. My associate David Jacobs has found that children first learning the numerals tend strongly to invoke one or the other: in other words he has found additional evidence, from a rather different quarter, for the children's formation of the original 'letters face right' generalization noted above.

It seems, then, that to account for how children master the semiotic system called the alphabet, or to account for how that semiotic system changes over time, 'generalizations' founded on psychosemiotic observation (in this case, extraspective rather than experimental) must be embodied in the semiotic grammar, which grammar thus gains a hope of modelling the grammar the people (children) apparently have in their heads. 'But', it may be rejoined, 'to such a task even extraspective evidence is adscititious, since any thorough semiotic analysis would discover these generalizations anyway.' Now, in a sense this is perfectly justified. Certainly it is hard to imagine that school-children or anybody else could unconsciously induce generalizations that the semiotic analyst, in time, would not turn up by ratiocination. This is not the problem at all. The problem is that there are vastly many generalizations that can be made about even so simple a semiotic system as the set of capital letters: and none of these generalizations offers any hints as to the likelihood of its being spontaneously derived by children learning the alphabet (or by anybody else). For instance capital letters 'A', 'M', 'T', 'U', 'V', 'W', and 'Y' are symmetrical on the vertical axis; 'B', 'C', 'D', 'E', and 'K' are symmetrical on the horizontal axis; and 'H', 'I', 'O', and 'X' are symmetrical on both axes.[13] Which (if any) of these symmetry properties are unconsciously realized by alphabet learners? In addition, 'O' and 'X' are radially symmetrical: is this generalization made? In addition, 'N', 'S', and 'Z' exhibit 'ambaxial' symmetry: they are symmetrical on both axes simultaneously but not independently (Watt, in press). Are these generalizations ever made by alphabet learners? For another instance, 'A', 'B', 'D', 'O', 'P', 'Q', and 'R' all contain enclosures: is this recognized? And, if any of these logically possible generalizations *are* made, are they made at the same level as the generalization 'letters face right'? In fact, the answer to this last question is already given, and it is 'no', since no child has ever to my knowledge been observed making errors in the direction of imposing erroneous symmetries, of whatever sort, or of 'closing' letters properly left open. (The historical fact that the Greeks symmetrized many theretofore-unsymmetrical letters testifies to the Greeks' wholly conscious love of symmetry, not to an unconscious process.)

If only psychological verification can establish which of the logically possible semiotic generalizations are in fact 'psychosemiotic generalizations', it may be equally true that not all psychosemiotic findings are of equal semiotic weight. For instance, it is well known and easy to prove that reversals of letters are harder to distinguish from their unreversed counterparts than are inversions from their right-side-up counterparts, at least when printed in rows (Wohlwill and Wiener 1964); but it is not clear how this finding should be incorporated into the semiotic grammar of the letters, or for that matter into any allied semiotic performance device. Here is yet another of the many *terrae incognitae* that lie in these waters.

6.3.2 In this section we will consider two factors which complicate the picture we have drawn so far. First, as can in fact be inferred from the discussion just preceding, 'knowing the letters' means 'knowing' rather different sorts of things, in fact may well mean having rather different sorts of 'knowledge', both in content and in mental (not to say neural) reality. Second, any discussion of psychosemiotic matters would be incomplete if it did not include some slight mention of the possibility that considerations of 'parsimony' may offer a short-cut from 'possible semiotic solution' to 'solution of psychological verisimilitude'. For variety's sake we will consider these questions in reverse order.

6.3.2.1 If we translated directly into iconics—that branch of semiotics that studies visual sign-systems—the conventional approach of Chomskyan linguistics, we should expect a characterization of the alphabet in these terms, it would seem: literates should have a 'competence', or very abstract characterization of the alphabet, as a cognitive reality; and they should also have (at least) two 'performance devices' for accessing and using that competence: one for visual discrimination or reading; the other for manual production, or writing. These are the analogues of hearing and speaking, respectively: when we assign both reading and hearing to the reception 'mode' and both writing and speaking to the production mode, the analogues seem rather close. Still, there are difficulties. The first is perhaps not hard to dispose of: it resides in the fact that the device ordinarily used for writing is not intrinsically tied to the production mode, since it can also be used for recognition, as of letters drawn on one's back or, for certain alexics, 'somesthetic' reading when other means fail (Watt 1979). One could account for such relatively rare 'reception' uses of what must still be essentially a 'production' device on the grounds that this represented a clear case of the actual case use of 'analysis-by-synthesis' (cf. Halle and Stevens 1959). A much more serious difficulty is urged by the fact that both of these 'performance devices' look and behave very like grammars.

Adopting the usage 'set of rules' as neutral between 'grammar' and 'device', we observe that the set of rules used for reading or recognition must specify a set of twenty-six visual patterns, or arrays or line-segments, to some of which certain holistic properties such as axial symmetry must be assigned. In contrast the set of rules used for writing must specify a set of twenty-six programmes, sequences of vectors or strokes. Of these strokes some will be visible (they will leave a trace on the page), others not. In Figure 6.1a (see p. 14) the dotted lines represent the invisible strokes; the unbroken lines represent, simultaneously, the visible strokes of the 'writing' rules and the line-segments of the 'reading' rules, the vectors of the 'programme' and the line-segments of the 'pattern'; or, to jump the gun, the 'phanemes' of the 'phanemic grammar' (Watt 1981) and the 'kinemes' of the 'kinemic grammar' (Watt 1980).[14]

To read and write in the conventional way, one needs both grammars: one needs to know both what an 'A' looks like and how to make one. True, an 'A' can be made in any number of ways; but knowing the *conventional* way of making 'A' is part of being in the culture. By the same token, one can know what a 'Γ' or 'Π' or 'Σ' looks like without knowing by what sequence of strokes they are made: yet knowing that is part of being a literate Greek.

How do considerations of parsimony bear on these two distinct grammars? Ambiguously. To take up a phanemic example first, we note that since a symmetrical letter like 'M' is properly characterized (or labelled) as 'monaxially symmetrical on the vertical axis', phanemic 'M' could be specified in either of two ways: (1) the entire letter could be specified, with the overall symmetry property then being calculated; or (2) half the letter could be specified, plus the overall symmetry attribute, with the remaining half then being calculated. In the first case a full specification of all of 'M's' line-segments would be identified as 'symmetrical on the vertical axis' by means of a rule of interpretation that would recognize all and only the letters so to be identified; while in the second case only half of 'M's' line-segments would be specified, but the whole (including the 'ghost' half, the half left unspecified) would also be identified, from the start, as 'symmetrical on the vertical axis'; then subsequently the 'ghost' half would be filled out by another kind of interpretive rule, actuated by the 'symmetrical' identification of the whole, which would convert the 'ghost' half into a mirror of the specified half. (Just such a rule is presented as 'Rule 8' of the phanemic grammar of the capital letters in 6.3.2.2 of Watt (1981).) So we are offered a clear choice between two competing solutions for 'M' and, of course, for every other vertically symmetrical capital letter. How do we choose? The second solution achieves an obvious saving, or parsimony, in that only half the letter need be specified, the remainder being 'inferred' or calculated via the second interpretative rule; yet, on the other hand, this calculation, since the specified half must be mirrored line-segment by line-segment in order to generate the 'missing' half, is apt to be rather laborious. In short, by achieving parsimony in one sense—that of the starting statement of 'M' and its ilk—we incur a diseconomy or inefficiency in another sense—that of how long or laborious the full derivation is that takes the 'starting' specification, applies rules of interpretation, and ends up with a full-fledged 'M' or the like. We could perhaps call the first criterion of parsimony, which minimizes what we must store in the mind, the criterion of 'archival' parsimony (it has been called many other things); and the second criterion, which minimizes how much labour must be expended to produce, from what is stored in the mind, an actual 'M' or whatever, the criterion of 'executive' parsimony (it has been called other things too).[15] Then the second solution appears to optimize archival parsimony at the expense of executive parsimony. And as the reader has probably already deduced, the first solution, in which the entire letter is specified and its symmetry then calculated, optimizes executive parsimony at the expense of archival parsimony. So now we ask: if we exert a higher criterion of 'approximation to psychological verisimilitude', which criterion of parsimony must we choose to optimize in making our forced choice between the first solution and the second?

Otherwise put, which criterion of parsimony is itself of greater psychological verisimilitude?

Notice that the last question touches the very nerve of the issue, for to claim that greater psychological verisimilitude is to be attained by optimizing a grammar by one or another parsimony-criterion —*ceteris paribus*—is to claim that the human mind itself, in forming its internal grammar, also optimizes by that criterion. Otherwise any such claim is flapdoodle.

What this means overall is that ascertaining which parsimony-criterion is to be used to optimize the phanemic grammar—or, if both criteria are to be applied but at different levels of abstraction, how those levels are to be defined—now becomes an area of lively interest in psychosemiotic research. Certainly the answer to this problem is by no means known. Nor is it known, leaving phanemic questions behind us, for the kinemic grammar either, even though there, one would think, since kinemic generations appear pretty directly on the page as kinemic productions, the criterion of executive parsimony should be uppermost. Certainly, in one sense, this is demonstrable, since over time a process of 'facilitation' appears to simplify the composition of letters, in effect *optimizing* the kinemic grammar as judged by the criterion of executive parsimony. Yet the same process also reduces the size of the compositional or kinemic programmes that one must store in the mind, so that it also optimizes the kinemic grammar by the criterion of archival parsimony. And in fact the kinemic grammar appears, in various ways, to be optimized in accordance with *both* criteria, one being the stronger at one juncture, the other at another. For instance, the conventional way of making an 'A', that shown in Figure 6.1a, is extremely inefficient when compared with the programme illustrated in Figure 6.1b, which in turn is not nearly so efficient as the programme illustrated in Figure 6.1c. Anyone using the 'conventional'

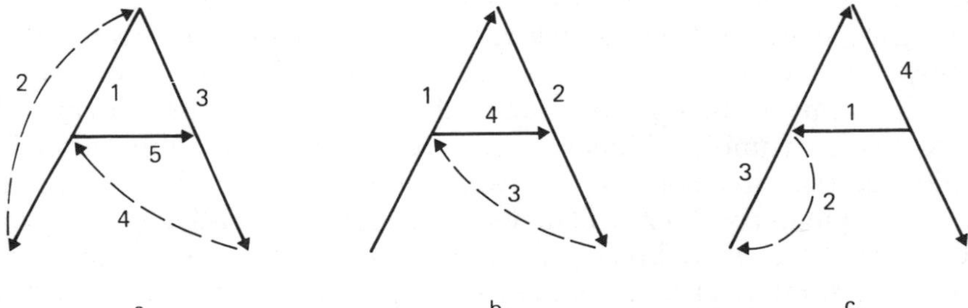

Fig. 6.1 Three ways of making an 'A'

programme of 6.1a, the five-stroke 'A', is not maximizing executive parsimony, clearly. Is he maximizing archival parsimony? The answer is 'Yes' if by using inefficient five-stroke 'A' he in some way manages to 'store less' in his mind as the kinemic aspect of what he knows about the dual nature (kinemic and phanemic) of the letters. And, in fact, just such a saving is achieved, since only five-stroke 'A', of the three of Figure 6.1, begins with the downwards stroke with which nearly all the other letters begin; only five-stroke 'A', then, fits into the kinemic grammar of optimum archival parsimony, the one in which the downwards direction of the initial stroke of almost all letters is left unspecified—a 'ghost' direction if you will—being supplied by an overall interpretative rule which supplies downwards direction to all such strokes.[16] So the conventional five-stroke 'A' does achieve greater archival parsimony, after all. Yet some people do use the four-stroke 'A' of Figure 6.1b: they sacrifice archival parsimony for greater executive parsimony, so it seems. We might even suppose that one might, as one is called upon to write more and more, faster and faster, 'graduate' from five-stroke 'A' to four-stroke 'A', as it were 'graduating' from archival to executive efficiency. By the same token the minimal 'A' of Figure 6.1c, which hypothetically the ancient Greeks used as a step towards the still more efficient but now phanemically altered 'A' of Figure 6.2a and then the curvilinearized version ('α') of Figure 6.2b, represents a further 'graduation', in this sense. Thus it seems that, at least in the kinemic grammar, at times the two parsimony-criteria are optimized together, while at other times—depending on whether or not speed-of-production is important—one or the other is clearly superordinate.

Whether this generalization will hold up through the next few years of semiotic theory-building and psychosemiotic experimentation, though, is another question.[17]

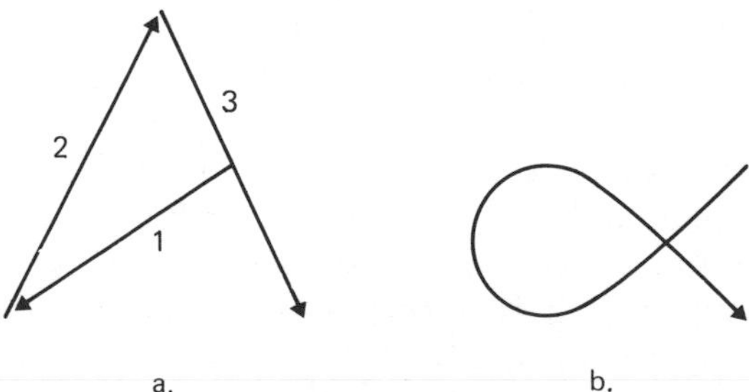

Fig. 6.2 Making 'A' and 'α' (phanemic elision)

6.3.2.2 Now we turn to the second 'complication' mentioned at the beginning of this subsection, namely, the possible disparity among the various sources of one's knowledge about the letters. Much of what one can say about this issue has already been implied by the foregoing discussion of the dual nature of that knowledge, reflected quite directly in the postulation, in Watt (1980) and Watt (1981), of two distinct grammars, the kinemic and the phanemic, respectively. For instance surely one knows very different sorts of things indeed when one knows that 'A' is symmetrical on the vertical axis, on the one hand, and on the other that 'A' begins with a downward stroke. The difference between these different sorts of knowledge is well handled, of course, by their being lodged in two different grammars; but this is an unusually clear case. Speaking intuitively, both of these sorts of knowledge seem different from knowing that a letter's augmentation ordinarily appears to its right, a piece of intelligence that, since an augmentation is realized both as line-segments and strokes, will be realized in the phanemic and the kinemic grammars, respectively.

If there are indeed different *kinds* of information entailed in knowing about the letters then it would not be surprising if people did not uniformly appeal to the same sorts of information in widely differing tasks. The tell-tale attributes that one looks for when trying to identify a letter visually, for instance, may not necessarily be the most salient characteristics of one's passive memory of the letters. Certainly we should be ever mindful of the possibly related fact, amply demonstrated by Goodnow (1971) and Millar (1971), that in knowing about the letters in different modalities (e.g., visual discrimination and motoric production), one knows very different things and will reveal that difference in how one behaves on differential experimental tasks (as see also Posner 1973). Or, to take another tack, the kinds of information that are 'redundant' (superfluous, predictable) vary greatly depending on what task is at hand: in recognizing an 'E' one could ignore, as completely redundant, the uppermost bar, for example, concentrating therefore just on the lower half of the presented letter. Yet when making an 'E' one cannot be so neglectful. In general, then, if people performed differently with respect to the English capital letters this would not be at all surprising, and would fit in well with what has already been found out about differential behaviour respecting other semiotic systems. For instance it is notorious that people behave very differently with respect to the English consonantal sounds depending on whether they are required to perform short-term memory tasks or to make inter-sound similarity judgements (Singh 1976: 115).

To some extent, variations in required task may prove to have been no less responsible for many of the striking disparities among experiments having to do with the alphabetic letters (no two of which are in full and joyous concord).

The preceding discussion leads us in an interesting new direction. It is by no means clear how a semiotic (iconic) account of the capital letters can accommodate the mass of psychological data on the letters that mounts steadily in the literature; but, among the various things that occur to me, one intriguing possibility stands out. This would exploit the function of 'redundancy' pointed out just above. Suppose some performative differences, in so far as they depend on utilizing different portions of one's overall knowledge of the letters, might be reflected *directly* in the letters' analysis in a particularly simple way: information used in some tasks but not in others could be included in the letters' analysis, at some level, as 'redundant'. Such a provision would be a simple and compelling way of modelling the analysis available in principle to the experimental subject, who on some occasions could tap only the 'non-redundant' information —for instance in a task requiring fast judgements (e.g., recognition under poor lighting conditions and/or with fast presentations)—but on other occasions make use of some or all of the 'redundant' information (e.g., when making more or less deliberated similarity judgements). Certainly, on any such hypothesis, very different patterns might result: that is, some letters dealt with as if they were highly similar on one task might on another task, demanding use of fewer redundancies, be dealt with as if they were quite different.

Such a 'Differential Redundancy Hypothesis' (hereafter, 'DRH') is easily illustrated. First, we'll invent a simple five-letter alphabet and then dissolve those letters into binary features, the better to compare them (see Table 6.2). Describing just their '+' values the six characterizing features are: (1) VEXILLARY (meaning, begins with a vertical line segment); (2) AUGMENTATION (has an augmentation); (3) AUG=DIAG (the augmentation is a diagonal line segment); (4) AUG = '/' (the augmentation is the line segment '/'); (5) AUG@TOP (the augmentation is at the top of the letter-space); and (6) AUG@BOT (the augmentation is at the bottom of the letter-space).

A few remarks about these features. First, if a letter is described as both [AUG@TOP] and [AUG@BOT] then the augmentation must be in the middle. Secondly, the first two features are completely redundant for this five-letter alphabet, since all letters have the same values for these two features. Thirdly, the fourth feature, AUG = '/', bears no value for the first three letters, and so is asserted

Table 6.2 Five letters factored into distinctive features

+VEXILLARY	+VEXILLARY	+VEXILLARY	+VEXILLARY	+VEXILLARY
+AUGMENT'N	+AUGMENT'N	+AUGMENT'N	+AUGMENT'N	+AUGMENT'N
−AUG=DIAG	+AUG=DIAG	+AUG=DIAG	+AUG=DIAG	+AUG=DIAG
AUG = '/'	AUG = '/'	AUG = '/'	+AUG = '/'	−AUG = '/'
+AUG@TOP	+AUG@TOP	−AUG@TOP	−AUG@TOP	−AUG@TOP
−AUG@BOT	−AUG@BOT	+AUG@BOT	−AUG@BOT	−AUG@BOT

to be redundant for those letters; for the last two letters, where it does bear a value, it is of course asserted to be non-redundant. Fourthly, the last two features are not redundant for any letter. In calculating redundancies for this little system, then, we will concentrate on the fourth feature: in what does its redundancy consist? In other words, from what *other* features can the value of AUG = '/', for those letters in whose specifications that feature has so far been left unvalued, be predicted? Well, for the first letter the value can easily be calculated from the fact that the augmentation of that letter is already specified to bc non-diagonal: hence, for this letter, the value of AUG = '/' must be '–'. More importantly, given the overall attributes of this illustrative alphabet as a whole, the value of the same feature can be calculated to be '–' for letter '↾' and '+' for letter '⇃'. This is because, since it seems proper to infer that neither '⎧' nor '⎩' can occur as well-formed letters in this system, to know that a letter has a diagonal augmentation and that it occurs at the top of the letter-space is to know that that augmentation must be '\', i.e., must be '–[AUG = '/']'; and the same comment holds, *mutatis mutandis*, when a letter is specified to have a diagonal augmentation at the bottom of the letter-space.

The calculation or insertion of the correct value of 'AUG is '/' ', for letters '↾' and '⇃', is handled easily by a redundancy rule like this:

$$[\text{AUG} = \text{'/'}] \rightarrow [\alpha\,\text{AUG} = \text{'/'}] \text{ in env} \begin{bmatrix} +\text{AUG=DIAG} \\ -\alpha\text{AUG@TOP} \\ \alpha\text{AUG@BOT} \end{bmatrix}$$

—or in plain words, 'the feature [AUG = '/'] must have the same value, for any letter already specified to be [+AUG=DIAG] and for which the features [AUG@TOP]'; or in plainer words still, 'if a diagonal augmentation is at the bottom it is '/', but if at the top it is the opposite.' Here, of course, we employ the abstract value 'α', ranging over '+' and '–', to achieve an economy of statement. Notice that 'Rule D' must not apply to the fourth or fifth letters, since for these letters the direction of the diagonal augmentation is not predictable; hence the specifications for these letters, in which the two features '[AUG@TOP]' and '[AUG@BOT]' have the *same* value, do not match the 'environment' which, in 'Rule D', is stated as a precondition for application of that rule.[18]

Since we have already determined that letter 'Γ' can have its value for '[AUG = '/']' calculated to be '–', by means of a rule which is so simple as not to deserve explicit statement here but which we might term '[unstated] Rule H', we are now able, using 'Rule H' for the first letter and 'Rule D' for the next two letters, to fill in the missing values. Since the values that were left unfilled could then be filled automatically (by applying rules), after they have been filled in they are 'redundant', precisely. So what we have done, then, is restore 'redundancies'. As originally stated the five letters were specified without redundant values for the feature '[AUG = '/']'; now, with those values calculated by applying 'Rule H' and 'Rule D', and duly inserted, those specifications look as in Table 6.3.

Now it is easy and natural to calculate inter-letter differences, either at the 'without redundancies' stage or at the 'with redundancies' stage, in terms of how many features, for any two letters being compared, have different values. (If two letters are being compared on a given feature and either or both of them has *no* stated value for that feature, that is counted as 'no difference'.) These calculations are exhibited in Table 6.4a and 6.4b. The 'before restoration' and 'after restoration' difference is perhaps best illustrated by boiling it down to just a single comparison. Signifying the concept 'distance [or difference] between ⇂ and ᚴ' as 'd (⇂,ᚴ),' and other like differences in like manner, we note that in the 'before' table, to the left, d(⇂, ᚴ) = d(⇂, ↾); but that in the 'after' table on the right, in contrast, d(⇂, ᚴ) < d(⇂, ↾). That is, someone using the 'before' table to judge inter-letter differences would judge the letter-pairs '(⇂,ᚴ)' and '(⇂,↾)' to be equally dissimilar; but using the 'after' table he would judge the first pair of letters to be less dissimilar to each other than the second pair are to each other.

The conditions, then, for scrutinizing a 'differential redundancy hypothesis' are easily met, even by a small and rather artificial alphabet like the one we have been using. With this in mind, let us take this speculation one next step. If we now imagine a hypothetical experiment consisting of two tasks on which people turn out to perform differently respecting this five-letter alphabet—say a task in which redundancies might expectably be ignored and a task in which they might expectably be put to use—then the differences determined by such an experiment might, with luck, lend themselves to explanation along the lines suggested here: depending on task, people heed or ignore the redundancies calculated by Rule H and/or Rule D. Without urging a fully mechanistic and rather silly view, we could say that, depending on task, people either use one or don't use the rules themselves.

If such an explanation should prove to have any merit in accounting for these phenomena it would also have a second merit in the eyes of semiotic analysts, I think, for it would proceed from a single unified analysis of this five-letter semiotic system, albeit from a unified analysis which can be accessed at either of two levels

Table 6.3 Five letters in distinctive features with redundancies restored

Γ	ᛚ	⅃	ᚴ	ᚳ
+VEXILLARY +AUGMENT'N −AUG=DIAG −AUG = '/' +AUG@TOP −AUG@BOT	+VEXILLARY +AUGMENT'N +AUG=DIAG −AUG = '/' +AUG@TOP −AUG@BOT	+VEXILLARY +AUGMENT'N +AUG=DIAG +AUG = '/' −AUG@TOP +AUG@BOT	+VEXILLARY +AUGMENT'N +AUG=DIAG +AUG = '/' −AUG@TOP −AUG@BOT	+VEXILLARY +AUGMENT'N +AUG=DIAG −AUG = '/' −AUG@TOP −AUG@BOT

Table 6.4 Inter-letter similarities expressed as shared features

(a) Without redundancies restored

	ᚳ	ᚴ	ᛚ	Γ
⅃	1	1	1	3
ᚳ		1	1	2
ᚴ			1	2
ᛚ				1

(b) With redundancies restored

	ᚳ	ᚴ	ᛚ	Γ
⅃	2	1	3	4
ᚳ		1	1	2
ᚴ			2	3
ᛚ				1

or 'stages'. We might further speculate that if a DRH is shown to have merit for alphabets it will very probably prove to have merit elsewhere in semiotics.[19]

Unfortunately these brief remarks explore this topic as far as current research can take us, and a little further. Beyond this we can note only that the kind of redundancies used illustratively just above are natural (indeed, inevitable) aspects of the kinds of iconic grammars for real alphabets that are presented in (Watt 1980; 1981).

6.3.3 We began this section, headed 'To defend it', with the intention of supporting the claim that for any semiotic system to achieve its optimal analysis it will typically be necessary to take into consideration various sorts of evidence of the kind that has traditionally been viewed as the province of the psychologist. I don't think there is anything very surprising about this general observation: but in the preceding pages I have tried to bring it down to earth and to show how it might be invested with some detail, and with some falsifiable predictions. Picking up a strand dropped earlier, we have noted that many historical changes in the history of alphabets seem due to uncorrected misrecollections. This general comment can now be tautened a little: the 'generalizations' discussed earlier are, in fact, the prime examples of such misrecollections; and, as will readily be seen, 'generalization' and 'redundancy' are but two sides of the same coin. That is, one generalizes, for a set of entities, a feature common to them all, which feature, when assigned to the entire set and ready to be imposed on each entity by means of a 'rule', is a redundancy. Otherwise put, to generalize is to acknowledge, for some set of entities, a quality which each entity possesses just by virtue of its membership in the set, hence a quality which would be redundant if stated for each entity individually. Continuing in this vein, we observe that the kind of uncorrected misrecollection under discussion here is the sort of 'over-generalization' that extends the membership of a set of entities by mistakenly including in that set an entity that stands outside it. This mistake involves two steps. First, an attribute of the 'outside' entity is forgotten, namely, the very attribute that differentiates it as 'outside' from the entities inside the set. (For instance, imagine an alphabet in which all letters are top-heavy except 'L', making 'L' the 'outside' entity in this respect, uniquely stigmatized as '–[TOP-HEAVY]'. Now suppose that this attribute '–[TOP-HEAVY]' is momentarily forgotten.) And secondly, the forgotten attribute is 'recovered', but mistakenly, the 'recovery' being of the *opposite* attribute, the dominant one exhibited in all the 'inside' entities, with the consequence that now the former 'outside' entity undergoes a change and is 'inside'. (Thus the opposed attribute '+[TOP-HEAVY]' would replace '–[TOP-HEAVY]' for 'L', changing 'L' into 'Γ' and making it an 'inside' or top-heavy letter.) This is an illustrative example of the process of 'homogenization' that appears to have operated quite often in alphabetic evolution (Watt 1979); it is related to the psychological process of 'assimilation' (Bruner *et al.* 1952).

To continue with an example used earlier, if all the capital letters having their augmentations to the right are 'inside' entities then 'J' is the one 'outside' entity; to forget where the augmentation of 'J' goes and then to supply this missing information by filling in the corresponding attribute of the 'inside' entities, is to put 'J' inside also by replacing it with '[. Notice that if one forgets where the augmentation of an 'inside' letter like 'F' or 'L' goes, but then supplies the missing information from the 'inside' set, the result is 'F' or 'L', with no change. Thus the process of 'generalization' (or 'homogenization') makes no claim at all that exceptions or 'outside' entities are more likely to be partially forgotten—indeed, to the extent that they are sore thumbs they may be *less* likely—rather, the claim is only that, once partially forgotten, an 'outside' entity recovers its missing attribute from the 'inside' set only on pain of moving into that set itself.

As was said long ago in a much-neglected paper (Bloomfield 1895), this tendency for set-properties to spread is a basic characteristic of some linguistic (and semiotic) evolution: in particular, of the 'advolutionary' tendency (Watt 1979) of elements of semiotic systems to become more like each other through 'over-generalization', a general trend which, viewed as a physical movement of elements towards each other, is the semiotic equivalent of gravity (Baudouin de Courtenay 1870).[20]

To assign an element to a group of elements having some attribute A_1 in common is to make it possible to extract A_1 from the specification of that element, as redundant to it, and assign A_1 to the group as a whole, by means of adding a rule which states A_1 as calculable for each member of the group. To assign a new and non-conforming element to this group is to 'forget' that it does not have attribute A_1 and to impose A_1 on the element anyway by making it newly subject to the rule that inserts A_1; the new member thus enjoys a gain in redundancy (and a loss in exceptionality, equivalent to the number of attributes that have to be specified for it in a fully non-redundant characterization).

The strands of the argument knit together at this point. Chief among the things that a semiotic account must capture are the attributes of the system that affect its history, both past and future. Those attributes are necessarily attributes of the system internalized by its users. Semiotics does its job in part by considering psychological evidence. Semiotics is psychosemiotics.

6.4 TO DISCARD IT

But if semiotics is psychosemiotics the latter term is superfluous and were better relinquished.

NOTES

1. In somewhat different form this paper was given at Burg Wartenstein in 1975, and has in some sense been 'in press' ever since. If this strains the reader's credulity, think what it does to mine. I have brought references up to date where this seemed imperative, and have made a number of other changes, but basically the paper is eight years old, and were best read with that fact in intermittent view. Beside this general caveat I should like to place a particular one: I now see the process of reconciling semiotic theory with psychological findings as even more complex an operation than I envisaged in 1975.

   For those already well familiar with the argument that semiotics (or linguistics) should ultimately seek reconciliation with psychological findings, the main novelty in the paper at hand is likely to prove section 6.3.2.2, where a notion of 'differential redundancy' is introduced as one aid to that reconciliation.

   I should like to acknowledge the wise counsel of Antonio Teixeira Guerra, of Quinta da Vela, Murfacem, Portugal; and of Rupert Pentweazle.
2. Zoösemiotics was named and brought into being by Sebeok, as see especially Sebeok 1977.
3. For instance, if a sign is more iconic in Peirce's sense is it more likely to be stored in the right hemisphere rather than in the left? Is it likely to be easier of access?
4. That both deaf children and chimpanzees master American Sign Language to a greater or lesser degree need not mean that both master the same parts or aspects of ASL, and so leaves open the question of the equivalence between their language capacities. For some caveats see Sebeok 1977 or Sagan 1980: 51-76. For a comparison of human and pongid ASL, see now Van Cantfort and Rimpau 1982.
5. As is well known, semiotics must endure the splendid misery of being founded on a text, Peirce's, which is needful of extensive Talmudic interpretation, with the result that there is always cause for worry that one is getting something wrong somehow. But the notion that Peirce considered himself a psychologist and (sometimes) semiotics a psychological discipline or psychology a semiotic discipline, does not hinge on a single quote, so

perhaps we are safe, if we bear in mind the appropriate doubts and qualifications (as see Fisch 1978: 55 f.).

6. The first comprehensive survey of the 'linguistic analogy' as such, and one of the most cautious ever, was Hymes 1970; see also Sebeok 1976: 66–9.

   By no means, incidentally, do I intend to imply that the path connecting linguistics and semiotics is a one-way street: Chomsky, for example, is only one linguist among many to have been influenced by Peirce (Chomsky 1975: 157–203; for comment see Sebeok 1977: 181).

7. See Chase 1973 for a broad view of current research in this area.
8. See, again, Sebeok 1977.
9. The evidence is presented in McCarter 1975. For the further history of this letter in the Greek epichoric alphabets, see Jeffery 1961. Note that since '⇃' disobeys *two* generalities concerning the Phoenician and Archaic Greek vexillaries ('if a letter begins with a vertical stroke then its augmentation follows' and 'augmentations are put at the top rather than the bottom'), it follows that it might undergo either or both of the indicated generalizations. If it undergoes both, it should change to '↾'; if only the first, it should change to '⇂'; if only the second, it should change to '↿'. The first and second of these new letters are well attested (Jeffery 1961); the third is not attested at all, to my knowledge, leading to the obvious open question.

   Note also that my 'homogenization' is the logical extension—and application to *all* members of a set of items-to-be-learnt—of Bruner's principle of 'assimilation' (Bruner *et al.* 1952). Within semiotics, or rather linguistics, the principle was discussed long ago by none other than Baudouin de Courtenay 1870; for another view of a quite similar process see Bloomfield 1895. And see further below.

   Aside from such general questions as the role of reversal in homogenizing trends, letter-reversals have long been studied by psychologists, as see Huttenlocher 1967 or Zusner 1970; for letter-reversals among children, see Frith 1971.

10. Since ten of the twenty-six capital letters (38 per cent) are unimpeachably right-facing, any child stands a better-than-even chance of having one such letter somewhere in his or her name, generally the first thing he or she learns to write.
11. It might occur to anyone taking a close look at these matters for the first time that the similarity of 'S' and 'Z' must reflect the similarity of the sounds /s/ and /z/. Maybe so, but the archaic forms of these two letters were 'ϟ' and 'I'.
12. The numerals '2' and '3' obviously face in a direction opposite to that faced by 'C', so that if 'C' faces right then '2' and '3' must face left. 'C' is of course begun with the curved stroke '↶', as are 'S' and every other letter beginning with a curve, even including 'O' and 'Q', which just as logically could begin anywhere. Thus for '2' and '3' the numeral generalization 'Numerals are the antithesis of letters' applies with special force, since '2' and '3' must begin with the stroke '↷', contrary to the practice with all of the corresponding letters. One might have supposed that '8' would begin with stroke '↷' to make it as numeral-like as possible; yet, at least in my own hand, it begins with '↶'.
13. In addition 'N', 'S' and 'Z' are distinctive as a set in that, while not displaying vertical and horizontal symmetries independently, they do exhibit 'ambaxial' symmetry (Watt 1980)—i.e., they are reflective on both axes

simultaneously (a transparency printed with an 'N', for example, if folded along its vertical axis and then also along its horizontal axis, produces a complete overlapping of lines).

For the present it remains a mystery that the vertically symmetrical letters cluster in the second half of the alphabet while the horizontally symmetrical letters cluster in the first half. As I've suggested elsewhere (Watt, 1981), this may be part of a *mystique alphabétique*, and so be best settled by appeal to graptomancy, so to term it.

14. That the production and reception aspects of language must to some degree be accorded separate and independent analyses is of course the major conclusion of a once widely read but now widely ignored classic of mid-century phonology: namely Fischer-Jørgensen 1952. But note that my 'executive'/'receptive' separation is by no means identical to Fischer-Jørgensen's production/reception separation, since e.g. my 'executive' modality is associated with both a productive (writing) and a receptive (somesthetic reading) performative capability.
15. For some discussion of executive (or 'computational') parsimony, see Chomsky 1972: 191 f.) and Watt 1974.
16. Since this interpretative rule fits in better with the kind of 'markedness' rules governing the quasi-predictability of, e.g., the initiating sequence of strokes '↓↑' (with the second invisible of course), it was omitted from the kinemic grammar of Watt 1980, but will appear in Watt, in preparation.
17. For further discussion see Watt 1974.
18. Stating that the features '[AUG@TOP]' and '[AUG@BOT]' must have different values, of course, is just one way (among many) of specifying that the augmentation must be either at the top or at the bottom.

    For the use of 'α' variables, see e.g. Chomsky and Halle 1968: *passim.*
19. That is, there may be cognitive structures and learning strategies that are peculiar to natural language, among semiotic systems, but it would be astounding if there were cognitive structures and learning strategies that were peculiar to alphabets (or writing systems in general or iconic systems in general). Not excluded, of course, is the possibility that a writing-system intimately associated *with natural language* might have a special psychosemiotic status, as has indeed been asserted for ordinary-font English printing (Bryden and Allard 1976).
20. See Jakobson 1980. 116 f. for elaboration.

BIBLIOGRAPHY

Baudouin de Courtenay, J. (1870), 'Izbrannye trudy po obscemu jazykoznaniji, I–II', Moscow, 1963; reference from Jakobson 1980.

Bloomfield, M. (1895), 'On assimilation and adaptation in congeneric classes of words', *American Journal of Philology*, 16, 409-34.

Bruner, J. S., Busiek, R. D. and Minturn, A. L. (1952). 'Assimilation in the immediate reproduction of visually perceived figures', *Journal of Experimental Psychology*, 44, 151-5.

Bresson, F. (ed.) (1974), *Problèmes actuels en psycholinguistique*, Paris, Centre National de la Recherche Scientifique.

Bryden, M. P. and Allard, F. (1976). 'Visual hemifield differences depend on typeface', *Brain and Language*, 3, 191-200.

Chase, W. G. (1973), *Visual Information Processing*, New York, Academic Press.

Chomsky, N. (1972), *Language and Mind, Enlarged Edition*, New York, Harcourt Brace Jovanovich.

Chomsky, N. (1975), *Reflections on Language*, New York, Pantheon.

Chomsky, N. and Halle, M. (1968), *Sound Pattern of English*, New York, Harper and Row.

Fisch, M. (1978), 'Peirce's general theory of signs', in Sebeok (1978: 21-37).

Fischer-Jørgensen, E. (1952), 'The phonetic basis for identification of phonemic elements', *Journal of the Acoustical Society of America*, **24**, 611-17.

Frith, U. (1971), 'Why do children reverse letters?', *British Journal of Psychology*, 62, 459-68.

Goodnow, J. J. (1971), 'Eye and hand: differential memory and its effect on matching', *Neuropsychologica*, **9**, 89-95.

Halle, M. and Stevens, K. N. (1959), 'Analysis by synthesis' in Walthen-Dunn and Woods (1959).

Huttenlocher, J. (1967), 'Discrimination of figure orientation: effects of relative position', *Journal of Comparative Physiological Psychology*, **63**, 359-61.

Hymes, D. (1970), 'Linguistic models in archaeology', in *Archéologie et Calculateurs: Problèmes Sémiologiques et Mathématiques*, Paris, Centre National de la Recherche Scientifique (Colloques Internationaux).

Jakobson, R. (1980), *The Framework of Language*, Ann Arbor, Mich., Horace H. Rackham School of Graduate Studies, University of Michigan (Michigan Studies in the Humanities 1).

Jeffery, L. H. (1961), *The Local Scripts of Archaic Greece*, Oxford, Clarendon Press.

McCarter, P. K., Jr. (1975), *The Antiquity of the Greek Alphabet and the Early Phoenician Scripts*, Missoula, Mont., Scholars Press.

Millar, S. (1971), 'Visual and haptic cue utilization by preschool children: the recognition of visual and haptic and stimuli presented separately and together', *Journal of Experimental Child Psychology*, 12, 88-94.

Peirce, C. S. S. (1977) (C. S. Hardwick, ed.), *Semiotic and Significs: The Correspondence between Charles S. Peirce and Victoria Lady Welby*, Bloomington, Indiana University Press.

Posner, M. I. (1973), 'Coordination of internal codes', in Chase (1973: 35-73).

Sagan, C. (1980), *Broca's Brain*, New York, Ballantine.

Sebeok, T. A. (1976), *Contributions to the Doctrine of Signs*, Bloomington, Indiana University Press (Studies in Semiotics 5).

Sebeok, T. A. (1977), 'Ecumenicalism in Semiotics', in T. A. Sebeok (ed.), *A Perfusion of Signs*, Bloomington, Indiana University Press (Advances in Semiotics), 180-206.

Sebeok, T. A. (ed.) (1978), *Sight, Sound, and Sense*, Bloomington, Indiana University Press.

Singh, S. (1976), *Distinctive Features: Theory and Validation*, Baltimore, University Park Press.

Van Cantfort, T. E. and Rimpau, J. B. (1982), 'Sign language studies with children and chimpanzees', *Sign Language Studies*, **34**, 15-72.

Walthen-Dunn, W. and Woods, L. N. (eds) (1959), *Proceedings of the Seminar on Speech Compression and Processing*, AFCRT-TR-59-198-Vol. II.

Watt, W. C. (1974), 'Competing economy criteria', in Bresson (ed.) (1974: 361-88).

Watt, W. C. (1979), 'Iconic equilibrium', *Semiotica*, **28**, 31-62.

Watt, W. C. (1980), 'What is the proper characterization of the alphabet? II: composition', *Ars Semeiotica*, 3, 3-46.

Watt, W. C. (1981), 'What is the proper characterization of the alphabet? III: appearance', *Ars Semeiotica*, 4, No. 3.

Watt, W. C. (in preparation), 'What is the proper characterization of the alphabet? V.'

Wohlwill, J. F. and Wiener, M. (1964). 'Discrimination of form orientation in young children', *Child Development*, 35, 1113-25.

Zusne, L. (1970), *Visual Perception of Form*, New York, Academic.

7 Two models of narrative structure: a consultation

L. M. O'Toole
Murdoch University, Perth, Australia

7.1 INTRODUCTION

The aim of this paper is not so much to present a finished argument as to offer for discussion two contrasting models for the analysis and interpretation of fictional narrative which may offer insights for the study of other semiotic systems. The different assumptions and methods underlying these models urgently need consideration and criticism by linguists and semioticians.

7.2 AN ANALYTIC MODEL

The first model is a type of multidimensional analysis which I have used for some time as a framework for the analysis and interpretation of Russian short stories. Starting from a provisional interpretation of the theme of a story, the text is analysed successively in terms of *Fable, Plot, Narrative Structure, Point of View, Character,* and *Setting.* The recurrence of certain elements of meaning in each of these structures and from the interaction between them tends to point to a reinterpretation of the theme. Subsequent, more delicate, analysis of stylistic features which have a function in relation to each structural level and of more pervasive elements of imagery and symbolism frequently leads to a further refinement of the interpretation (O'Toole 1971, 1972, 1982).

The method is explicit and descriptively adequate to the extent that each dimension of structure represents a given closed set of options from which the writer selects: the reconstruction of the *Fable*, the original sequence of events underlying the story, reveals the extent to which he has chosen to change the sequence (through flashback or anticipation), to dispose the events unevenly through the text and to omit certain actions or events. Through the analysis of *Narrative Structure* we can map the trajectory of the story's action through complication, peripeteia, and denouement. The placing of these moments, their degree of explicitness and their relationship to the framework of Prologue and Epilogue may be crucial to our interpretation of the theme. These structures of the action will clearly influence and be influenced by the author's choice of features of *Character* and *Setting*. All four dimensions will be intimately dependent on the author's chosen *Point of View* at a given moment in the text: does the reader learn of some events prior to those comprising the action through narratorial flashback or through the dialogue, thoughts, soliloquies, or dreams of the characters? Is the peripeteia physical or psychological and, if the latter, is it manifested in the actions or behaviour of the main character or an accessory, or even through some significant adjustment of the setting?

It is, perhaps, misleading to refer to this as a 'levels' analysis (as in O'Toole 1971, 1972) since the levels of structure are not comparable to the distinct levels of phonology, grammar, and semantics analysed by linguists. They are more analogous to simultaneously operating systems of options in a systemic grammar where selections from networks of meaning potential select combinations of features from the syntactic, lexical, and phonological systems. Thus a certain ideational content in the *Theme* will be realized through a particular pattern in the core of a story's *Narrative Structure*, rather as 'process-participant relations' realize the central ideational content in a sentence. A similar parallel seems to exist in the psychological strategies for the production-perception of narrative texts and of sentences between other structure systems as well. To tabulate and oversimplify:

Narrative Text		**Sentence**
Narrative Structure	=	process-participant relations
Point of View	=	mood, modality, aspect
Plot	=	subordination and causal relations
Fable	=	temporal structure; tense and time adverbials; coordination
Setting	=	characterization of time and place
Character	=	characterization of participants

The relationship may be made clearer if we label features in the sentence below which also happens to be the kernel of a famous narrative text:

PV C F NS P NS P F NS
Apparently Red Riding Hood was shaken but unhurt by her encounter with the
PV C S PV S F
big bad wolf in the woods that sunny day.

However primitive this analysis, it is clear that options are not selected independently of each other; as in a systemic grammar where the function system networks are to be thought of as wired 'in parallel' (Halliday 1971: 338). On the other hand, it is as true of text structure as of sentence structure that certain units tend to be the vehicles for particular functions. A slight expansion of our kernel narrative with a somewhat exaggerated functional focus on each unit may help to make this clear:

Functional focus	
F:	**Once upon a time** there was a little girl called Red Riding Hood who **used to take** cakes to her granny **every week.**
S:	**The woods she had to walk through** were **full of pretty flowers** and **on sunny days** she would stop to pick them.
P:	One day a wolf spotted her and asked her where she was going. She told him she was taking cakes to her granny because she was ill, so he bounded off to get there first.
C:	She was a **very sweet and innocent little girl** and he was a **very cunning wicked wolf.**
NS: (Complication) (Peripeteia) (Denouement)	She went into the cottage and **offered the cakes to the wolf** who **she thought was her grandmother**, but he **tricked her and gobbled her** up whole. Fortunately, a passing woodcutter **came in, killed the wolf** and **released Red Riding Hood.**
PV:	When Red Riding Hood went up to the bed **she was surprised** at **how** her granny **had changed:** – **What** big eyes **you have,** granny! – **All the better** to see you with, **my dear!** – **What** big ears **you have, granny!** – **All the better** to hear you with, **my dear!** – **What** big teeth **you have, granny!** – **All the better** to eat you with, **my dear!** And **with these words** the **cruel** wolf **bounded** out of bed and **gobbled** up **poor** Red Riding Hood **in one mighty gulp!**
Theme:	Innocence is risk.

We should note that even in such an artificial text there is room for individual interpretation depending on how one analyses the narrative structure. If one preferred the theme of this children's bedtime story to stress 'security' rather than 'danger', one would see the complication as being the gobbling up, the peripeteia as the wolf being killed, and the denouement as the heroine being released. (Theme: 'Don't worry, daddy usually gets there in time'.)

A primitive story like Red Riding Hood will serve, of course, for clarifying theoretical issues, but it hardly puts the model to the test.

In my article 'Narrative structure and living texture' (O'Toole 1976) I applied this model in an attempt to synthesize the results of a collective discussion of Joyce's *Dubliners* story, 'Two Gallants'.[1]

The conclusions reached through this analysis may be summarized briefly. A first postulation of the theme as 'exploitation' (the girl by Corley, Corley and Lenehan by each other, Ireland by an alien oppressor, and the reader by the narrator) seemed to be borne out by analysis of the syntagmatic levels of Fable (temporal) and Plot (causal). In reconstructing the Fable, the time sequence in which the original events took place, we find that it differs from the actual story in three significant ways: (1) in sequence: the necessary biographical information about Corley is provided by the narrator after the introduction of Lenehan and after Corley's own account in flashback, of his earlier meetings with the young woman (both time sequence and use of narrator here are conventional enough techniques); (2) in the mode by which we learn of the events: the sparse information we glean about Lenehan's life and character is relayed to us by the narrator from the views of him of his drinking companions (whom we never meet) and, later, from Lenehan's own musings; (3) in the atemporal disposition of the information through the first two-thirds of the text, after which a strictly chronological order is observed. In other words, the reader is highly dependent on the flawed, even masked, viewpoint of Lenehan for much of his knowledge of what is happening. This is even more critical in terms of plot where the true nature of Corley's intentions is masked by recurrent 'dummy-word' references ('bring **it** off', 'on **that point**', 'Corley's **adventure**', 'the **result**') until the final epiphany of the gold coin. This reveals a Narrative Structure which is virtually squeezed into the last eighth of the story, the essential peripeteia on the level of action being the reversal of the normal transaction of courtship and prostitution: Man uses Cash to acquire Sex → Man uses Sex to acquire Cash. But a close study of Point of View reveals that the action is wholly refracted through Lenehan's consciousness and this opens up a parallel reversal on the psychological plane: Lenehan, the admiring audience and disciple, has become voyeur, yet the vicarious gratification he seeks is not sexual but financial. Joyce's Dublin is even more corrupt than we had feared. An appraisal of Corley's and Lenehan's characters in the light of the story's title and the hints about the 'gallant' appearance and behaviour suggest that the deeper theme which permeates the story at every level is 'gallantry unmasked'. Every aspect of Corley and Lenehan, their appearance, their attitudes, and their actions is a subversion of a whole code of assumptions built up through a genre of literature over several centuries (though Joyce was himself well aware that the code of gallantry already held the seeds of its own subversion). This revised statement of the theme as 'gallantry unmasked' is the starting-point for the application of our other model.

7.3 A GENERATIVE MODEL

The second model I wish to test against Joyce's story is newer and more original, less dependent on categories from traditional literary criticism, and more challengingly problematic than the analytic one described above. It aims to be more rigorous in its methods, more explicit in its formulations, and more universal in its application.

Its proponents, Alexander Zholkovsky, a semanticist, and Yuri Scheglov, a literary structuralist (who both lived and worked in Moscow until 1978-9, but now work at Cornell and Montreal Universities respectively), see the whole literary text as being generated from a deep underlying theme through a repertoire of 'expression devices' which constitute a kind of generative grammar of text structure. After a somewhat provocative introduction to this notion in a popular academic literary journal in 1967 under the title 'A Structural Poetics is A Generative Poetics' (Zholkovsky and Scheglov 1967) they have applied it to the frame narrative in Sherlock Holmes stories (Scheglov 1968), to the 'Matron of Ephesus' anecdote in Petronius' *Satyricon* (Scheglov 1970), a Somali folk-tale (Zholkovsky 1970a) and a sketch for a film sequence by Eisenstein (Zholkovsky 1970b). The implications and problems that the model raises for poetic theory and method have been elaborated in detail in five long preprint articles published through the Russian Language Institute of the Soviet Academy of Sciences (Zholkovsky and Scheglov 1971, 1972, 1973, 1974 and Zholkovsky 1975).

The authors have described the relationship between Theme, Expression Devices, and Text as follows (1972: 6-7):

> Semantic models of language are a formalization of the well-known truth that language is a vehicle for transmitting thought. Similarly the approach to art which we are developing through our
>
> Theme —— *Expression Devices* ——→ Text
>
> model rests on a quite traditional notion of the nature of art which Leo Tolstoy expressed as follows: 'Art is a human activity whereby one man, consciously and making use of well-known external signs, transmits to others the sensations that he feels and they are infected with these sensations and experience them too'. (Tolstoy 'What is Art?'). If we adopt this view we may find a similarity between art and language

a. in being a kind of mechanism, a transformer; which
b. is set in motion by information of some kind (thoughts, feelings . . .); which
c. is transmitted by the mechanism using externalized signs.

The crucial distinction is

d. that the aim of art is not merely to transmit information but to *infect* with it; whereas with language it is sufficient for the listener to receive, comprehend and learn what is being communicated, with art he has to be penetrated by the communication; it has to capture the depths of his being, to become a part of his own experience.

We propose to attempt to fix this rather elementary notion of art in the following concepts. The information to be transmitted (the author's inmost thoughts, feelings, predilections, and intentions) is labelled the *Theme*. The mechanism which brings about the 'infection' of the receiver with the theme, that is, the mechanism for translating the declarative ('uninfectious') theme into a literary text is a repertoire of *Expression Devices*. Each of these is a rule for transforming elements of the Theme (or the results of previous transformation) in such a way as to *preserve the meaning but heighten the artistic expressiveness* ('infectiousness'). At the point of entry to an ED is some element; its output is an element (or a number of elements) synonymous with the first but more 'infectious'. (It is theoretically vital to separate clearly the semantics (theme) from the expressiveness (devices) in order to describe a complex of problems covered by diffuse labels such as 'artistic meaning', 'artistic expression', and so on; only such a rigorous separation makes it possible to explore the interesting relationships between theme and ED.)

Just as the structure of a sentence is described in a generative grammar by its transformational history, i.e. its derivation from a kernel structure through standard transformations, *we propose to regard as a description of a literary text the derivation of that text from a theme through the Expression Devices.* In other words, the ED are standard units for formulating the correspondence between a literary text and its meaning (theme). *The Text is a Theme plus ED. The Theme is a Text minus ED.* This postulate implies that the theme is a kind of semantic invariant of all the relative elements, aspects, episodes, etc. of the text, while the ED are ways of artistically varying the theme (according to the characteristic of EDs formulated above of preserving the meaning, while heightening the degree of expressiveness).

By this rather bold set of claims Zholkovsky and Scheglov have not only raised a host of problems about using generative models for poetics as powerful as ones used for studying sentence structures, but have, perhaps, put their finger on the central problem of semantics in a generative model. How could any model claim to produce 'all and only the well-formed structures' of a work of art? And however pervasive the deep Theme of the story, how could it possibly account for the syntagmatic meanings which are produced in the surface structure of an essentially linear art form like prose narratives?[2]

The Expression Devices which Zholkovsky and Scheglov have isolated so far are the following (I have added a conventional symbol after each label for reference in the examples):

1 CONCRETIZATION (REALIZATION) (→): one element X is replaced by a more concrete element (or combination of elements) which includes all the denotata of X, i.e. a general case is replaced by a particular one, a genus by a species, a species by a member, a whole by one of its parts, e.g. 'egoism' → 'conceit'; 'entrance' → 'door'; 'danger in the woods' → 'big bad wolf'; 'Red Riding Hood used to take cakes to her granny' → 'One day she took cakes to her granny'.

2 MAGNIFICATION (<): element X is replaced by an element which exceeds it in some dimension, i.e. in size, intensity, duration, etc., e.g. 'day' < 'week'; 'once' < 'many times'; 'what big ears you have, granny!'—'All the better to hear you with!' < 'What big teeth you have, granny!'—'All the better to eat you with!'

3 REPETITION (//): one element is replaced by several others more or less identical with it: 'door' // 'door 1', 'door 2', 'door 3': 'What big eyes you have, granny!'—'All the better to see you with!' // 'What big ears you have, granny!'—'All the better to hear you with!' As the last examples in 2 and 3 make clear, REPETITION (which is a kind of MAGNIFICATION in number) must be distinguished from MAGNIFICATION proper whereby an element is replaced by only one other element; 'eyes—so see' and 'ears—to hear' are both equally neutral semantically, whereas, 'teeth—to eat you' MAGNIFIES the general statements into a specific threat.

4 MULTIPLE REALIZATION (VARIATION) ({): one element X is replaced by several new elements each of which includes all the denotata of X, but which are strongly distinct from each other, e.g. 'modern technical equipment' {'electric shaver', 'motorbike', 'tape recorder': 'touching' {'embracing', 'wounding'; 'dallying in the woods' { 'picking flowers', 'listening to birds', 'talking to woodcutters'.

5 CONTRAST (/): one element X is replaced by a pair of elements X and Anti-X which are opposites in some respect, e.g. 'black' → 'black' / 'white'; 'death' → 'life' / 'death'; 'granny' (i.e. security) → 'granny' / 'wolf' (i.e. 'security' / 'danger').

6 ANTECEDENCE (↣ or ↢): one element X is replaced by a pair, X and Pre-X, where Pre-X precedes X in the text and is in some respect an incomplete version of X, a lack of X or an Anti-X, e.g. 'Holmes' client arrives' ↣ 'a cab is heard pulling up', 'steps are heard coming up the stairs', 'there is a ring at the door', 'the client appears'.

Direct ANTECEDENCE (anticipation) (↣) includes all kinds of forewarning, prophecy, tragic irony, and other kinds of foreshadowing: e.g. 'Red Riding Hood's mother always told her not to stop in the woods and to look out for the big bad wolf'.

REVERSAL (↞) is really a combination of ANTECEDENCE and CONTRAST. It is the mechanism underlying all peripeteias in narrative structure, but it also produces smaller scale oppositions such as 'granny' ↞ 'wolf-granny' and 'axe (for cutting wood)' ↞ 'axe (for killing and chopping open wolves)'.

7 COMBINATION (+): two elements X and Y are replaced by a single element which includes all the characteristics of X and Y, e.g. 'touch' + 'pain' → 'wounding';
'innocence' + 'trust' → 'gullibility'.

7a AGREEMENT (ↀ): element X is replaced by a new element which includes all the characteristics of X and a certain characteristic P which pertains to element Y. Clearly most metaphors are produced by this mechanism.

8 ABBREVIATION (- - -): element X is replaced by some part of X such that all the information contained in X which is needed for the theme expressed by X may be reconstructed, e.g. metonymy and synecdoche.

Zholkovsky and Scheglov have pointed out that cases of transformation or derivation often arise where two Expression Devices combine in a given step, or where (as we saw with MAGNIFICATION and REPETITION) the boundary between two EDs is hard to establish. However, their many examples of the derivation process in action and its application to episodes in works from many genres, periods and cultures indicate that this model 'works' to the extent that it explicates many systematic structural relationships in a text and produces many new and valuable insights into latent meanings and that it has a rare degree of universality.[3]

Where their generative model particularly needs testing, however, is on a complete and acknowledged work of literature. They have successfully used many separate episodes from Ovid, Petronius, Molière, Conan Doyle, Jules Verne, Pasternak, and Ilf and Petrov to illustrate and explore the functions of the Expression Devices, but the only full derivation of a whole literary Text from its Theme has been that carried out on a maxim by La Rochefoucauld (their 1972 paper). As that derivation of a four-line text took some fifty pages to expound, it is a foolhardy task indeed to attempt to derive a seven-page classic by James Joyce in three diagrams and some notes. Hopefully, however, some detailed explanation of the diagrams will help to clarify many steps in the synthesis. Like my other published attempt to apply this model (O'Toole 1975) to a complete work, Conan Doyle's 'The Sussex Vampire', there will inevitably be oversimplifications and steps missed out. The subtlety and elegance with which Zholkovsky and Scheglov probe the semantic interstices of every theme and stage in the derivation would be hard to emulate. What may be clearer in the type of treatment presented here is the relationship between various stages in the derivation and the larger structures of Character, Narrative Structure, and Point of View.

As we said earlier, we will take as *Theme* the notion '*gallantry unmasked*'. (And a quite full analysis of a work is clearly needed in order to isolate a usable Theme before any synthesis can be attempted. Nor do the Russian authors make clear at what stage one decides to abandon a particular theme in favour of another; that is, how confident is the researcher of the monovalency of his Expression Devices? The derivation could be going awry because of ambiguity about the *order* in which they apply, about the degree to which they may be *combined*, or about the uniqueness of the *results* of, for instance, operations like MAGNIFICATION or CONTRAST—problems not entirely unknown to generative linguists!) We then isolated ten components of the traditional concept of 'gallantry' which seem to play a role in the story (see Figure 7.1).

As so often happens, the story's title takes on greater and greater significance as we explore more deeply, for our 'two gallants' represent through their appearance, speech and actions virtually all aspects of the traditional code of gallantry. Like the Three Musketeers, they contrast strongly with, while being strongly dependent on, each other. Not being quite up to strength, and belonging to Dublin in the twentieth century rather than Paris in the sixteenth, most of their gallantry is flawed.

The traditional gallant was bold and decisive in action; in Corley this is magnified into rudeness, egoism and exploitation, while in Lenehan it is reversed into weakness, doubt and anxiety (see Figure 7.1, box a) which is connected to certain neurotic symptoms which can be traced as stemming from other aspects of gallantry. These will be discussed below in relation to Figure 7.2: the gallant was eloquent and subtle in speech, free and independent in his life-style and a loyal comrade; as we shall see, almost all of these qualities have been significantly inverted in both Corley and Lenehan.

In Figure 7.1 we can see how the gallant theme of chivalry to women (box e) is concretized into the most conventional of courtship rituals, each phase of which is ironically reversed. From the first magic encounter ('where did you pick her up, Corley?') with a fair damsel ('I spotted a fine tart') and a fond farewell ('and said goodnight,

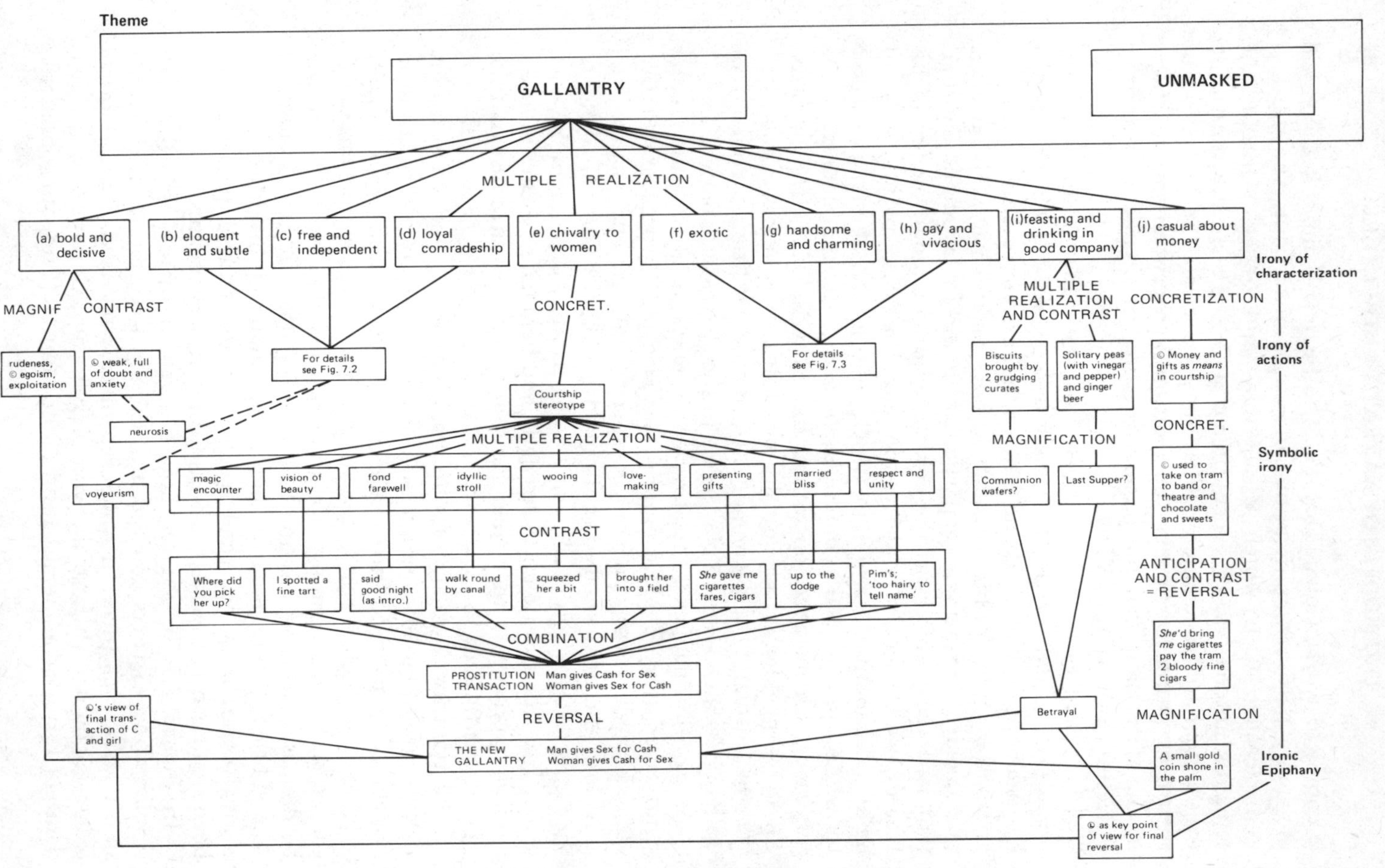

Fig. 7.1 Gallantry unmasked: a generative chart

you know'—the standard way of *greeting* a prostitute!) via a first idyllic stroll ('We went for a walk round by the canal') and a first timid contact ('I put my arm round her and squeezed her a bit that night') to the ecstasy of love-making ('We went out to Donnybrook and I brought her into a field there'), not, we will have noted by now, with a pure and virginal dairymaid but with a slavey who 'told me she used to go with a dairyman'! Even the presentation of gifts was in reverse, by her to him, and the gifts were second-hand ('two bloody fine cigars—O, the real cheese, you know, that the old fellow used to smoke'). The ultimate dream of marriage and family bliss sets the ironic seal on this cynical 'romance';

'. . . I was afraid, man, she'd get in the family way. But she's up to the dodge!' 'Maybe she thinks you'll marry her', said Lenehan. 'I told her I was out of a job', said Corley.

All these inversions of the gallant tradition of courtly love combine to make up a transaction that is doubly ironic: it is not just that love has been redefined as prostitution, but that prostitution itself has been turned upside down: in this travesty of a relationship it is the man who gives sex for cash and the woman who gives cash for sex.

Of all the reversals in the story, this is the reversal that most ruthlessly 'unmasks gallantry'. Yet the essential actions in this plot are never seen because we have to rely first on Corley's cynical account of the affair and later on Lenehan's heavily obstructed (physically, intellectually, and morally) point of view for all our information about it. If we follow the realization of the key 'gallant' qualities in Figure 7.2, it is clear that they are realized (inversely) most fully in Lenehan, the observer, not in Corley, the man of action.

The 'eloquent and subtle' quality (box b) is CONCRETIZED directly in the text as Lenehan's lively speech which is revealed in such idiomatic phrases as 'that takes the biscuit', REPEATED three times and MAGNIFIED into the rhythmic and exotic 'That takes the solitary, unique, and, if I may so call it, *recherché* biscuit!' and the complex subordinate structures of Lenehan's speech. But the words CONTRAST with the voice 'winnowed of vigour' in which they are uttered and it is the negation of eloquence and subtlety which predominates for the rest of the story, CONCRETIZED into a paragraph of extraordinary vacuity describing Lenehan's wanderings and conversation with two friends after his meal. The placing of this conversation in the story and the minute detail of who said what to whom and where accentuate its total lack of content, apart from some incidental names of places and people.[4] Vacuousness,

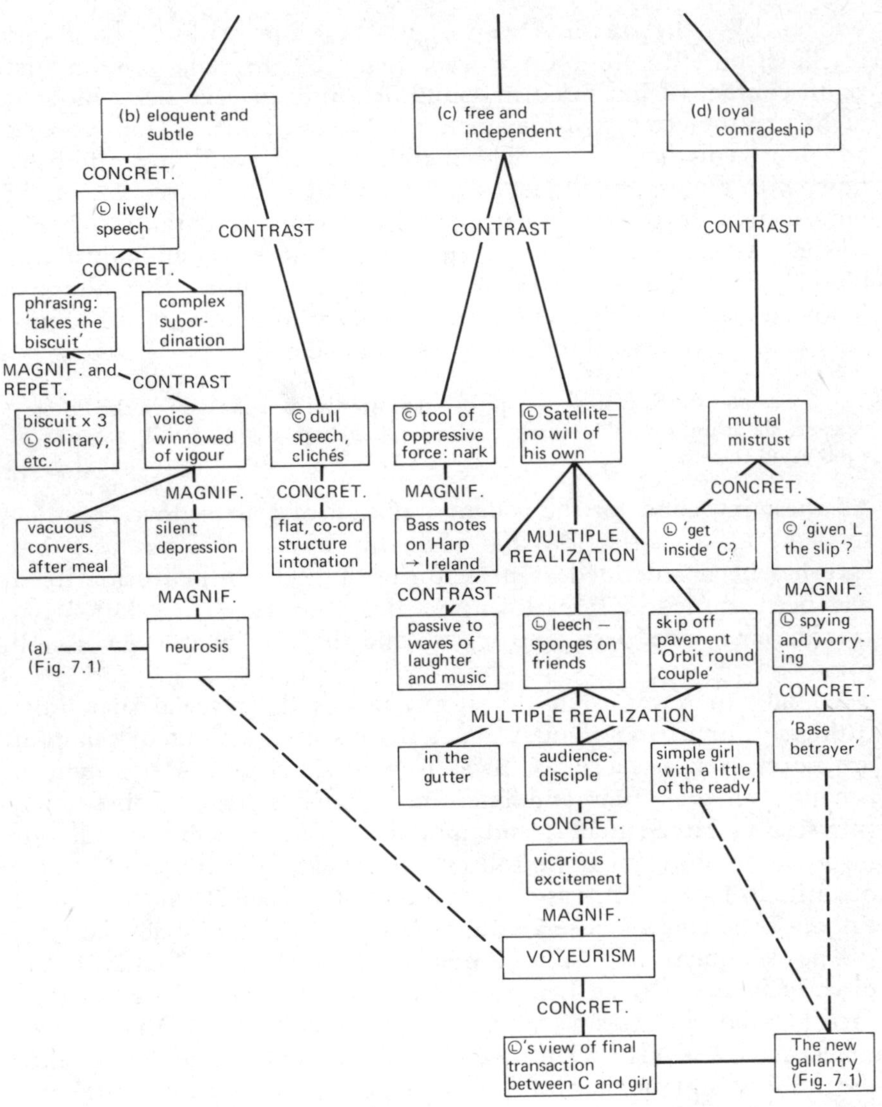

Fig. 7.2 Gallantry unmasked: first detailed analysis

like circularity is realized formally in the story. Lenehan's silent depression at this point has a neurotic quality by the time Corley returns with the girl.

Corley might appear at first sight to have some of the freedom and independence (box c) we expect from a gallant man of action. But there are strong hints that he is an informer to the police. This

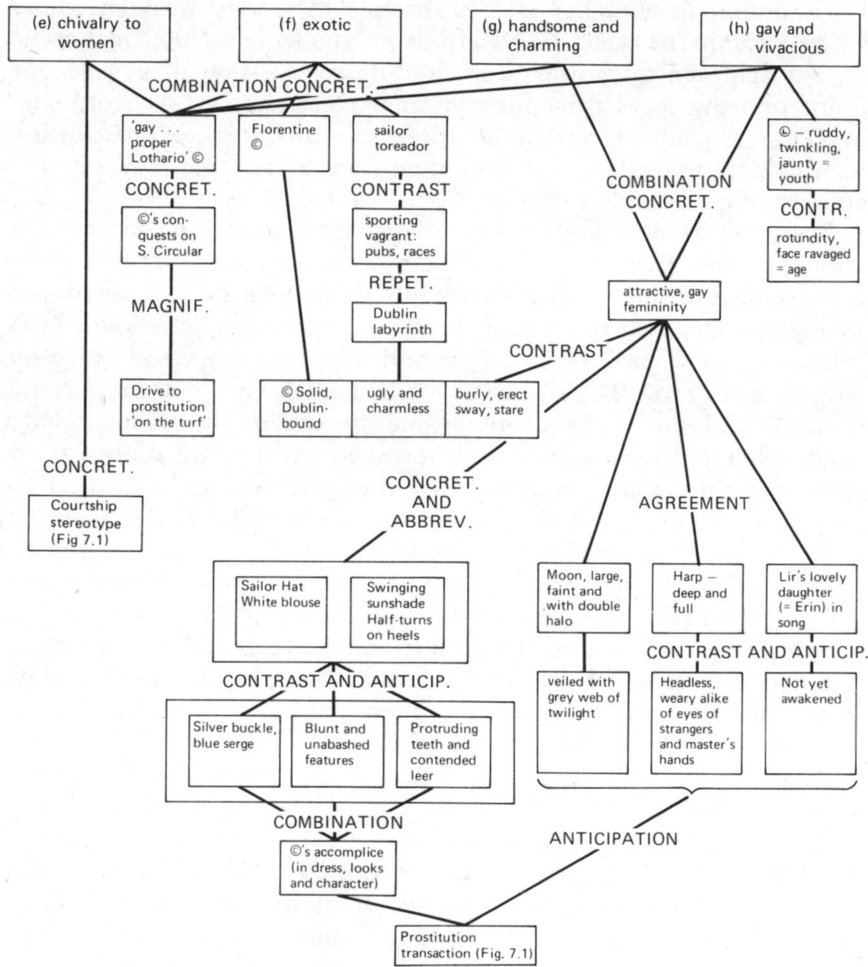

Fig. 7.3 Gallantry unmasked: second detailed analysis

alien quality seems to be MAGNIFIED in the symbolic harp music where the heavy bass notes seem to mark the heavy tread of the 'copper's nark'. Lenehan's lack of independence becomes more significant as the story progresses. He is a satellite to the globular Corley as he skips off the pavement or describes an orbit around the couple; he is known as a 'leech' who sponges on his friends; most revealing is his total passivity to the music and to the waves of laughter which seem to break over him in a passage where virtually every verb involving Lenehan is passive. His dream of happiness is to sponge off 'a simple girl with a little of the ready', but in reality he is bound as audience and as disciple to Corley through whose seedy exploits he gains his vicarious excitement. By the final scene he has achieved the ultimate in satellite roles—that of *voyeur*. His point of view is essential for the final reversal since the gold coin in Corley's palm represents not only the inversion of prostitution (Corley's transaction), but the inversion of *voyeurism*: only the glimpse of gold satisfies Peeping Tom Lenehan.

Even the ironic manifestation of gallant feasting and drinking in good company (see Figure 7.1, box i) strengthens the ironic epiphany. If Lenehan's earlier meal of 'some biscuits which he had asked two grudging curates to bring him' suggest communion wafers, his later solitary meal of peas with vinegar and pepper and washed down by ginger beer have the bitterness of a Last Supper. Both portend betrayal. All the ideals of the romantic dream of gallantry have been subverted, unmasked, and betrayed by the end of the story save one: the loyal comradeship of the gallants is still intact. Both may have feared treachery ('would he give him the slip?'; 'Are you trying to get inside me?') but they are bound indissolubly together. Just as the tradition of courtly love was indebted to the 'troubadour-gallant' for its knowledge of the noble deeds accomplished by the 'knight-gallant', so we are indebted to our 'voyeur-babbler', Lenehan, for our knowledge of the noble deeds of the 'soldier-like' Corley. There are *two* gallants and for their existence (since 'gallantry' is a fantasy) they depend on each other.

As we have indicated, only four of the ten 'gallant' qualities appear to be realized directly in the Text: (b) *eloquence and subtlety* in Lenehan's speech early in the story; (e) the notion of *chivalry* (Corley as Lothario); (f) *exoticism* in Corley's aspiration of the first letter of his name 'after the manner of Florentines' and Lenehan's faintly maritime aspect and toreador fashion of carrying his waterproof; (h) *gaiety and vivacity* in a certain initial liveliness in Lenehan's movements and behaviour. Most of the multiple realizations of 'gallantry' are realized only in reverse: we are conscious of 'what might have been' (boldness-decisiveness-independence-loyalty-glamour) by implicit CONTRAST with 'what is' (egoism-vacillation-satellitism-mutual mistrust-ugliness). As can be seen at the extreme right of the Diagram, the 'unmasking' element of the Theme works at the level of characterization: almost every line in the portraits of our two 'gallants' is drawn with irony. The operation of EDs such as MAGNIFICATION and MULTIPLE REALIZATION then intensifies the negativity of the portrayal by showing the gallants' *actions* in an ironic light: Lenehan's enthusiasm turns out to be fraught with anxiety, Corley's earlier amorous conquests have turned to prostitution: his latest brings him presents; our first impression of a pretty, demure girl (see Figure 7.3) turns out on (Lenehan's) closer inspection to be a good match both physically and morally for her 'knight errant'. The symbols of moon, harp, and song (*Silent O Moyle*, whose words we appear to be expected to know) provide both an ironic commentary on the episodes in which they appear and an ironic anticipation of the poignancy and comedy of the final reversal. The small gold coin is both a CONCRETIZATION + CONTRAST + MAGNIFICATION of a true gallant's attitude to money and the crucial epiphany which reverses all our expectations about the outcome of the plot and illuminates every detail of the story with its glow.

7.4 CONCLUSION

I shall continue to prefer an analytical model for my own work, since it leads more readily (and less ambiguously) to reasoned interpretation. Though less formal and explicit in its operations, it still seems to keep a firmer rein on productive intuitions than does the highly formal step-by-step derivation of the synthetic model. Nor does it wholly submerge general theoretical problems of literary structure and the way we perceive it in a sea of interpretative detail. In any case the analytical model is as much a representation of the realization of semantic options as is the generative model. A system-network representing options for the depiction of Character might look like the following:

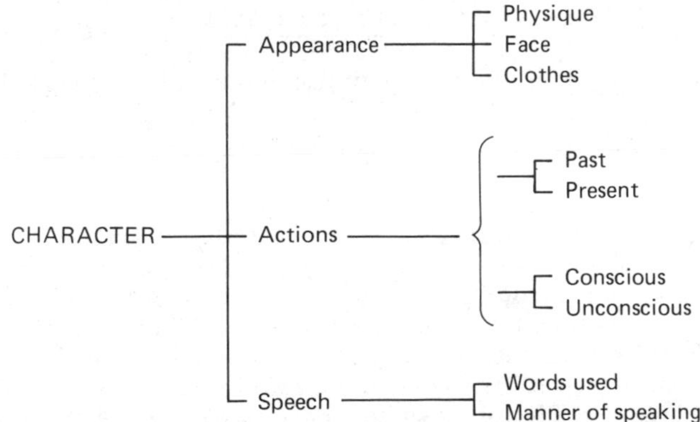

Fig. 7.4 A system network for Character

Point of view, on the other hand, might require the following network of options:

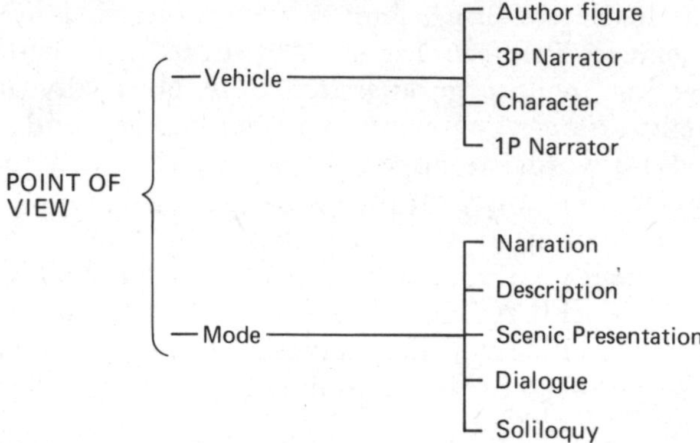

Fig. 7.5 A system network for Point of view

Ultimately, then, these models are not opposed. Concretization in the generative model is similar in its operation to the realization of deep meanings in surface structure in a systemic model. While it is common enough in literary criticism to work 'from the outside-in' as with my analytical approach, working 'from the inside-out' as do Zholkovsky and Scheglov demands a degree of semantic alertness and subtlety which prompts many new intuitions. To derive a whole literary Text from a complex underlying Theme requires one to maintain an overall grasp of the structure and content of the work which brings out many new relationships. The Expression Devices reflect, perhaps, universal psychological mechanisms of text production and perception of considerable validity. The very starkness of their hypothesis that

$$\text{Theme} \xrightarrow{\textit{Expression Devices}} \text{Text}$$

is, I think, a major challenge to semioticians of language, literature, and culture.

NOTES

1. The group analysis of this story was held during a symposium at Thaxted, Essex in February 1975. The symposium on 'Structures in Literary Texts' was organized jointly by the Department of Language and Linguistics at the University of Essex and the Neo-Formalist Circle. While the author is indebted to his fellow participants in the discussion for many acute and valuable insights and interpretations, he must accept the main responsibility for the shortcomings of their synthesis into an integrated view of the story's theme, narrative structure, and linguistic texture.
2. These problems were among the valuable comments and criticisms made by colleagues during the discussion following my paper at Burg Wartenstein. They are further discussed in O'Toole 1978.

3. It was pointed out that the Expression Devices, once they have been adequately tested, provide a powerful and relatively precise tool for the comparative study of literature, whether in terms of period or of genre. They may, moreover, have even wider relevance as universals in forms of ritual and other areas of folk culture.
4. Mention was made in discussion of the use of a similar device in *Anna Karenina* and *The Magic Mountain*. There are clearly times when a passage achieves its significance in a literary work by being drained in this way of semantic content, reflecting the boredom of Anna's life with Vronsky once the romance is over, or of life in a sanatorium, or of the 'poet-troubadour' waiting for the action to begin.

BIBLIOGRAPHY

Chatman, S. (ed.) (1971), *Literary Style: A Symposium*, London, Oxford University Press.

Fowler, R. (ed.) (1975), *Style and Structure in Literature: Essays in the New Stylistics*, Oxford, Basil Blackwell.

Greimas, A. J. (ed.) (1970), *Sign–Language–Culture*, The Hague, Mouton.

Halliday, M. A. K. (1971), 'Linguistic function and literary style: An inquiry into the language of William Golding's *The Inheritors*' in Chatman (ed.) (1971).

O'Toole, L. M. (1971), 'Structure and style in the short story: Chekhov's "Student" ', *Slavonic and East European Review*, 48, No. 114 (January): 45–67.

O'Toole, L. M. (1972), 'Structure and style in the short story: Dostoevsky's "A Gentle Spirit" ', *Tijdschrift voor Slavische Taalen Letterkunde*, 1: 81–116, The Hague, Mouton.

O'Toole, L. M. (1975), 'Analytic and synthetic approaches to narrative structure: Sherlock Holmes and "The Sussex Vampire" ', in Fowler (ed.) (1975: 143–76).

O'Toole, L. M. (1976), 'Narrative structure and living texture: Joyce's "Two Gallants" ', *PTL: A Journal for Descriptive Poetics and Theory of Literature*, 1: 441–58.

O'Toole, L. M. (1978), 'What price rigor?', *PTL*, 3: 429–35.

O'Toole, L. M. (1982), *Structure, Style and Interpretation in the Russian Story*, London and New Haven, Yale University Press.

O'Toole, L. M. and Shukman, A. (eds) (1971), *Russian Poetics in Translation*, Oxford, School House, Somerton, and Holdan Books.

Rey-Debove, J. (ed.) (1973), *Recherche sur les systèmes significantes*, The Hague, Mouton.

Scheglov, Yu. K. (1968), 'Opisanie struktury detektivnoi novelly' (A description of detective story structure), *Preprints for the International Symposium on Semiotics* (Warsaw 1968), reprinted in J. Rey-Debove (1973: 343–72).

Scheglov, Yu. K. (1970), 'Matrona iz Efesa' (The widow of Ephesus), in Greimas (ed.) (1970: 591–600).

Zholkovsky, A. K. (1970a), 'Somaliiskii rasskaz "Ispytanie proritsatelya" (opyt porozhdayuschego opisaniya)' (The Somali story 'Testing the Oracle' (an attempt at a generative description)); *Narody Azii i Afriki*, 1: 104–15.

Zholkovsky, A. K. (1970b), 'Porozhdayuschaya poetika v rabotakh S. M. Eizenshteina' (Generative poetics in the writings of Eisenstein), in Greimas (ed.) (1970: 451–68).

Zholkovsky, A. K. (1974), 'K opisaniyu smysla svyaznogo teksta', V. Ibid. *Vypusk*, 61.

Zholkovsky, A. K. and Scheglov, Yu. K. (1967), 'Strukturnaya poetika-porozhdayuschaya poetika', *Voprosy literatury*, 1: 73-89.

Zholkovsky, A. K. and Scheglov, Yu. K. (1971), *K opisaniyu smysla svyaznogo teksta* (Institut russkogo yazyka AN SSSR, predvaritelnye publikatsii, *Vypusk*, 22, I: 'Ponyatiya temy i poeticheskogo mira' (the concepts of 'theme' and 'poetic world'). English translation in O'Toole and Shukman (1971: 4-50).

Zholkovsky, A. K. and Scheglov, Yu. K. (1972), Ibid. *Vypusk*, 33, II: 'Tema i priyomy vyrazitelnosti. Primer vyvoda khudozhestvennogo teksta iz temy' (theme and expression devices: an example of the derivation of a literary text from a theme).

Zholkovsky, A. K. and Scheglov, Yu. K. (1973-4), Ibid. *Vypusk*, 39 and 49, II and IV, 'Priyomy vyrazitelnosti' (expression devices).

8 Relations between environmental and linguistic structure

Donald Preziosi
State University of New York, Binghampton, U.S.A.

We are distinguished from the bulk of the biosphere by virtue of the fact that over the past million years we have elaborated a growing series of extensions to our organisms whose developments have shifted evolution from our bodies to our extensions, thereby tremendously accelerating the evolutionary process. It is suggested, moreover, that the elaboration of these extensions has, in turn, modified our bodily structures in the direction of our present condition (Hall 1966).

The set of such extensions comprises an extremely rich, highly dynamic assemblage under continuous transformation, re-evaluation and reorientation. Each new construct potentially offers a re-evaluation of the universe of knowledge or some fragment of it. This assemblage of extensions is capable of continually revealing itself anew in fresh and unexpected ways that are in essence inexhaustible.

The position of the built environment as a central component or matrix in this cultural assemblage has been long noted but seldom appreciated to any profound degree. In part, this situation is due to three factors: to the very great apparent complexity of environmental structure *vis-à-vis* other cultural ensembles; to a misreading of its conceptual boundaries and intersections with other ensembles; and to a pervasive belief, especially among theoreticians of environmental structure, that the relationships between built form and other cultural systems are of a deterministic nature.

The study of the human environment—the built world—may be said to define a conceptual space formed by the intersection of certain key issues in human psychology, anthropology, sociology, and communication theory. As a coherent inquiry, the study of environmental structure (which study we might term architectonics)[1] focuses upon the complex relationships between culture and physical form.

The forms of dwelling or settlement are not simply the result of physical forces or of any single set of causal factors, but are rather the consequences of a broad range of sociocultural interactions (Rapoport 1969). Furthermore, the relationships between geographical, economic, and survival factors and the forms of human settlement are not deterministic in nature. The wide differences in built form across the face of the earth are much more closely tied to dynamic ensembles of cultural factors than to any of the aforementioned. Moreover, differences may be observed not only in the manner whereby humans conceptually represent the world around, but also in the very ways of perceiving that world (Yi-Fu Tuan 1974).

We take here the position that environmental structure comprises a complexly-ordered system of relationships (which we have elsewhere termed *formal syntax*; Preziosi 1975) directly and indirectly observable in sensory products or artefacts. This system of relationships is not coterminous with the sum of environmental artefacts.

Environmental structure may be composed of existent portions of a landscape both built and used. Furthermore, we will consider that individuals themselves may become transitory artefacts through the use of bodily decoration, ritual movement, and linguistic scoring. Often, environmental structuration may involve an absence or near-absence of spatial artefacts (Rapoport 1972). Indeed, a theory of environmental structure will necessarily have to take into account the fact that dwelling or settlement may not involve interventions in landscape beyond patterns of bodily orientation. We acknowledge that perception is in essence construction and reconstruction, and hold that the non-built environment becomes artefactual due to our perceptual intervention.

Thus, we consider that the core of the architectonic phenomenon is not necessarily tied to environmental artefacts; though its presence is pervasive in nearly all human societies (Marshall 1960), the built world is not a necessary component of environmental structure:

> It takes the women only three-quarters of an hour to build their shelters, but half the time at least the women's whim is not to build shelters at all. In this case they sometimes put up two sticks to symbolize the entrance of the shelters so that the family may orient itself as to which side is the man's side and which the women's side of the fire. Sometimes they do not bother with the sticks. [Marshall 1959]

Consequently, architectonics as a field of enquiry overlaps the traditional boundaries of disciplines which have focused severally upon the history of built form, the properties directly and indirectly manifested or realized by built form, environmental cognition and perception, 'man-environment' relations, 'kinetics', and studies of the nature of spatial appropriation and behaviour in individuals and groups, and environmental symbolism.

It has become increasingly clear in recent years that a number of important structural equivalences exists between certain aspects of the behaviour of organic systems, systems of linguistic and para-linguistic communication, and the organization and functioning of artefact ensembles (Preziosi 1975). A good deal of current research on environmental structure has both explicitly and implicitly held that this study cannot remain entirely self-centred and independent of work in those areas of human knowledge concerned with the multifarious aspects of human communication and interaction. Indeed, it is largely by seeing the built world as a component in a dynamic, interactive cultural ensemble that its unique properties may be more finely isolated.

Attempts to integrate work in cognate areas with the study of environmental structure are still in their infancy. All too often, these many diverse attempts to work in a comparative manner have little more in common than a clumsy and insensitive translation of the methods and data-language of other disciplines into environmental structure (Collins 1965). Whether or not there is a 'grammar of vision' (Gregory 1970), 'architecture' is not language or a language in a sense directly equivalent to verbal language.

The time is past due when we should focus fully upon environmental structure without all the worst of the constraints imposed by literal translations of work in cognate areas of cultural study. Yet we should also remain in touch with some of the original insights and intuitions which have led the study of the environment into flirtations with information theory, systems theory, structuralist anthropology and linguistics, and semiotics. While much has been learnt over the past couple of decades, the tricycle won't support the elephant. Rather than replacing broken tricycles with new ones, we should begin in earnest to design a vehicle which will.

In this chapter we shall attempt to sketch the broad outlines of the parameters of architectonics through a consideration of its relational boundaries with the ensemble of culture as a whole, and with its immediate boundaries with linguistic structure. We have already begun the former task through a consideration of the structural nature of the cultural ensemble in general, and will continue to return to this question. We shall now turn to a consideration of the latter task.

Environment and linguistic structure are not directly comparable on what might be called levels of manifestation or realization. A word, sentence, or unit of discourse does not in any physical or material way resemble a built space, building, or any other fragment of the built environment, however partitioned. But are the two terms of this abortive equation the correct terms? In other words, might it be more useful to suggest some resemblance between built form and, say, recorded speech acts (on the one hand), and what we have termed above environmental structure and verbal language or linguistic structure?

That is to say, might it not be possible to consider that the built environment bears a similar relationship to the cognitive properties and culturally-embedded rules and organizations of human spatial behaviour that written or otherwise recorded speech bears to the cognitive organizations underlying speech—i.e., grammatical structure (however modelled)? Seen from this perspective, a building or a city might be considered as a quasi-permanent record of behavioural stage-directions or scorings, a rich, multi-channel set of directions suggesting culturally appropriate spatial behaviours, orientations, and interactions. A building may be seen as offering parameters on social interaction, of opening up certain possibilities and constraining others.

Clearly, the built world 'speaks' in this way, among others, and it has long been noted that the built world presents particular transformations and embeddings of a culture's knowledge of itself and of the world. Leaving aside for a moment the nature of the connections between artefacts and their intended or effective 'meanings' (Mackay 1970), we might draw certain analogies between built environments and animal displays (von Frisch 1974) or (a somewhat better analogy) between buildings and what have been recently termed 'sematectonic' artefacts of certain animals (Wilson 1975).

The analogies are suggestive, but in the final analysis misleading. Let us consider, in general, that communication is a process wherein the behaviour of one individual organism alters the probability of behavioural acts in other organisms (of the same or differing species). By sematectonic communication is meant the evocation of any form of behaviour or physiological change by the evidence of work performed by other organisms: the mere sight of nests constructed by a species can acquire a communicative function and serve as a 'petrified display signal' (Wilson 1975); structures built by animals can be the most durable signal source of all, becoming a means for the increase of information (over displays and call-systems).

The analogy is misleading in the sense that it overlooks what appear to be profound differences between non-human signal systems (as currently understood) and systems of communication evolved by humans, which are by and large built on an underlying property of 'duality' (Hockett and Ascher 1964). In other words, in human language, units which signify are inherently arbitrary in form; meaning in human language is a property of the relational connectivity between elements rather than a property of the elements themselves.

Even the most cursory consideration of environmental structure will reveal the same property of arbitrariness or of 'semi-autonomy' (Preziosi 1975) between built forms and their cultural and cognitive connotations, meanings, functions, usages, etc. The spatial structure of a building is as arbitrary as the acoustical structure of a word, and as variable cross-culturally. There may or may not be 'archetypal forms' cross-culturally; this issue is as vexed as that of 'universal grammar' in verbal language (Eliade 1959; Nitschke 1974); we will return to comment on this problem below.

We might say, then, that the built world shows an equivalent relationship to 'animal architecture' that human language shows to animal communication. It also appears that an equivalency may be shown to exist on another axis: the built world is to environmental structure as speech acts are to grammar. But here, the analogy is not quite so patent: it appears that we must carefully distinguish between speech acts. Consider that for hundreds of thousands of years, humans used the environment (both built and unbuilt) in much the same way that we now also use written texts—for the storage of information. Indeed, it is important to bear in mind that writing is clearly an outgrowth of a number of systems for recording information (as well as speech), including pictorial representation and symbolization, calendrical notation, and other environmental marking devices.[2]

It is equally important to bear in mind that the development of systems of recording speech has had a profound feedback effect upon other forms of informational storage, including architecture, for the use of the built environment for the storage of information is consciously developed by a number of cultures (Yates 1966). One of the functions of the built world, in its palaeolithic origins and today, is as a memory bank (Preziosi 1976). Greek and Roman orators consciously trained themselves to make of portions of the built world ideograms or visual mnemonic devices in delivering long arguments in public places.

So, the built world, like a written text, stores information. Similarly, it is internally cross-referencing; portions of the built environment refer to other portions of this ensemble of forms. It is under continual transformation; the imposition of a new construct in a built environment reverberates with other, extant constructs. Patterns of formal orderings may come into being, suggesting that forms have a quasi-life of their own. Such patterns are colloquially referred to as 'style', which may involve formal harmonies over many different levels of environmental organization, harmonies which may be consciously or unconsciously elaborated. But note that patterns of formal harmonies *may* come into being in the history of an environmental ensemble—suggesting that patent stylistic orderings may not be properties of built form but rather characteristics of certain ensembles of built form. Just as the existence of built form is not universal in all cultures, so also patent stylistic harmonies may not be found universally.[3]

However, the built world cannot be compared directly to either written texts or speech acts, but will be seen as in some way comparable to both. Let us be clear about what we are doing: we are saying that from the point of view of a certain analogic structure, the built world, in such a binary, linearized equation, comes out as apparently equivalent to speech acts and records of speech acts more or less simultaneously. A visual metaphor: consider a space in projective geometry within which speech acts and texts are two separate points which project onto the same plane, built form. In other words, what we are saying is that within the constraints of a linearized equation, the aforementioned equivalency seems plausible. But as we shall see, there may be other ways of conceptually representing this set of relationships which are not as rigid. The above may simply be an artefact of our initial starting position.

It is important at this point to observe how radically environmental and linguistic structure diverge on the side of forms of manifestation or realization. Speech acts do not remain frozen in the air like word-balloons in cartoon strips, to be observed the following morning. But records of speech acts may remain, like neon signs in Las Vegas. The construction of a built form may involve the labour of generations of slaves, or merely the bending down of a branch by a single hand, done in an instant. An environmental artefact may endure as long as millenniums, or as briefly as an open umbrella in a rainstorm, a game of chess played with real individuals, or a parade down Broadway.

So, we see an important difference between linguistic and environmental forms with respect to *duration*. However, such differences are minimizable. Other differences are patent: both systems contrast with respect to scale, and to the nature of the media involved.

Speech acts are chiefly auditory phenomena; built forms are chiefly spatio-massive. A system of built form may incorporate anything palpable; speech acts are limited to the range of soundings which the human body, and particularly the vocal tract, are capable of generating. Speech acts occur in a linear stream over time, while built forms occur in a tripartite space-manifold in time, involving simultaneity of decoding as well as linearization: the manner of 'reading' an environmental display is a function of the geometry suggested (but not determined absolutely) by a given form. When an architectural historian refers to differences between, say, the conceptions of space in a Roman versus a Greek building, an important part of what is being referred to is a difference in the suggested manner of reading each assemblage. A given construct may in fact be 'readable' from a single, central point (as for example is often the case with centralized Renaissance dwellings, where from a single central point the organizational geometry of the totality becomes clear), or readability may be a function of certain spatial passages through a construct (which may be reversible), or it may involve deliberate ambiguities, hierarchical embeddings, and complex spatial geometries not easily verbalizable, but none the less palpable: this does *not* necessarily place environmental forms more in line with 'poetic' usage in verbal language (in the sense of the poetic function of communication in Sebeok 1962). Indeed, this equation is more misleading than useful, and arguments along this line inevitably reduce to the values of class struggles in certain societies. We should rather recognize that the built world serves a variety of communicative functions; a case can easily be made for architecture as emotive, phatic, cognitive, conative, metacommunicative, and poetic (Sebeok 1962).

Thus, despite wide differences in medium, duration, scale, and the geometries of internal structural organization, there appear to be groups of overlapping functions present here. In other words, there is a certain amount of redundancy between these two cultural ensembles. This is apart from a consideration of the continuous interactive relationship between speech acts and built forms arising from a positional simultaneity (we speak within built and/or appropriated environments, and much of speech—and of built form—is simultaneously cross-indexed with the other). Certainly, a reasonable case can be made for the survival value of such redundancy as an increase in the strength of a signal and its staying power, an increase or amplification of information. A simple analogy may be made with certain animal displays accompanied by calls: despite important differences in the organization of the analogized systems in humans and other species, the resultant redundancies serve to increase information in both cases.

Consider the potential differences in the following statements:

1. Leave me alone.
2. Step over that line and I'll knock your block off.

The 'line' in (2) may be (a) unindicated bodily; (b) a movement of the eyes downward to the ground; (c) a movement in the air by a finger or hand; (d) a line in the sand made by a foot; (e) a doorway; (f) a street or neighbourhood markers; (g) the barbed-wire boundary of a nation-state; and so forth. Conative statements made by a man in a costume sharply different from those of everyone else in a group, sitting on a golden chair in a certain kind of space, has, within the patterns of expectation held in common by a given cultural group, potentially more power than identical statements made by one's fellow bus-passenger.

It is important to stress the potentiality of this, however; as will be amplified below, the principle of duality (or gratuity or semi-autonomy) in the organization of linguistic and environmental systems precludes the determinism inherent in the simultaneous call-displays of some other species. Nor are the resemblances between cities and beehives any more than superficial.

At any rate, it is clear that much of the content of verbal language is environmentally referential, and that much of environmental form is linguistically evocative. We should take care to stress both sides of this statement, and to emphasize that a redundancy exists here (as noted above). It is important to resolve the bind within which *either* language *or* 'visual thinking' are held to be *the* 'central component' of a culture (Jakobson 1973; Arnheim 1971), or that one or the other provides a master key to the *Zeitgeist* of a given culture. Students of language as well as of the environment have by and large been equally provincial on this matter.

At the beginning of this chapter, we referred to environmental structure as a central component or matrix of the cultural assemblage. But it is not *the* central component any more than verbal language is. We have become what we are as a species through the interactive evolution of linguistic and environmental structure, the two lenses of a stereoscopic construction of realities. It may well be as important to stress the role of language and environmental structure in perceptual activity as much as their role in communication (Jerison 1976). Any consideration of the origins of either of these systems must account for the role of the other in its development (Preziosi 1976).

We have so far touched on a set of differences between linguistic and environmental forms, and a number of functional redundancies between them. It is necessary to turn our attention now to a consideration of the possibility that there may exist a number of underlying structural or organizational equivalencies in both ensembles.

Recall that earlier in this chapter (p. 48–50) we elaborated a general distinction between built form and environmental structure, which suggested analogies with the distinction between speech acts and linguistic structure (grammar). Later (see pp. 52–4) we explored some of the ways in which this analogy might not hold. Let us here suggest a number of crucial areas of structural equivalency.

We are concerned with what might be termed the *design features* of both systems (Hockett 1960). We have suggested above that environmental structure comprises a system of relationships indirectly observable in spatial products (built form). It is also clear that the relationships between built form and environmental structure, as well as those between physical form and culture, are not deterministic in nature.

The forms of inhabited environments are various and may or may not involve constructional intervention beyond simple bodily appropriation. We do not necessarily posit the existence of a single set of invariant properties underlying any given environmental assemblage.

An environmental array is not clearly analysable into discrete elements in an ordinary, linear sense. As we have seen above, a building presents series of simultaneously occurring components which, depending upon scale and physical configuration, are readable backwards or forwards, upwards or downwards, and inside to outside, whether or not there is embedded in the assemblage a set of clues or stage directions (which can be anything from seemingly obvious modular transformations of formal components to graphic glossaries —arrows, colour codings, etc., to verbal labellings such as 'please check your coat on the right' or 'entrance to the book stacks on third level').

Thus, while members of a fairly cohesive cultural group will reveal a shared knowledge regarding 'proper' reading usage of an assemblage, the essential arbitrariness of the signals ensures a degree of freedom in decoding the assemblage. Essentially, the forms of an environmental assemblage are blank with respect to significance, acquiring significance chiefly in relation to sets of expectancies projected by a culture, which itself is composed of ensembles in dynamic and changing interaction. I live in a fake Victorian apartment complex and sleep in a room which I know from various formal clues was intended to be the 'dining-room' of the apartment. I do this because I like to wake up with the sun streaming in in the morning on this (east) side of the building. Nothing prevents me from doing this; the formal constraints are fairly loose (I could not fit my mattress into the bathroom—though I could sleep in the bathtub). If I lived in a traditional culture where the social constraints against sleeping in the dining-room were very great, such constraints would be potentially as powerful as certain formal constraints (like the size of the bathroom).

But in any case, these are by and large 'as if' constraints; they operate with a seeming necessity projected upon a generic arbitrariness. This is not to suggest that there may be no 'architectonic universals'; such universals as may exist should clearly be referred to as underlying properties of form or formal relations, rather than the simple iteration of, say, courtyard houses in twenty-five different cultures and climates across the globe.

In other words, the study of environmental structure has as its focus the underlying *properties* of built (and appropriated) forms; the *relationships* established within formal assemblages rather than the identities of physical forms themselves. This study is concerned with the reading of graded messages and the elaboration of techniques for separating out simultaneously-occurring signals. The forms of an environmental array are seldom met in isolation, but typically comprise portions of a dynamic, on-going, interactive process which is unique at a given place and time (Proshansky, Ittleson and Rivlin 1970).

It is this interactive, mutually-defining nature of environmental forms which is crucial to an understanding of our task. We require an analytic perspective which is powerful enough to account for a series of simultaneously embedded, mutually defining, continuously transformed structures which at base are organized in ways inherently more complex than the linearly-generated elements of verbal language.

But note that we have not necessarily precluded by the above description an equivalency or equivalencies between the design features of environmental and linguistic structure (rather, it is simply much more apparent how difficult a task this has been). Indeed, as we shall see, one of the most important developments in the study of environmental structure in recent years has been the elaboration of a relational analysis which promises to be adequate to the task of handling the complexities of environmental structure in a non-trivial way (Preziosi 1975). Although this work is still in its beginning stages, it has already suggested that deep level equivalencies in design features can be demonstrated for the two systems in question, and that these equivalencies are consonant with certain cognitive and biological expectancies.

It is important to stress that the equivalencies which have been emerging between linguistic and environmental structure have to do with fundamental aspects of the design of each system and only secondarily with manifested aspects of the systems. In other words, whether or not a case can be made on a surface level for a series of correspondences between language and architecture, such apparent correspondences are primarily an artefact of shared equivalencies in the fundamental design of each system.

Environmental and linguistic structures comprise groups of performances regulated by codes or rules whose deep level organizations are normally minimally present in the consciousness of performers. Both are employed for purposes of the construction of realities and the conveyance of information, and may be conceptually represented as polysemous projective planes for the mapping of social interactions, employing distinctive methods, media, and contrastive logics arising out of fundamental differences in temporal ordering and spatio-temporal segmentative routines. To say that architecture is language transformed or that language is architecture in Flatland (better, Lineland; Abbott 1952), is to miss the point alluded to earlier on pp. 52-4.

One of the chief breakthroughs in the study of environmental structure in recent years has been the demonstration that however large a given corpus (Preziosi 1975) of built forms, however materially diverse its set of manifested forms, such diversity may be shown to arise from the result of the combination, recombination, and transformation of a rather small number of formal entities (properties) definable in terms of their patterns of interrelationships. A corpus of built forms is open-ended diachronically and diatopically, and is the result of a transfinite set of possible realizations and transformation of a rather small number of formal entities (properties) definable in terms of their patterns of interrelationships. A corpus of built forms is open-ended diachronically and diatopically, and is the result of a transfinite set of possible realizations and transformations of a small number of components (bundles of properties) upon which a certain geometry or group of restricting operational regulations or constraints are imposed.

Moreover, the number and identity of kernel formal properties varies from place to place and over time. Consider an ecological niche (E) in which two distinct cultural groups are settled. Variability may be observed between groups (A) and (B) with respect to:

(1) inventory of materials (which may, however, also be identical);
(2) methods of construction (which may also be identical);

(3) the social significance or connotation of certain formal groupings (which may be identical despite differences in use of building materials);
(4) underlying properties of built forms (which, nevertheless might be similar);

in other words, variability may be observed across all dimensions of environmental organization, despite, say, a shared language and social system; and, conversely, an identity of environmental organization may be observed across differences in social organization and linguistic structure (Rapoport 1969).

Environmental structure comprises a complexly-ordered system of relationships, the core of which has been termed *formal syntax* (Preziosi 1975). The geometry of this organization is distinctive to environmental structure, and contrasts with the various syntactic organizations proposed for linguistic structure in recent times.

Such a system reveals (1) sets of items or formal properties of space; (2) sets of relationships among these; and (3) a set of rules or laws obeyed by the latter. All of these are limited in number for a given corpus. For example, a given corpus will be seen to reveal about twenty formal spatial properties on a given space-manifold (see below), relationships among these properties such as conjunction, disjunction, equivalency, implication; and corpus-specific rules such as 'formal item x will reveal conjunctive relations with h and g under conditions C', and so forth.

In contrast to the organization of formal entities in lingusitic structure, kernel 'items' in environmental structure are organized on a tripartite space-manifold: that is to say, there are found three perspectives or axes of organization for formal items. These axes (termed 2-space, 3-space and 4-space) define three sets of formal regulatory organizations, so that, for example, from the perspective of 2-space, a certain set of formal properties is operable. But from the perspective of 3-space, a corpus reveals a different, partially-overlapping set of formal kernel properties.

These three sets of formal regulatory organizations reveal a binary oppositional frame between mass-forms and space-forms, as well as combinatory mass-space transformations that can be modelled or represented as shown in Figure 8.1. A given corpus of forms is composed of a complex geometry of interrelationships whose 'elements' are transformed as one passes from one 'level' or perspective (or dimension) to another. These perspectives are semi-autonomous and co-existent, mutually defining and embedded, and exhibit equivalent regulatory operations and realizations. Thus, in 3-space, a given

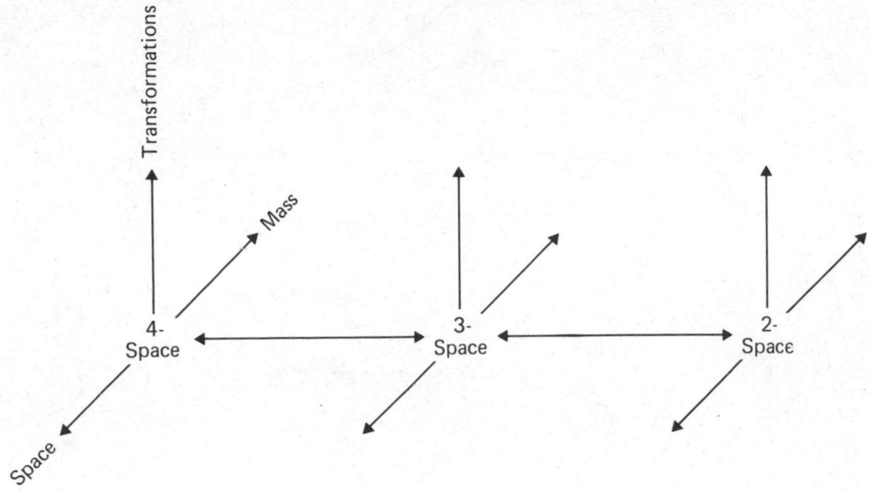

Fig. 8.1 Formal syntax

corpus manifests a set of relational properties of space which may be displayed as a list of 'items' such as $(h = l = w) + (h = l = w)$, etc. ($h$ = height, l = length, w = width). The 'items' are in fact tridimensional ratios or relationships without regard to absolute size or scale. From the perspective of 2-space, the corpus 'decomposes' along different lines (namely, according to topological properties). It is found to be convenient to summarize these internal bundles of properties by letter symbols, which may then be portrayed in larger groups of relationships by means of a graphic alternation between symbols or nodes and connecting links of different kinds, signifying relationships of conjunction, disjunction, equivalency, etc. (The development of a relational calculus is described in Preziosi 1975.)

Figure 8.2 might portray the formal syntax in a given corpus. We have noted above the significance of the fact that the number of 'kernel formal "items"' for any given corpus is not only finite but rather small; among several dozen corpora analysed to date, the number of 'items' seldom exceeds a score for any of the three space-manifolds, a situation which clearly finds an equivalency in linguistic structure, notably at the 'phonemic' in nature except in the most generic sense, regarding the apparent *manner* of their formation of mutual definition. There is, in other words, an apparent equivalency in structural design of each system at this level, but with

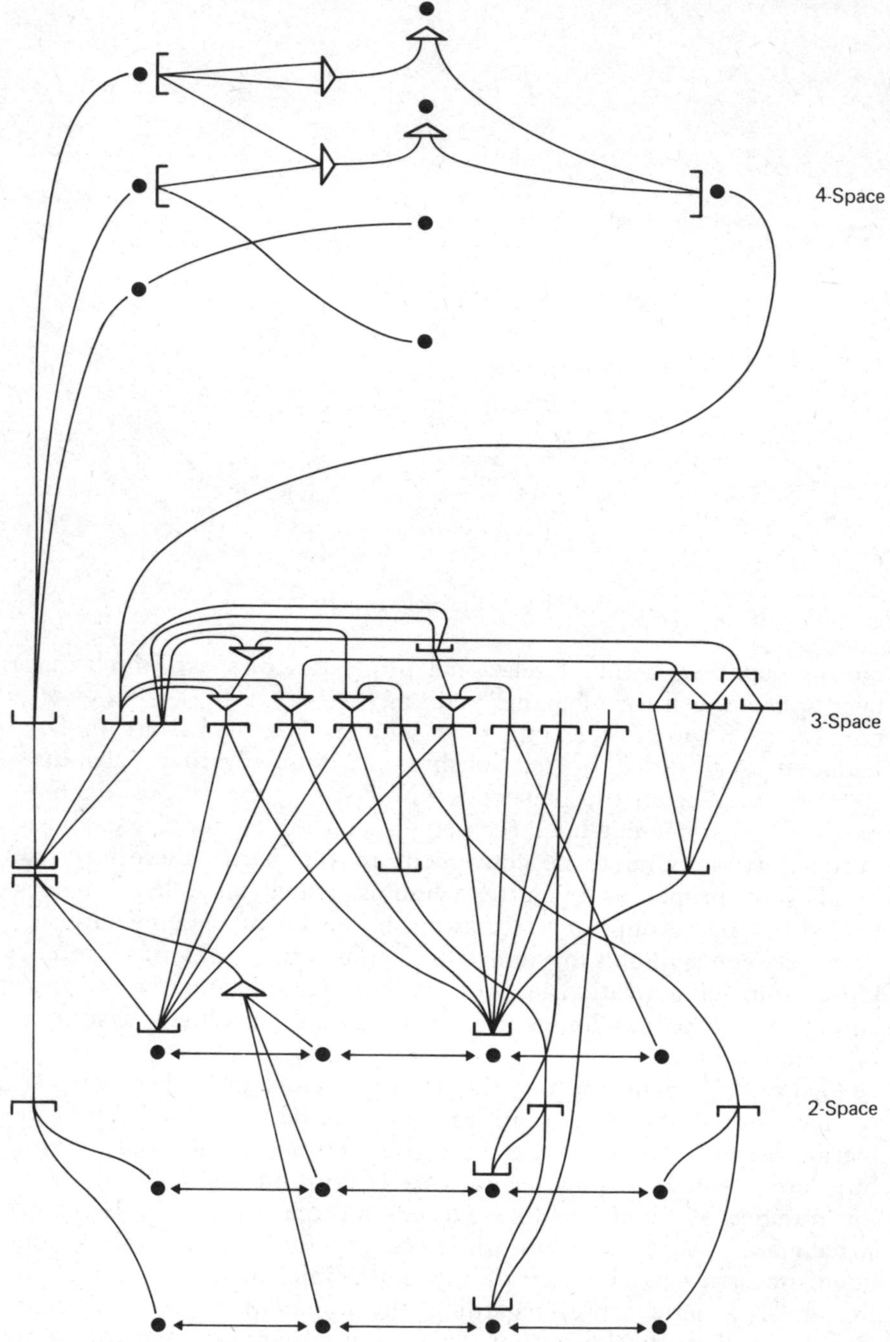

Figure 8.2 Formal syntax in a given corpus

this observation we should bear in mind that in every other way (internal structure of the entities, behaviour in ensembles, relationships to other ensembles) they are profoundly different. A phonemic-morphemic analogy between the two systems quickly self-destructs.

It is important to remember that we are discussing properties of form and their interrelationships and are in no direct way considering the details of material form. In other words, the same formal syntax will hold for a given spatial configuration whether realized in brick, stone, wood or other material. The latter can be referred to what clearly emerges as a semi-autonomous 'level' of organization of environmental structure, characterized by its own internal geometry or syntax. This aspect of environmental form has its own semi-independent reality, manifesting differing rates of change and duration over time *vis-à-vis* formal structure.

For a detailed discussion of the nature of material organization, see Preziosi 1975; for our purposes here we will note that 'material syntax' refers to the organization of structures of manifestation or realization, and that as such the specific properties of material form are the consequence of a dual projectivity—in other words, a series of heuristic routines designed to relate properties of formal structure to extra-architectural cultural ensembles. Material organization comprises highly ordered routines involving materials, textures, colours, specifics of size, scale and modulation, as well as programmes or scores of constructional realization. Each of these routines is a dual function of formal organization and extra-architectural constraints (indeed all the constraints that may be imposed upon the realization of forms by other cultural factors).

An analogy might be drawn between material organization and so-called 'surface structure' in verbal language; but here the analogy ends: the details of material organization in environmental structure are vastly more complex than those of linguistic 'surface structure', and more highly subject to extra-formal constraints. A corresponding situation in verbal language might be that where one's idiolect changed from place to place and even over time in the same place.[4]

At any rate, it is clear that both organizational strata or organizational perspectives have their own conditions of what might be termed well-formedness. Strictly speaking, the ensemble of formal and material organization is a partially-ordered set or poset (Preziosi 1975).

We have seen that in environmental structure, information is preserved in the connectivity of syntactic networks or reticula, and that the notion of entity or item is strictly a function of the perspective (level, stratum, dimension, axis) one is looking from. This property of *conditional elementarity* is common to both environmental and linguistic structure, and indeed a case can be made for equivalent behaviours in various organizations of matter, down to the molecular level (Preziosi 1975; Monod 1971).

Another important recent development has been the emergence of an apparent equivalency between the organizational geometry of the central core of the architectonic phenomenon—what we term here formal syntax—and the tripartite equilibration of spatial concepts observed by Piaget and others in the development of the human child (Preziosi 1975; Piaget and Inhelder 1967).[5] While this may not appear to be unexpected in a general sense, the elaboration of the specifics of formal syntax in environmental structure came about independently.

We have observed that environmental and linguistic structure are employed together and separately for purposes of the construction of realities and the conveyance of information, and may be conceived as polysemous projective 'planes' for the mapping of social interactions. This is not to say, of course, that both ensembles are passive receptacles for the conveyance of cultural meaning; the very flexibility and plasticity of linguistic and environmental systems of human cognition argue for their evolution as analogous to that of other sensory integrative or reconstructive systems, which are known to be modifiable by early experience.

Realities are the creation of the nervous system; models of possible worlds, which enable the nervous system to handle the enormous amount of information it receives and processes. The conscious experience is essentially a construction of nervous systems for handling incoming information in simple, consistent ways (Jerison 1976). The basic constructs of human conscious experience are objects in space and time. Realities are specific to a species.

How is it possible to speak of 'meaning' in dealing with environmental structure? We began this chapter with the observation that the study of environmental structure is chiefly concerned with the complex relationships between culture and physical form (i.e., the built world). We would see environmental structure as a system which relates expression or form to content or meaning. It is understood here what is meant by built form; what does or can built form(s) mean? We can say that forms refer to other aspects or components of cultural ensembles (including linguistic ensembles), and that environmental structure is a complex device for making such connections.

As a whole, a culture is a vast, integrated, cross-indexed semiotic in which can be recognized a number of subsemiotics (Lamb 1976), including language, environmental form, conceptual, perceptual, and motor structures, etc. It may be proposed that the organization of a cultural ensemble at least in part resembles some sort of relational network not unlike that proposed for environmental structure (or linguistic structure). It is clear that the relationships between various ensembles of a culture are not deterministic (Davenport 1976).

To say that an environmental form 'means' is to say it stands in one or more relationships to other things. A given form is 'meaningful' (relates) on at least three main axes: with respect to a linked series of like constructs preceding and following in time; with respect to the perceptual and biological constraints of human geometry; and with respect to all other forms extant at the same time in the same (or connectible) context(s).

If culture is seen as a dynamic, interactive, *relational* system or assemblage, then clearly 'meaning' occurs throughout the system, and every isolable or isolated component in such a system is meaningful in some way.

This is not to say that for any given individual, everything is equally meaningful; the creation of a self involves the construction of a reality (as described above) which is hierarchicalized from the perspective of the individual. Each individual provides a perspectivity on the whole of society and its cultural resources, much like a component in a holographic image which preserves a view of the whole from its positional perspective.

Ensembles within culture are all interconnected, and may be considered separate only in the special sense that we as observers can recognize (draw) boundaries (Lamb 1976). We would propose that the boundaries between environmental structure and other cultural systems are in some way equivalent to boundary conditions prevailing between subsystems within environmental structure itself—say between formal syntax and material syntax. Since it is clear in our relational view of the cultural ensemble as a whole that systems within such an ensemble are semi-autonomous, then groups of systems form partially-ordered sets (posets).

We have until now not discussed the possibility of the existence of a third layer or stratum in environmental structure alongside formal and material syntax, namely something corresponding to a 'semantic' level or organizational geometry. We have elsewhere (Preziosi 1975) made a case for such an organization, but the proposal therein is only summarily and partially outlined. What is clear, however, is that such a level of organization would position itself between the (core) formal syntax and extra-environmental structures

—i.e., other cultural ensembles. In other words, a 'semantic' level of organization would be a 'surface structure' in a manner equivalent to material syntax.

However—and this is an equally important point—it would seem that its *orientation vis-à-vis* the other two subsystems is in some way *perpendicular* to them both, to allow (in our conceptual representation) for simultaneous connection with both formal and material syntax. This of course is simply an artefact in the geometry of our model on a page, and a convention which is intended to portray something of the nature of the simultaneous interaction of material and formal items with extra-environmental ensembles (see Figure 8.3).

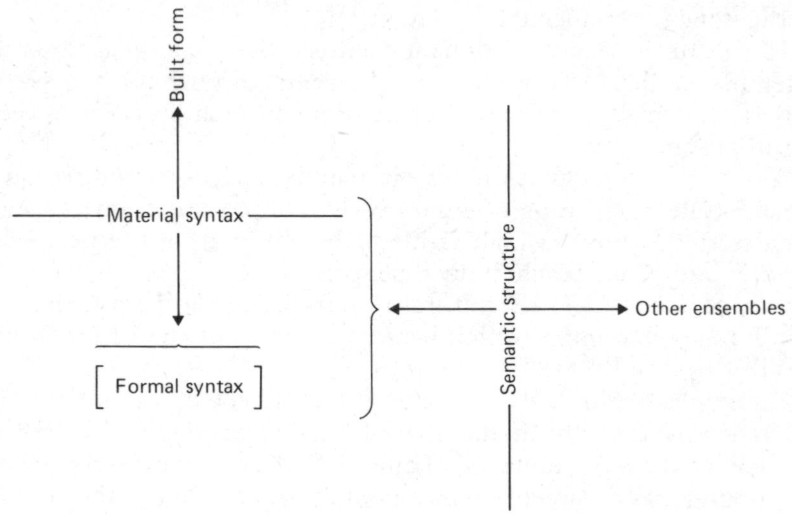

Fig. 8.3 Semantic structure and other organizational levels

'Elements' or items of semantic structure may be *any* isolable formal or material items in a corpus, and transformations of these. Semantic structure may be considered as a reordering of properties of material and formal relationships. Just as the rules of a material syntax provide a series of orderings which can be said to transform formal relationships into physical form, so also may it be seen that semantic structure comprises a series of regulations for the projection of formal relationships on to other cultural ensembles (and vice versa).

The relationship between semantic structure and the other two organizational levels is again one of semi-autonomy, for it is demonstrably the case that identical semantic geometries may underlie disparate formal representations (Preziosi 1975).

We might conclude by summarizing our observations regarding relations between linguistic and environmental structure. It would appear that the two ensembles share certain features of underlying design. Both reveal properties of conditional elementarity, both are built upon an organizational property of duality or semi-autonomy, and both comprise a limited stock of kernel relational entities which generate a transfinite number of realized physical forms. Both reveal thc presence of isolable groups of equivalent properties (syntactic levels).

It is clear that environmental and linguistic structure differ greatly in the direction of structures of manifestation (built form, speech acts), and that equivalencies become more frequent in the direction of core organizations and behaviours.

Our experience has been that it is largely through an understanding of broader configurations of cultural interactions, through an appreciation of culture as a dynamic, interactive, *relational* ensemble, that the unique properties of isolable components of that ensemble —whether environmental or linguistic structure—can be more clearly seen. These 'extensions' of ourselves, to recall an image which began this chapter, behave like waves in a medium; a wave is a singularity of a medium, and its existence is dependent upon corresponding changes in its context. Ensembles within culture are not independent of the conceptual space surrounding them, and function like reifications of connections between ensembles.

Architectonics is emerging from what might be considered a 'natural history' phase in its development, where what passed for theory was essentially semantic manœuvring to obtain a maximum congruence of classifications. One of the chief faults of environmental theories has been the quality of untestability. One of the chief hopes for architectonics is that its theoretical models can be disproved.

NOTES

1. One of the problems with not having a common term to cover the range of related issues common to current research is the perpetuation of often unnecessary specialization under headings such as 'environmental psychology', 'architectural history and theory', 'kinesics', 'environmental cognition/perception', 'environmental symbolism', and 'man-(sic) environment relations' (not to speak of similar headings with the term 'urban-' prefixing the phrase). Of course, we cannot wave a magic wand and dispel the unnecessary overlappings. Nevertheless, it seems not unreasonable to refer to a broad range

of common interests in this area by means of the adjective *architectonic*, which by and large has little specific reference in the field today, and to refer tentatively to a common range of interests described by such properties as *architectonics.* Architectonics has as its subject matter the phenomenon of environmental structuration in general, and its primary task is to account for the occurrence and behaviour of environmental forms in cultural contexts. One of its chief goals is the elaboration of theoretical models to describe the relations between environmental form and other aspects of culture. It is by definition a semiotic inquiry, and is concerned with configurations of meaning in cultural ensembles from the perspective of environmental structure.

2. In its origins as a device for the cognitive construction of realities, environmental structure, it may well be fruitful to consider the built world as a simplification and coherence of groups of stratagems of disparate character, rather than simply an elaboration of a single, less complex stratagem (like sematectonic devices employed by other species). On this subject, see Preziosi 1976 (forthcoming), *The Origins of the Built World.*
3. Any more, say, than the concept of 'symbol', the existence of which is not recognized cross-culturally apart from a generalized symbolicizing mechanism common to human cognitive structure (Sperber 1975).
4. The analogy is not very clear; at any rate, there seems to be nothing quite equivalent in language to a situation in environmental structure where the details of manifested form can be so arbitrary and subject to changes which have little or nothing to do with formal prescriptions. It is as if one is playing a game over time in which the rules may remain more or less constant, but the tokens or markers on the board are replaced at irregular intervals by turnips, cabbages, elephants, and trees.
5. There is a rich body of work in this area in recent years; a more detailed discussion may be found in Preziosi 1975, along with a representative bibliography.

BIBLIOGRAPHY

Abbott, E. (1952), *Flatland* (6th edn.), New York, Dover.

Arnheim, R. (1971), *Visual Thinking*, Berkeley, California.

Collins, P. (1965), *Changing Ideals in Modern Architecture*, London, Faber.

Eliade, M. (1959), *The Sacred and Profane*, New York, Harper.

Gregory, R. L., (1970), 'The Grammar of Vision', *The Listener*, 19 February.

Hall, E. T. (1966), *The Hidden Dimension*, New York, Doubleday.

Hockett, C. F. (1960), 'The Origins of Speech, *Scientific American*, September.

Hockett, C. F., and Ascher, (1964), 'The Human Revolution', *Current Anthropology.*

Jakobson, R. (1973), *Main Trends in the Science of Language*, New York, Harper.

Jerison, H. J. (1976), 'Palaeoneurology and the Evolution of Mind', *Scientific American*, January.

Lamb, S. M. (1976), 'Semiotics of language and culture: a relational approach', this volume, pp. 71–100.

Mackay, D. M. (1970), *Information, Mechanism and Meaning*, Cambridge, Mass., MIT Press.

Marshall, L. (1959), 'Marriage Among !Kung Bushman', *Africa*, 29, No. 4.
Marshall, L. (1960), '!Kung Bushman Bands', *Africa*, 30, No. 4.
Monod, J. (1971), *Chance and Necessity*, New York, Knopf.
Nitschke, G. (1974), entire December 1974 issue of *Architectural Design.*
Piaget, J., and Inhelder, B. (1967), *The Child's Conception of Space*, New York, Ballantine.
Preziosi, D. A. (1975), *Architecture and Cognition: Toward a Relational Theory of Environmental Structure* [See Preziosi, D. A. (1979), *The Semiotics of the Built Environment*, Indiana, Indiana University Press, *Ed.*]
Preziosi, D. A. (1976), *The Origins of the Built World* [See Preziosi, D. A. (1979), *Architecture, Language, and Meaning: The Origins of the Built World and its Semiotic Organization*, The Hague, Mouton, *Ed.*]
Proshansky, H. M., Ittleson, W. H., and Rivlin, L., *Environmental Psychology*, New York, Holt, Rinehart & Winston.
Rapoport, A. (1969), *House Form and Culture*, Englewood Cliffs, N.J. Prentice-Hall.
Rapoport, A. (1972), 'Australian Aborigines and the Sense of Place', in proceedings of the Third Environmental Design Research Association (*EDRA III*), Los Angeles.
Sebeok, T. (1962), 'Coding in the Evolution of Signalling Behaviour', *Behavioural Science*, 7, No. 4.
Sperber, D. (1975), *Rethinking Symbolism*, Cambridge, Cambridge University Press.
Tuan, Y. (1974), *Topophilia*, New York, Harper.
von Frisch, K. (1974), *Animal Architecture*, New York, Harcourt, Brace, Jovanovich.
Wilson, E. O. (1975), *Sociobiology*, Cambridge, Mass., Belknap.
Yates, F. (1966), *The Art of Memory*, Chicago, Ill., Chicago University Press.

Part III
Relating culture and language

9 Semiotics of language and culture: a relational approach

Sydney M. Lamb
Rice University, Houston, U.S.A.

9.1 INTRODUCTION

The aim of this paper is to suggest the possibility of extending certain techniques from structural linguistics to structural anthropology. Like other structuralist approaches to culture (e.g. Pike 1967), it explores the hypothesis that the form and organization of linguistic information are to be found also in portions of the cultural information system not commonly considered as included within language. It is natural that structuralism should have developed in linguistics earlier than in other areas since language is evidently less complex than culture, hence more easily subjected to formal analysis.

The particular type of structuralism that I find most useful has evolved in part from several important ideas of Louis Hjelmslev (1961). Most important is his insistence on the primacy of relationships as opposed to substance. One implementation of that proposal is briefly sketched below in section 9.2.

Also of great value is Hjelmslev's notion of catalysis. This concept is quite unrelated to the catalysis of chemistry. In Hjelmslev's use of the term, which is quite close to its etymological meaning, catalysis is similar to but opposite from analysis. It differs in that it involves a building up of that which is not directly observable rather than a breaking down of that which is; the latter is of course analysis;

> . . . linguistic theory prescribes a *textual analysis*, which leads us to recognize a linguistic form behind the 'substance' immediately accessible to observation by the senses, and behind the text a language (system) consisting of **categories** from whose definitions can be deduced the possible **units** of the language. The kernel of this procedure is a catalysis through which the form is encatalyzed to the substance, and the language encatalyzed to the text. [Hjelmslev 1961: 96]

Thus the attempt to understand linguistic structure, in a Hjelmslevian context, requires first the recognition of a structure lying behind the linguistic data, of which the data are manifestations or 'outputs'. The job of this type of structuralist, then, is not just to tabulate or classify or talk about the outputs of linguistic structure. Nor is it just to devise lists of rules which collectively generate outputs of linguistic structure. To do that is merely another way of classifying these outputs.

Of course, the process of catalysis requires that analysis of linguistic data also be done. The analysis must be done first (or, in practice, alongside the catalysis). The linguistic data are the raw material for the analysis. The results of the analysis are the raw material for catalysis.

9.2 LINGUISTIC STRUCTURE AS A RELATIONAL NETWORK

The recognition . . . that a totality does not consist of things but of relationships, and that not substance but only its internal and external relationships have scientific existence . . . may be new in linguistic science. The postulation of objects as something different from the terms of relationships is a superfluous axiom and consequently a metaphysical hypothesis from which linguistic science will have to be freed. [Hjelmslev 1961: 25]

Although Hjelmslev himself never took this step, the possibility of actually charting these structural relations has presented itself as an attractive challenge to a small group of investigators during the past twenty years. The process of relational catalysis begins with observing the relationships that can readily be seen in the linguistic data. Some examples are shown in Figure 9.1. In these diagrams the vertical dimension relates to the fundamental distinction between form and meaning (or expression and content, in Hjelmslev's terminology): the downward direction is toward form (expression), the upward towards meaning (content). Thus, in some contexts the expressions **big** and **large** are alternatives for the same content (Figure 9.1a). Of course there are also uses of **big** for which **large** is not an alternative (for example, in **I'd like you to meet my big sister**): thus we need to add the additional information shown in Figure 9.1b, which includes an either-or node of opposite direction from that of Figure 9.1a, since we have two alternative content functions which **big** can express. As Figure 9.1c illustrates, we evidently have to recognize also a both-and type of relation (requiring a different type of node in the relational network) for the sake of (1) the combination of expression elements which as a unit expresses a meaning (commonly with a specified sequence of these elements required), and (2) the combination of content elements which, taken together as a unit, has an expression.

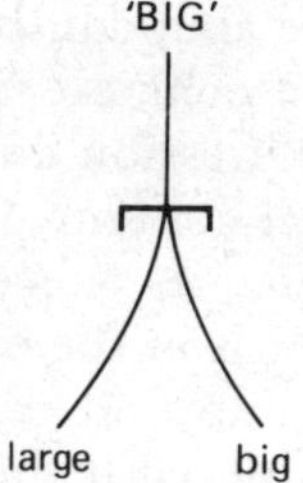

(a) Diversification
(alternative expressions)

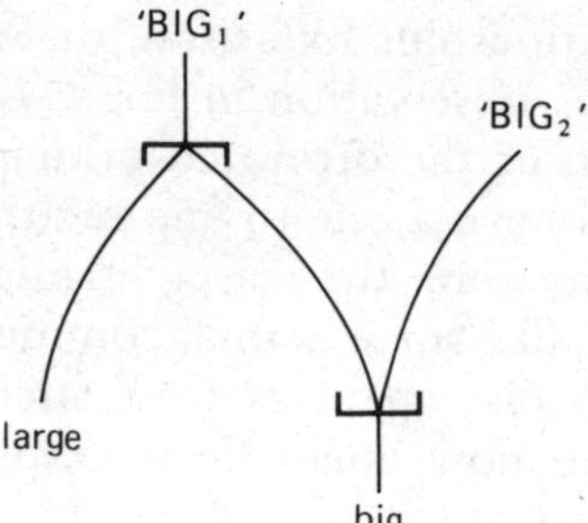

(b) Diversification
with neutralization

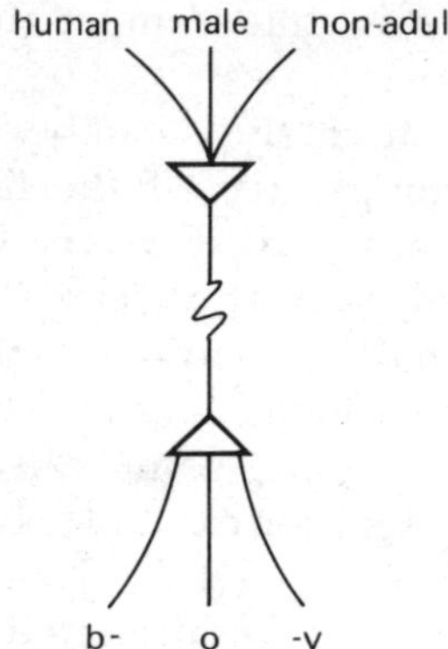

(c) Both–And Relations. The wavy line in the middle indicates the presence of intermediate connections not shown

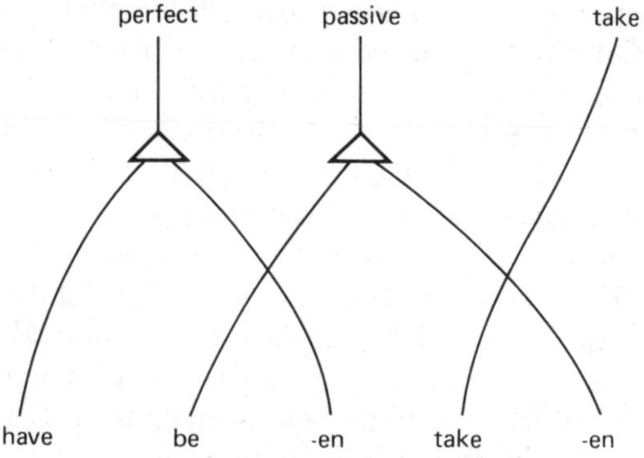

(d) Anataxis (ordering discrepancy)

Fig. 9.1 Diversification and anataxis

Relationships like those of Figure 9.1, which are abundantly available for observation in linguistic data, provide the concrete demonstration of the oft-noted principle that units of expression do not in general have a one-to-one relationship with units of content. Indeed, if such were the case, linguistic structure would be exceedingly simple, like some animal communication systems. It is in the observation of discrepancies from such a simple relationship that we begin to learn how linguistic structure is organized. Along with the types of discrepancy illustrated in Figure 9.1, we may recognize the special case of diversification in which one of the possibilities on the expression side is zero (nothing); this is called zero realization. And the special case of neutralization in which one of the possibilities on the content side is zero is called empty realization. For example, **do** is empty in **I don't know.**

The findings of relational catalysis can be stated with, as yet, only limited assurance. The complexity of the linguistic structure is so great that interpretation has played a very large role in the studies that have been presented over the years, and (as with cognitive studies in general), different interpretative stances have led to different results. Nevertheless, some rough ideas and first approximations are available (along with, no doubt, some mistakes) in some twenty years' worth of literature (see, for example, Lockwood 1972, Makkai and Lockwood 1973, Bennett 1975, Johannesson 1976, 1980). At the same time, we should be prepared to recognize that the assumptions and notational techniques used in these preliminary explorations in relational catalysis may have been faulty in some respects, so that the results may have to be revised as the techniques become more refined.[1]

In studying the relational structure of language, a fundamental step is the postulation of the elementary relations into which more complex relations can be analysed. Figure 9.1 above illustrates one such proposal.[2] The investigator may then map out various configurations of these relations that are needed to account for linguistic data; this is the process of relational catalysis: the relational structures are encatalysed to account for the observed data. And for a structuralist interested in formal systems it is then natural to proceed to a second level of investigation: to analyse the structures of the relational networks (themselves purely formal structures) that are encatalysed in the first-level investigation. It is in the course of this second-level investigation (which in practice is carried on simultaneously with the first) that the relational theoretician may identify the various strata of linguistic structure and their internal composition.

The study of this layering, of stratification, is rather complex, and the evidence has led to a variety of interpretations (Lamb 1972)[3] but it appears that the variation comes from the criteria used rather than from differences between languages. That is, with a given set of criteria for drawing stratal boundaries we find the same number in different languages around the world. There is, in other words, great uniformity among the world's languages in this respect. The number of strata is either three or four, depending upon the criteria used (earlier versions with more than four are possibly no longer accepted). In the view that accepts four strata they are called phonemic, morphemic, lexemic, and sememic. In the three-stratum view, morphemic and lexemic are seen as two branches, as it were, of a single stratum (some might say that the two are conflated, in this view).

Part of the difference in point of view hinges on the point of whether some of the linguistic relationships should be considered as interstratal or as belonging within one stratum or another. In either case there is, of course, structure within the stratum. Perhaps most important is the syntactic structure or tactics, which controls arrangements and co-occurrence possibilities, For example, the tactics of the phonemic stratum (or 'phonotactics') of a language specifies the general structure of syllables and of phonological words and phrases. Other structural patterns, involving relations of the kind illustrated in Figures 9.6 and 9.7 below, can be considered as belonging within the same stratum as the adjoining tactic pattern.

9.3 LINGUISTIC STRUCTURE AS A SYSTEM OF SIGNS

> That a language is a system of signs seems *a priori* an evident and fundamental proposition, which linguistic theory will have to take into account at an early stage. Linguistic theory must be able to tell us what meaning can be attributed to this proposition, and especially to the word **sign**. [Hjelmslev 1961:43]

9.3.1 In the preceding section a distinction is made between different phases of analysis and catalysis. Although, as mentioned, the various phases are not actually performed at distinct times nor in a fixed order, there is a logical order: (1) analysis of data; (2) selection (postulation) of a small set of elementary relations that can form the basis of the catalysis; (3) catalysis (construction) of networks of relations to account for the data; (4) analysis of the structure of these networks. Other phases, not yet mentioned, are also possible: (5) using the results of (4) to make improvements in hypotheses constructed for earlier phases; and (6) construction of hypotheses concerning operations upon or in relational networks to account for the fundamental linguistic processes of (a) speaking and understanding, (b) addition of new concepts, new complex lexical items, etc. (short-range diachrony), (c) language acquisition, and (d) longer-range diachronic changes. Such operations on the networks might include activation of lines and nodes of the network, the addition of new lines and nodes, the withering or gradual fading away of lines and nodes under certain conditions, and the addition of blocking elements which block certain lines. It might also be necessary to posit a gradience of lines or nodes with respect to their ease of activation or of transmitting impulses.

Let us turn our attention now to phase (4), the analysis of the structure of relational networks. One type of analysis, mentioned in the last section, is the macroscopic analysis of a whole linguistic network into its major sections, called strata. (Of course, a whole linguistic network has never been constructed for any language, nor is it likely that such a feat will ever be performed. The structuralist must operate with fragments of networks and perform generalizations to arrive at hypothetical abstract structures. Thus phase 4 is not an actual analysis of an actual network, but a 'thought-analysis', analogous to a thought-experiment.)

The other type of analysis which immediately suggests itself is at the other end of the scale of size. It involves the examination of the lines and nodes of a network to determine whether they appear to be organized into clusters or other units of some kind intermediate in size between the individual lines and nodes (at the microscopic end) and the strata (at the macroscopic).[4] This type of analysis results in the discovery of a unit which is quite reminiscent of the traditional concept of the linguistic sign.

9.3.2 The first significant level of organization above that of the elementary relations may be called the *nection* (as in connection). It can be characterized by the following series of definitions (slightly revised from the original in Lamb 1966: Chapter 3):

9.3.2.1 In a relational network, any point at which lines connect is a *node.* The nodes may be taken as loci of the elementary relations.

9.3.2.2 A node has two sides: a *singular side*, at which one line connects, and a *plural side*, at which more than one line connects (Figure 9.2a).

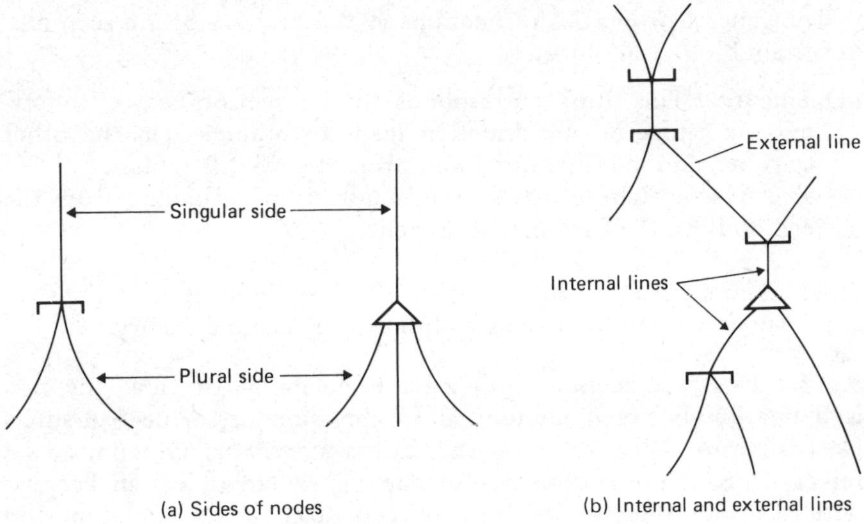

Fig. 9.2 Defining the nection

9.3.2.3 A line which connects the plural sides of two nodes (or the plural side of a node with a boundary of a network) is an *external line*. Any other line is an *internal line* (Figure 9.2b).

9.3.2.4 On every external line there is a *nection boundary* (at one end or the other, or in the middle).

9.3.2.5 A *nection* is a continuous portion of network bounded by nection boundaries.

9.3.3 The following general features of nectional structure may be deduced from these definitions:

9.3.3.1 A well-formed relational network consists entirely of nections.

9.3.3.2 A nection has one and only one line connecting the singular side of one node to the singular side of another node (unless there exist special cases at network boundaries). This line may be called the *nection centre.*

9.3.3.3 On either side of the nection centre, branching is present in one direction only. That is, moving outward from the nection centre, at every node crossed, the passage is from a singular side to a plural side, until a nection boundary is reached.

The general properties of nections (9.3.3.2, 9.3.3.3) are seen also in certain biological objects:

(1) The tree. The trunk corresponds to the nection centre; following the trunk in one direction leads to branches, in the other to roots, and in either direction, property 9.3.3.3 applies.
(2) The neuron. The centre is the major axon extending from the cell body to the first axonal branch.

9.3.4 We may now turn to consideration of the notion of the sign, as it may be viewed from the standpoint of relational theory.

9.3.4.1 First, in keeping with a relational point of view, the sign is a relation between content and expression or, in de Saussure's (1916) terms, between a *signifié* and a *signifiant*. Of course, we reject de Saussure's depiction of the sign as an object in keeping with the fact that, as he himself recognized, it is a relation and not an object (Figure 9.3).

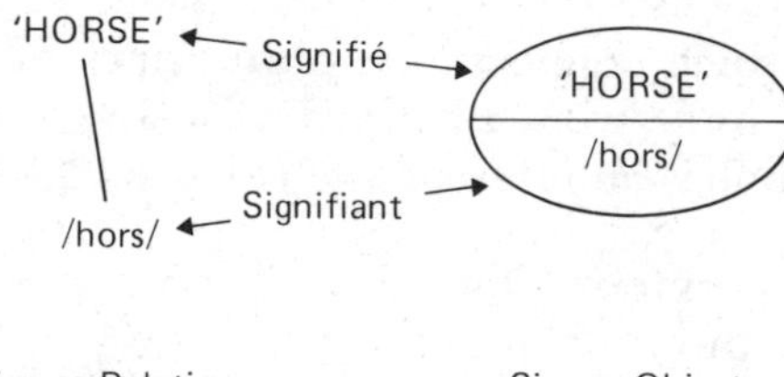

Fig. 9.3 Two views of the sign

9.3.4.2 As is well known, the *signifiant* (or *signans*) is in general complex (Figure 9.4).

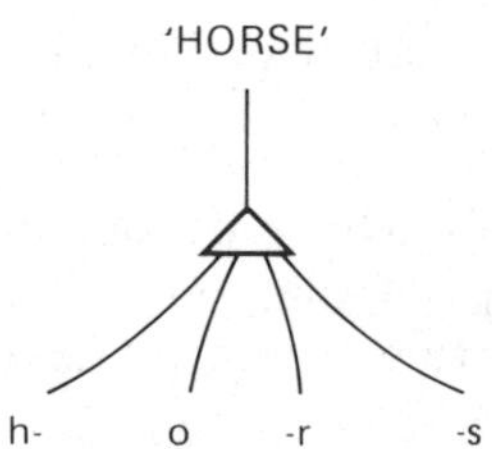

Fig. 9.4 Complex *signifiant*

9.3.4.3 But a linguistic sign generally also has a tactic function, in the tactics of its level (Figure 9.5a).

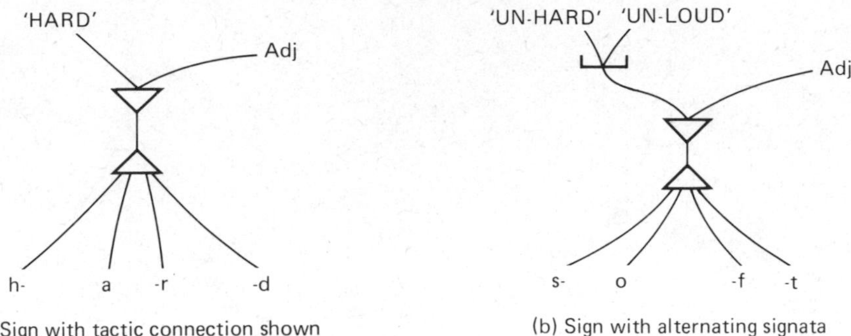

(a) Sign with tactic connection shown

(b) Sign with alternating signata

Fig. 9.5 Complex *signifié*

9.3.4.4 A sign is often a sign for more than one *signifié* (Figure 9.5b).[5]

9.3.5 Thus it is apparent that a sign, if we identify its most salient characteristics, is representable as a nection in a linguistic structure as relationally encatalysed. But to say that is quite different from saying that all linguistic nections represent signs since there are also other types of nections. Let us now take a look at some of them.

9.3.5.1 Perhaps closest to the sign of the generally recognized type is that whose expression side is connected to other signs rather than directly to phonological units. Some examples are shown in Figure 9.6. If simple signs (like 'black' and 'stand') can be called morphemes, those which are above them (like 'understand' and 'blackboard') might be called hypermorphemes, and those of the more general class which includes both of these may be called lexemes (see also Conklin 1962 and references cited there). They correspond to the units generally recognized as lexical items.

It should upset no one if the notion of 'sign' is extended to include hypermorphemes along with the lower-level morphemes.

9.3.5.2 When the network is analysed into nections, alternation is seen to involve external lines, hence internection connections. Consider the alternation of ^{M}/gud/ and ^{M}/bet/ (of *better*) as realizations of ^{M}/good/ (Figure 9.7). Notice that ^{M}/gud/ and ^{M}/bet/ are both nections, and that ^{M}/good/ is also a nection (not fully shown in the diagram).

It is apparent that the nection labelled ^{M}/good/ is like those of the hypermorphemes considered above, except that its downward connections into the lower-level morphemes are in an either-or relationship to each other rather than a both-and sequence. Perhaps

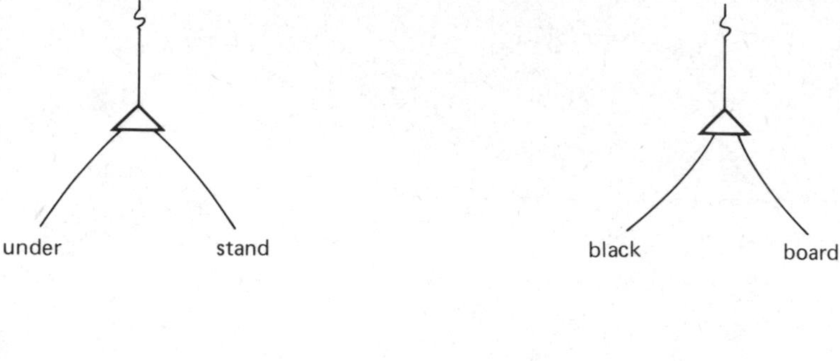

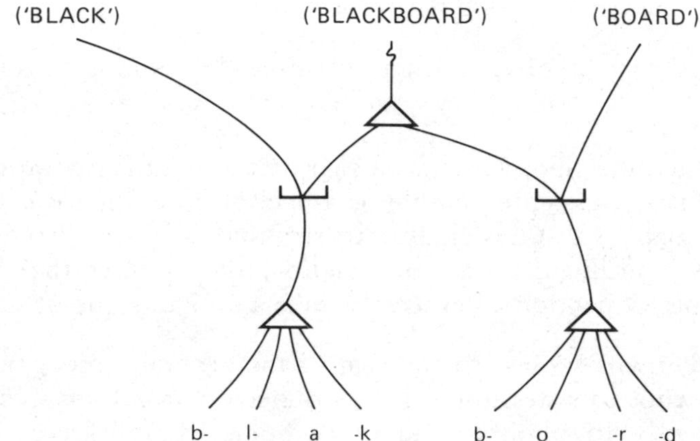

Fig. 9.6 Hypermorphemes (and their connections to lower-level morphemes)

this difference is not too great to allow us to consider that this ^{M}/good/ is also a type of linguistic sign. We can then also permit ourselves to call this ^{M}/good/ a lexeme. The remainder of the figure comprises part of the syntax of morphemes (or 'morphotactics').

9.3.5.3 Tactic patterns are easily seen as composed of nections, with tactically 'upward' connections to functions and 'downward' connections to (nections representing) units, classes of units, and constructions. I would now like to argue that it is possible to view tactic nections as signs without unduly stretching the traditional notion of the sign. We should first be clear about a distinction between two types of tactic nection which differ with respect to their first downward branching from the centre: the syntagmatic (or constructional) and the paradigmatic (or taxonomic). Examples are shown in Figure 9.8a.

The upward connections of tactic nections are to their functions.

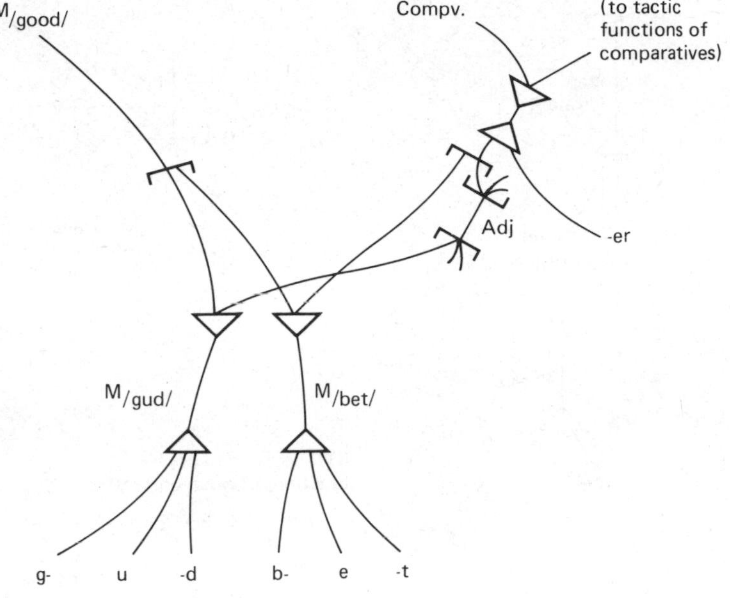

Fig. 9.7 Morphemic alternation

In previous work in relational linguistics it has generally been taken for granted that these functions are in general tactic rather than semantic. For example, prepositions have tactic function in prepositional phrases (Fig. 9.8b).

Another possibility, that they might also have meanings (that is, semantic functions) has been given insufficient consideration. Bloomfield's system (1933) did give recognition to constructional meanings. A tactic nection (either syntagmatic or paradigmatic) with meaning was, in Bloomfield's terms, a *tagmeme* (not the same as Pike's tagmeme, which is less directly relatable to nectional analysis), and one without meaning was called a *taxeme*. (The meaning of a tagmeme was called an *episememe*.) Strangely, this part of Bloomfield's theory was not used by him or anyone else, as far as I know, except that Hockett's Item-and-Arrangement model (1954) included provision for constructional meanings. The alternative is to suppose that the notion of constructional meaning is in general superfluous and that all of the meaning of, say, an English declarative clause can be accounted for by the meanings of its constituents. By contrast, the standard interrogative clause (for yes-or-no questions) seems clearly to involve a purely tactical device for expressing a meaning, so some provision must be made for connection from tactics directly to meaning; but such cases have been considered

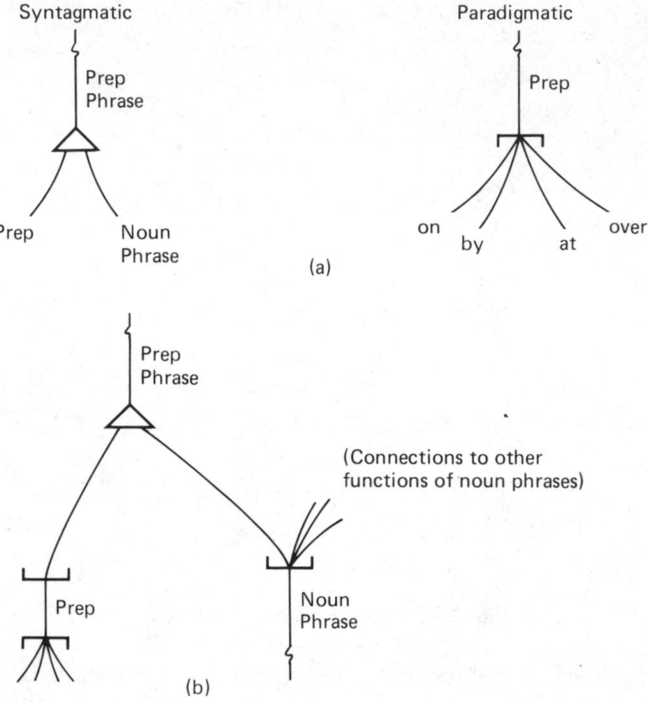

Fig. 9.8 Tactic nections

exceptional. It may be, however, that Bloomfield's tagmeme, long since discarded (or never adopted by structuralists) was valid after all.

Consider the English construction exemplified by *redhead, redcap, whitecap*, etc. It seems clear that the meanings of these forms are not entirely accounted for by the meanings of the constituents: a redhead is not a head but a person having a red head. That is, an important part of the meaning is to be assigned to the construction itself (Figure 9.9).

Now consider the construction exemplified by such forms as *red-headed, silver-tongued, dim-witted*. Do we say that since there is a suffix *-ed* in *red-headed*, it is not necessary to assign any constructional meaning, on the grounds that the meaning not accounted for by *red* and *head* may be assigned to *-ed*? Or do we say that here too we have constructional meaning and that this construction differs from the previous one in having a *marker* (namely, *-ed*). These two alternatives are shown in Figure 9.10, the former as Figure 9.10a, the latter as Figure 9.10b. Both diagrams include the construction

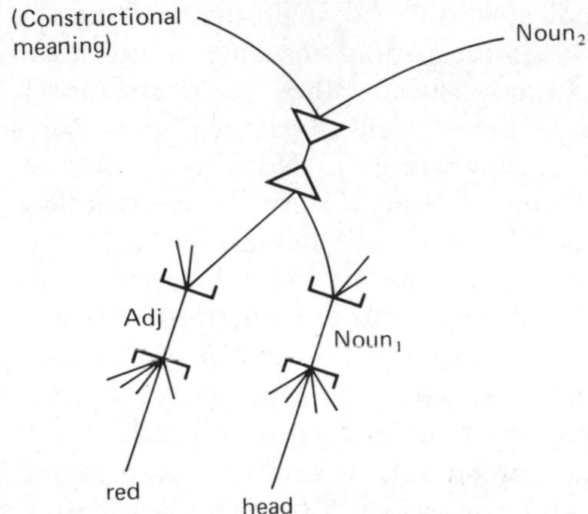

Fig. 9.9 Construction with constructional meaning

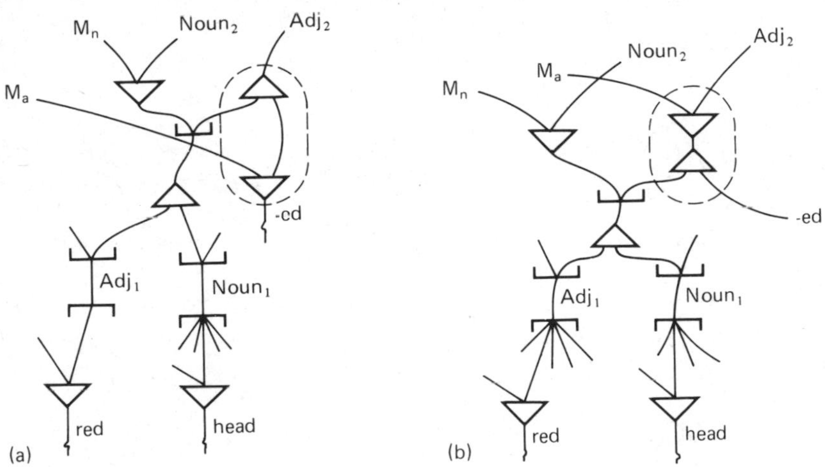

Fig. 9.10 Construction with meaning and marker

of Figure 9.9; the point labelled 'M_n' is the same as that labelled 'constructional meaning' in Figure 9.9. These diagrams are the same except for the parts enclosed in dotted lines.

The catalysis shown at the right may be preferable, since it provides a closer parallel between the adjectival (e.g. *redheaded*) and nominal (e.g. *redhead*) constructions. It also seems to work better for encoding and decoding, but as these processes have not yet been formally specified, no argument based upon them can be regarded as conclusive. In addition, the catalysis of Figure 9.10b provides a neater nectional structure (a single nection for the encircled portion) as well as a simple formal account of the intuitively apparent distinction of presupposition: the *-ed* presupposes the adj-Noun combination, but the latter does not presuppose the former ('selection' in Hjelmslev's terms). (Note that a treatment of *redhead*, etc., along the lines of the adjectival construction at the left is possible, if a 'zero' suffix is encatalysed to bear the additional meaning, so that no meaning need be assigned to the construction; but such a catalysis seems rather contrived.) Now it would appear that, the same presuppositional situation being present, the corresponding treatment should be used generally for constructions involving affixes—and indeed this consideration may provide (finally) a formal explication of the intuitively apparent distinction between affixes and non-affixes.[6] (This is the treatment already used for the comparative construction in the example of alternation above, Figure 9.7.)

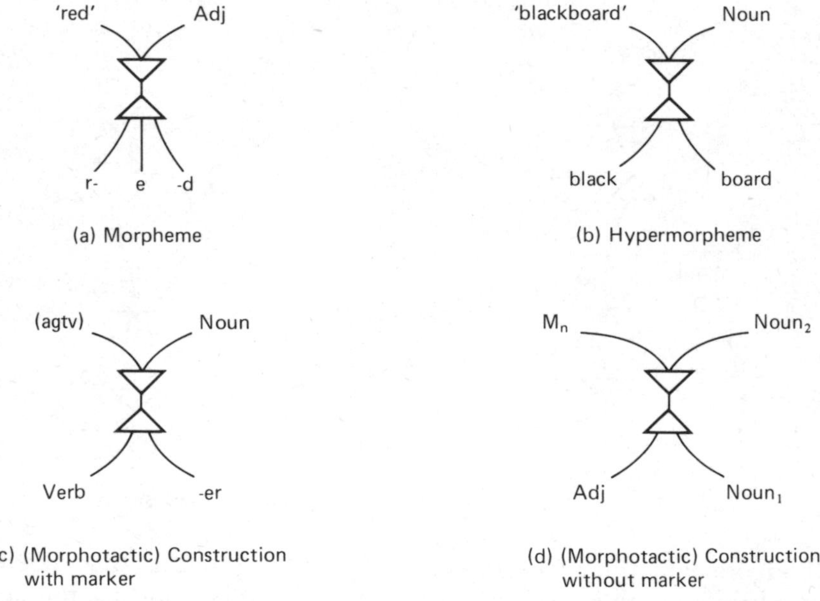

Fig. 9.11 Some types of linguistic signs

Now let us compare tactic constructions (catalysed as indicated above) with signs (Figure 9.11). We see that they are very similar indeed, and that constructions with markers are intermediate between signs of the familiar type and constructions without markers. All of these types of nections share the general properties shown in

Figure 9.12. On the expression side, the connections can be to specific elements or to classes (or to further tactic constructions, hence indirectly to classes); the nections of the latter type we have been accustomed to calling tactic constructions. But the difference is not in the form of the nection itself but only in what it is connected to—and in either case the connections are to or toward expression. It may therefore be reasonable to consider that tactic nections with meanings are also signs—and that may include all tactic constructions in the lexico-grammatical system.

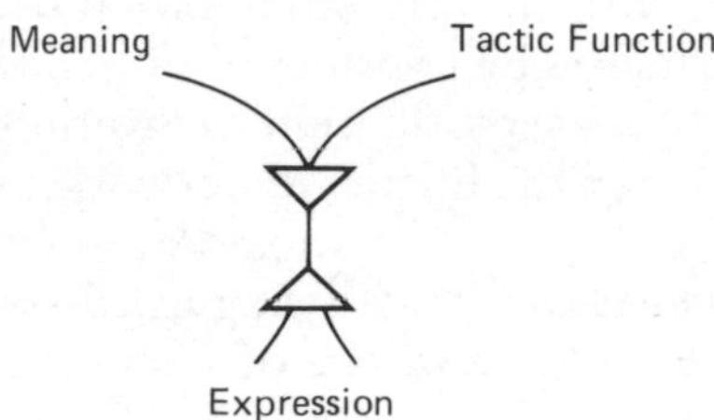

Fig. 9.12 General properties of the signs of Figure 9.11

If, as Bloomfield proposes, there are class meanings associated with (some?) tactic classes, then the corresponding nections are not unlike those already considered. That such class meanings do exist is suggested by the old high school English teacher's much maligned semantic definition of 'noun' as 'the name of a person, place, or thing'. On the expression side, such nections would have an either-or node instead of the both-and seen in Figure 9.12. In this respect they are similar to the nection for ^{M}/good/ discussed above (Figure 9.7). Thus one might also include these paradigmatic nections under a broadened scope of the traditional concept of sign.

9.3.5.4 On the other hand, in phonotactics at least, and perhaps to some extent also in grammar, there is evidently another type of nection which is concerned only with sequencing: at a given position or set of positions in the syllable, for example, there is a particular set of possibilities for what can come next (Lamb 1980). Nections with this type of function differ in two ways from those discussed so far (which fit more or less well with a somewhat broadened concept of the sign). First, they have one-way lines—that is, they are orientated in one direction only, from the 'before' to the 'after', in keeping with the fact that speech is in general linear in time—whereas signs provide connection both from content to expression and from expression to content.[7] Second, they do not connect expression to content, nor even two syntactic levels to each other, as both ends are at the same level: they only connect two stages within a sequence of possibilities at the same level of structure.

It therefore seems much less appropriate to extend the concept of sign far enough to include such nections.

Also in phonology are the nections corresponding to the phonemes. They are like the nections which resemble signs in being bi-directional and in having an up-and-down orientation, but their upward connections are not to meanings except in a greatly broadened sense of the term meaning, although they are *toward* meaning (via morphemes). Such nections, while in form very much like those which correspond to signs, might nevertheless be considered not to fall within the scope even of a broadened concept of 'sign', because of their location in the expression stratum of the linguistic network.

9.3.6 It is mentioned above that a linguistic structure, as relationally encatalysed, is made up entirely of nections. We have now seen that some of the nections correspond closely to the traditional concept of the linguistic sign, while others correspond less closely but might be included in the scope of a broadened concept of the sign, and still others might fall outside even this range even though they are very close to, and in some cases formally indistinguishable from, those which correspond closely to the traditional concept. There is in any case a tantalizing relationship between the sign and the nection.

There is also an important difference not yet sufficiently emphasized. The nection is a purely formal entity within an abstract relational system, and the term 'nection' is thus a technical term. The term 'sign' is certainly a technical term in the work of many semioticians, but it is also a vague term and one which is almost too versatile for technical use. It is used both by those who think of the sign as an object and by those who see its essence as connection; used both with reference to linguistic data and with reference to the system which lies behind the data (of which the data are outputs). Thus it will probably enhance discussions of relational semiotics if the terms 'sign' and 'nection' are kept clearly distinct.

It is then perhaps justifiable to consider the nection an important concept in the type of study which might appropriately be called relational semiotics, important in just the way that the concept of sign is important in the general field of semiotics.

If it is also meaningful to assert that the concept of the nection incorporates the essence of the notion of the sign, then it seems reasonable to conclude that a linguistic structure, as relationally encatalysed, is made up of relational configurations having the formal properties of signs. It appears that (recalling the passage quoted above from Hjelmslev) linguistic theory does indeed tell us what meaning can be attributed to the proposition that a language is a system of signs. In case this conclusion seems too obvious to mention, let me point out that it is quite contrary to that at which Hjelmslev himself arrived:

> Languages, then, cannot be described as pure sign systems. By the aim usually attributed to them they are first and foremost sign systems; but by their internal structure they are first and foremost something different, namely systems of figurae that can be used to construct signs. The definition of a language as a sign system has thus shown itself, on closer analysis, to be unsatisfactory. It concerns only the external functions of a language, its relation to the non-linguistic factors that surround it, but not its proper, internal functions. [Hjelmslev 1961: 47]

9.3.7 Semiotics is by definiton the study of sign systems. That language is a proper object of semiotics has never been doubted, but this proposition can now be given a meaning in the context of a formal semiotics based on relational catalysis.

If we now ask what are the objects, other than languages, with which relational semiotics is concerned, we could try to answer on the basis of the traditional concepts of semiotics, or on the basis of substance or function, but we would then get involved in problems of defining substance or function. It would weaken the theoretical structure if such a definition were to be based on some criterion other than a formal one. The basis would have to be imported from outside the theory.

The alternative that is in keeping with the approach adopted at the outset of this paper is to specify the objects of semiotics by means of their form. A possible proposal would be that, for relational semiotics, any system composed of nections is a semiotic. A more stringent proposal that might be more in keeping with traditional approaches to semiotics would require also that the network as a whole, by virtue of the way its nections are interconnected, have a formal structure similar to that of a linguistic structure.

As indicated above, linguistic systems have an up-and-down orientation according to which connections leading upward are to meaning or function or significance, while downward connections are to the things having significance. In language, the latter are expressions. In extending this type of catalysis to systems other than language, we can add substance other than speech, such as artefacts, people, and flora, fauna, and other features of the environment, as well as motor activities. Such substance, of whatever type, may be considered to lie at the bottom of a network that is encatalysed to it, and the upward direction, away from that substance, is toward content, function, or significance. It may seem that function or significance is becoming criterial, despite the above argument against such a thing. In fact, however, it is the downward direction that is specified, and up is merely defined as the opposite of down. Downward is specified, in terms of the cognitive systems of members of a society, as toward sensory-motor apparatus; while upward is away from sense and motor organs. It is from this specification that we can explicate the notion of function, or significance.

9.4 CULTURE AS A SEMIOTIC

> Linguistic theory is led by an inner necessity to recognize not merely the linguistic system, in its schema and in its usage, in its totality and in its individuality, but also man and human society behind language, and all man's sphere of knowledge through language. [Hjelmslev 1961: 127]

We are now ready to turn to the question of whether culture can be subjected to semiotic analysis. The question can be answered affirmatively by demonstrating that various properties of culture can be accounted for by relational catalysis. Whether or not all properties of culture can be so treated is a more difficult question, to which no answer will be attempted here, but the limit, if there is one, has not been reached in the preliminary steps of this study.

9.4.1 Activities

Perhaps the most obvious characteristics of a culture are the activities in which members of the society characteristically engage. Activities are processes, and their essential property is sequence: an activity or process is a sequence of subprocesses; that is, it is relationally syntagmatic. It follows that activities are hierarchically organized, as can easily be verified by observation.

Consider the dinner in American culture. It consists of several courses, as shown in Figure 9.13a, in which the tiny circle represents zero, indicating that appetizer and soup are optional. Each course is a subprocess: the food is served, it is eaten, and the dishes are cleared away. The eating is a further subprocess (Figure 9.13b), and putting the food in the mouth is also a complex process. And so forth.

Looking in the other direction, we can see that the dinner functions

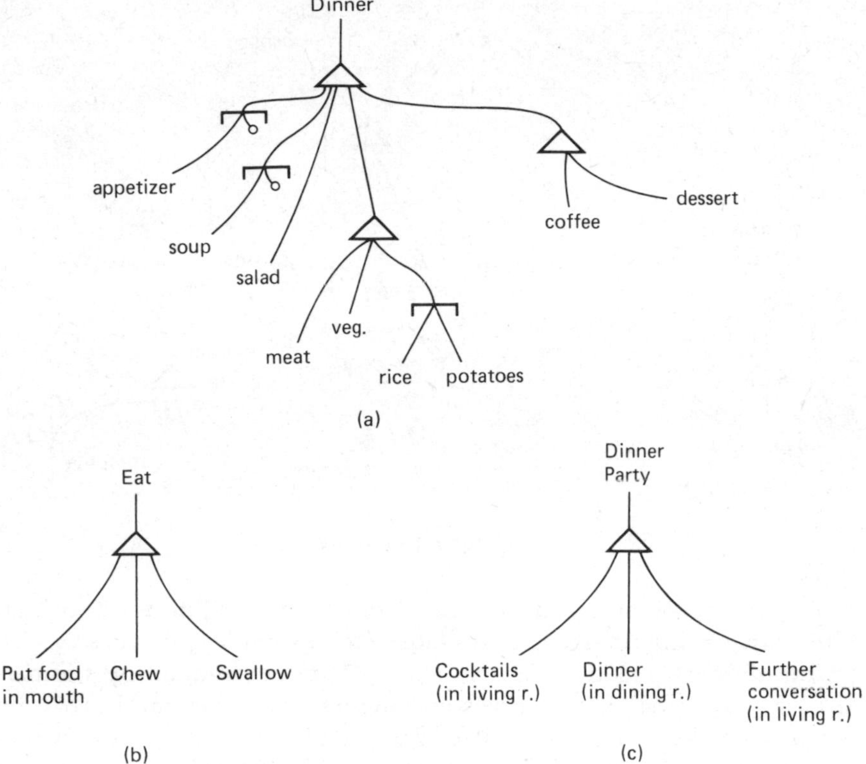

Fig. 9.13 The dinner

as a part of various higher-order processes, such as the dinner-party (Figure 9.13c). And the dinner-party is a component of a still higher-level construction: first the guests must be invited; then the party; then the house and the dishes have to be cleaned.

In dealing with hierarchical structure of activities it is convenient to borrow some terminology from computer programming, an area in which hierarchically organized process is, as it were, the name of the game. Programmers speak of programs, subprograms, routines, and subroutines.

The structure of activity that is humanly organized (and hence culturally important) as opposed to random appears to be characterizable in terms of relational modules of the general form shown in Figure 9.14a. These modules (with variety, of course, in the number of connecting lines and other properties that nections may have) are nections. Like nections of linguistic structure, they are, as mentioned above, organized in hierarchies. One further point is that

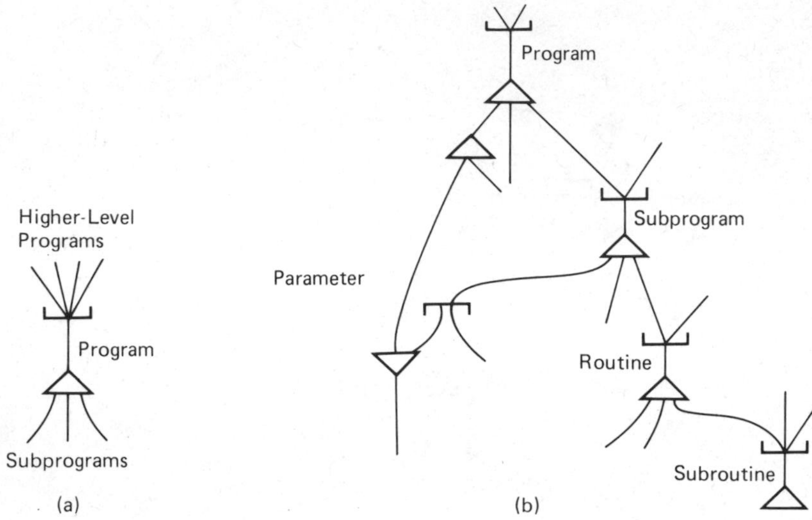

Fig. 9.14 Programs

a process (program, routine) may have choice points, at which alternative subprocesses are available (for example, potatoes or rice in the dinner) and that the choice is often determined by the particular step being executed in some higher-level program. Borrowing again from the terminology of computer programming, such choice-determiners may be called parameters (Figure 9.14b). In Figure 9.14b, the choice is indicated as an ordered 'or' node (used also in Figure 9.7); the line which goes straight through is for the usual case; the one at the side is for the special case, taken if the indicated condition is present (cp. Lamb 1966, Lockwood 1972).

9.4.2 Social Groups

Another important property of any culture is social organization—the people of a society are organized in various social groups. Let us consider the nuclear family—the prototypical social group—as an object for relational catalysis.

The information encatalysed in Figure 9.15 may be represented verbally as follows (roughly from top to bottom): a nuclear family is a part of one or more larger groups (e.g. extended family) and may have various properties and functions in the society; the family is made up of parents and (optionally) children; the parents consist of two people, a woman (the mother) and a man (the father), comprising a married couple; this unit has other properties or functions

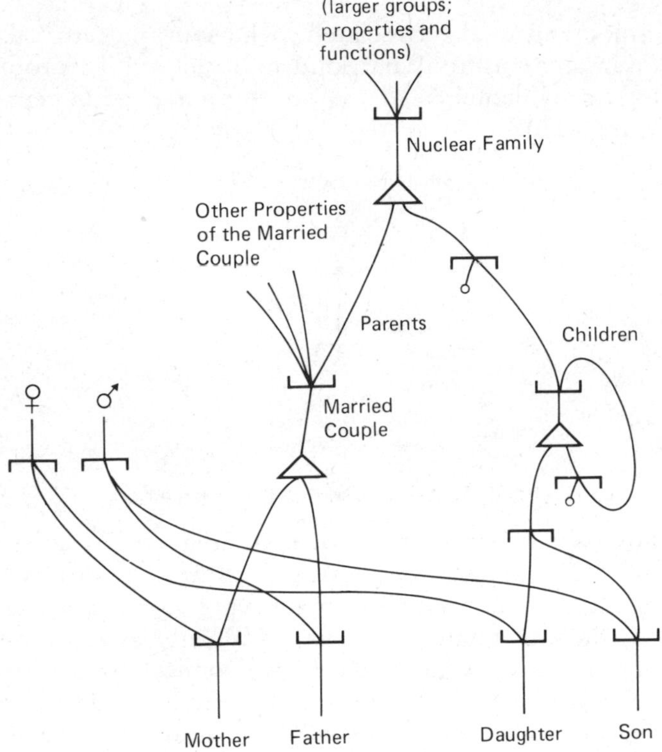

Fig. 9.15 The family

besides its essential participation in the family (for example, they went through a marriage ceremony at one time); as already mentioned, children are optional; if there are any, any beyond the first is likewise optional, and in the (recursive) structure shown no limitation is present on the number of possible children (i.e. possible iterations at the loop); each child is either female (a daughter) or male (a son).

It is clear that this structure, too, is composed of nections, and it requires little or no stretching of the imagination to see these nections as signs in the sense of having significance or function. Thus a boy has function or significance as son within a nuclear family; a married couple has cultural function/significance as parents of a nuclear family; and so forth. This observation perhaps bears out what is suggested above, that our notions of function and significance are related to the 'upward' direction (i.e., away from the sensory-motor 'substance').

9.4.3 Roles and Behaviour Patterns

Societal roles and their associated behaviour patterns also form a structure in any culture. What kind of structure? This too is easily represented as a hierarchy of nections, each nection representing a role (Figure 9.16).

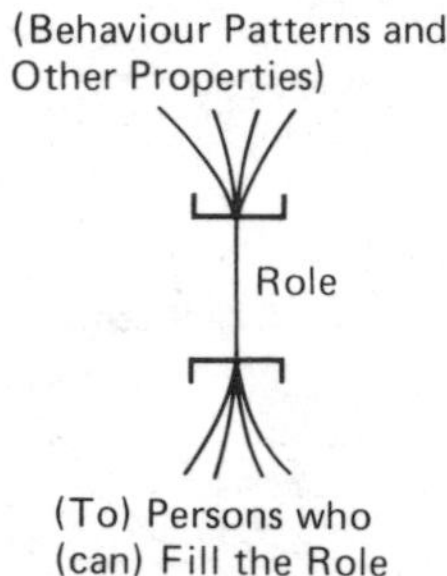

Fig. 9.16 Roles and behaviour patterns

That this type of structure, too, is multilayered is illustrated by the role of military men in American culture. The downward connections from this role lead first to subtypes of military men (army, navy, etc.), then to further subtypes, and only after following the connections through several levels do we connect to nections representing individual members of the society. Similarly, the upward connections lead to higher-level roles and through them to the behaviour patterns and other properties of these higher-level roles. Other features of this type of structure (such as cross-cutting subcategorizations of military men) are mentioned in 9.4.4 which treats the general structural pattern of which the role and behaviour structure is just a part. We may note also that the specification of behaviours involves activities, which are treated above (9.4.1). These various types of cultural subsystems, in other words, are indeed shown to be interconnected in the relational network, just as we would want them to be.

9.4.4 Taxonomies

Any culture imposes upon its members a way of classifying the phenomena of their world. All of the objects, people, plants, and animals, both imaginary and real, abstract concepts, institutions, roles, etc. are taxonomically organized on the basis of similarities which the culture considers important. The taxonomic structure obviously has multiple levels, and the units present at any level have the type of formal structure discussed in 9.4.3, as the structure of roles in a society is no more than a type of taxonomic structure.

As an example to aid the discussion of features of taxonomic structure, let us use a portion of the taxonomy of plants as part of the knowledge of a typical member of American society (Figure 9.17).

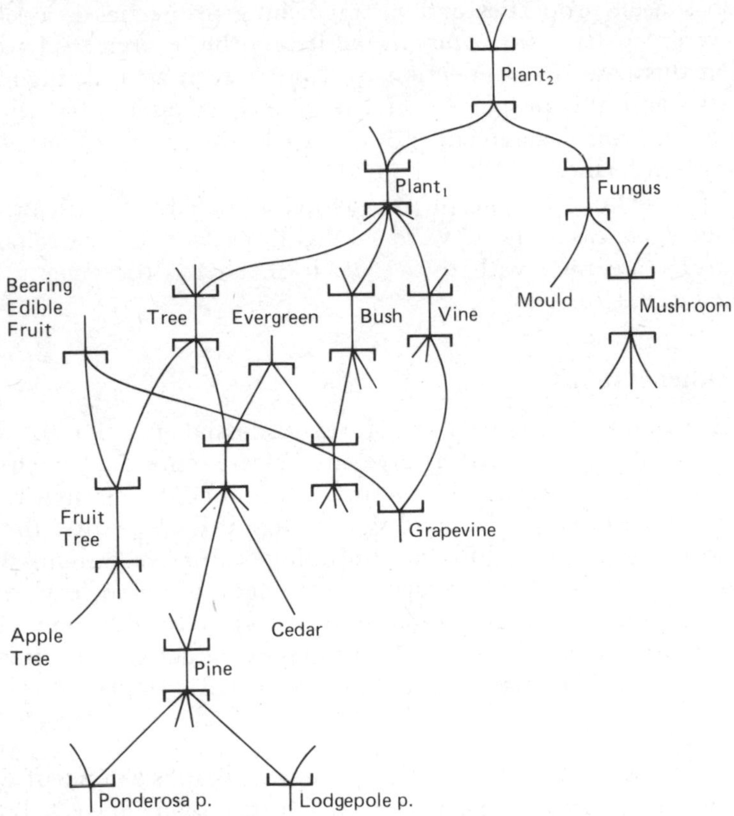

Fig. 9.17 The taxonomy

In keeping with the general orientation discussed above, lines lead upward to or toward properties/functions/significance and downwards to individuals and classes of individuals exhibiting the specified features. This illustration includes two examples of 'cross-cutting' classification: (1) the grouping of some plants as evergreens conflicts with subgrouping into trees and bushes; (2) likewise the grouping of plants which have edible fruit cross-cuts other groupings. As the diagram shows, such cases are easily handled with relational network notation.

We may also take note of the distinction between shared properties and distinguishing features. Evergreen trees are distinguished from other trees by being evergreens; the properties which they share with other trees need not be connected directly to the nection for evergreen trees, since this nection is connected to the **tree** nection, which is, in turn connected (directly and indirectly) to the properties which evergreens share with other trees. Notice also that the distinction beween shared properties and distinguishing properties is a relative one: evergreen trees are *distinguished* from other evergreens by being trees; in this case the connection to 'tree' is seen as a distinguishing property; and the properties of evergreens, given by the upward connections from 'evergreen' (not shown in the diagram) are *shared* by evergreen bushes.

The properties of some plants involve culturally significant activities. In such cases the upward connections lead to the relational structures concerned with those activities, having the general form sketched in 9.4.1.

9.4.5 Other systems

And in general, the various structures discussed in 9.4.1–9.4.4 are interconnected portions of a large integrated semiotic, which may perhaps be called conceptual structure. The conceptual structure constitutes only a portion of a culture, although it is apparently the portion most studied by cultural anthropologists. Other systems which must be included are the language (or languages) of the society and the various perceptual systems (visual, auditory, etc.). In addition we must recognize one or more systems governing motor activity, distinguishable from the activity structures of the conceptual system (9.4.1).

9.4.5.1 Language

Wherever, in any of the conceptual patterns, there is a concept which has a name or label in the culture (such as **dinner, dessert, family, mother, mushroom, pine** in the structures sketched above), the relational network has, *ipso facto*, a connection to a lexeme, which of course is a part of the linguistic system. Thus we can say, about the relation of the language to the conceptual system of a culture, that (1) they are interconnected relational networks, or semiotics, forming subportions of a larger semiotic; and (2) their formal structures, as encatalysed relationally, are quite similar. The relationships between the linguistic and conceptual systems are discussed further below in section 9.5.

9.4.5.2 Perception

We should be prepared to recognize that one culture may differ from another to some extent with respect to the various perceptual systems. It seems obvious that people of all cultures have a great deal of common perceptual structure, based on general properties of brain structure; but it is also apparent that differences can exist from one culture to another, not only because members of different societies are subjected to different kinds of artefacts and other stimuli but also, and more important, because perceptual structure is to a large extent learned and that learning is culturally conditioned.

Preliminary attempts suggest that the various perceptual modalities can be subjected to relational catalysis, and the resulting networks appear to have formal structures quite similar to the linguistic system. The support for this claim, however, will have to wait for another paper.

9.4.5.3 Motor structures

All people walk, but Chinese people walk differently from Americans. All people use facial expressions and hand gestures, but those of Italians are different from those of the English. As with perception, it appears that each culture imposes a certain distinctiveness upon systems having general properties given by the biological structure of human beings. (That observation applies also, though a little less obviously, to language: all people have languages, and there is much in common among the structures of all the world's languages.)

Again, and with apologies, I omit the demonstration, but preliminary study suggests that this area too can be accounted for by relational catalysis. The principles that apply are like those involved in the activity structures of the conceptual network (9.4.1).

It is appropriate to question, at this point, whether the motor structures are really distinct from the activity structures of the conceptual system. Perhaps, it might be argued, the former are just the lower levels of the latter. A full answer will have to await the evidence that can be provided by some detailed relational catalysis in these areas; but it seems evident that an important distinction is to be recognized between 'knowing' what an activity consists of (conceptual relations) and having the ability to perform the activity. Now in the case of activities at lower levels (i.e. where the corresponding neural structures are close to the muscles), such as walking, the information is represented only in the motor modality, except for those individuals who have made an intellectual study of walking; while for higher-level activities, such as the dinner, the information specifying the overall structure of the activity is present only in the conceptual system; so that in this case 'knowing' what the activity consists of does indeed confer the ability to perform in one of the roles involved. But at intermediate levels (perhaps that of eating, for example) there are similar but distinguishable representations in both systems.

The distinction between the motor and conceptual levels thus appears at first glance to resemble a stratal distinction within linguistic structure. Thus, between the phonemic and morphemic strata we can distinguish higher-level structures that are represented only at the morphemic stratum, lower-level structures (involving phonological components) present only at the phonemic, while in between there is an area of overlap but with different treatment at the separate strata: morphological words as opposed to phonological words, morphons as opposed to phonemes, etc.

9.5 LANGUAGE AND CULTURE

You see, people tell us from the time we are born that the world is such and such and so and so, and naturally we have no choice but to see the world the way people have been telling us it is. [Don Juan in *Castaneda 1972: 299*]

A culture as a whole may be characterizable as a vast integrated semiotic in which can be recognized a number of subsemiotics, one of which is the language. Let us now focus on the relationship of the language to the rest of the culture.

Since the language is intricately connected to the rest of the culture (9.4.5.1), it can be considered separate only in the special sense that we as observers choose to recognize a boundary—and such a boundary, to be valid, must be recognizable in the form of the relational network, rather than on the basis of some external criterion. In work with linguistic structure we recognize important boundaries between strata—for example, between the phonemic and morphemic strata. On what basis? The boundary between the morphemic and phonemic strata is easily recognizable in that it amounts to the summation of thousands of boundaries between nections. On the upper side of the boundary are nections that can be called morphemes (cp. Figure 9.5 above). Their lower connections are to points in the phonotactics.

Such a boundary appears to be present between the lexicogrammatical system and the conceptual system. Is this the boundary between language and the rest of culture? The conceptual system, which includes most of the structures discussed in the preceding section, is surely within the scope of what most anthropologists would call culture; but although much of it lies outside the scope of what linguists have customarily concerned themselves with, at least until very recently, it also covers a great deal of the kind of structure most linguists would include within language, such as the syntax of processes and participant roles.

This system, termed the conceptual system up to now in this chapter, appears in fact to be none other than that which has been called the sememic stratum in some of the work in cognitive linguistics (e.g. Johannesson 1976). If these interpretations are correct, the conclusion is that, far from finding a boundary between the jurisdictions of anthropology and linguistics, we find them even more closely intertwined, if that is possible, than did, e.g., Sapir. In other words, as linguistics pushes farther and farther in its studies of what is needed to explain the structure of the clause, it finds itself right in what used to be considered the preserve of the cultural anthropologist.

If we look beyond the sememic (conceptual) stratum, however, we find a boundary that is perhaps more significant. Here we find that the connections are to several other systems, the other modalities—visual, auditory, kinesthetic, kinesic, etc. As indicated above, these systems are within the territory of the cultural anthropologist in so far as they include culturally determined structure; but they are clearly outside the language.

The boundaries between the conceptual system and the various perceptual and motor systems may well be like the stratal boundaries in linguistic structure, except that we encounter a slight problem of direction, the problem of 'which way is up?' According to the policy adopted earlier in this paper, sensory-motor 'substance' is at the bottom, and the direction away from it is *ipso facto* upward. It is this upward direction that corresponds to what semiotically-inclined people are tempted to talk about with such terms as meaning, significance, and function. The problem—which concerns us only momentarily as a problem since it has an obvious solution—is that if we go upward from the bottom of, say, the visual system and continue in the same direction into the linguistic system, we go into the top of the latter and, still continuing in the same direction, out the bottom. The solution is simply to see this pathway as similar to that from one end of an arch to the other.

It appears that the conceptual system is at the top of the various perceptual and motor modalities and is what integrates them and interrelates their information processing. But it is also part of the language. It occupies a central position between the lexico-grammatical system and the perceptual and motor systems, by virtue of which it not only interrelates them but also is dependent upon them for much of its structure. In fact, it acquires its structure, in the information system of the individual, largely through the use of language. Indeed, the very presence of a lexeme in a system produces an automatic assumption that a concept is represented by it. That this is so may be built into the structure of the human information system: following a pathway upwards from a percept leads to a concept. Continuing in the same direction leads to lexeme, which can be taken as a more abstract concept, even though it is in fact nothing but a label. Thus lexemes can automatically get imbued with the status of high-level concepts!

This property and another—the conceptual system's segmentation and categorization of all experience—tend to limit the ability of any human, of any culture, to perceive reality directly. And these properties are evidently built into our instruments for knowing—our minds. Perhaps one of the most important contributions of future work in relational semiotics will be a greater understanding of the ways in which our instruments for knowing the world actually get in the way of that task.

We may then be in a better position to practise techniques for seeing things as they actually are.

NOTES

1. Between 1975, when the first version of this paper was prepared for the Wenner-Gren Symposium, and the beginning of 1983, I have found certain infelicities in some of the assumptions and notational devices that have been used in the so-called cognitive-stratificational school during the decade from 1965 to 1975, when most of the literature of this school appeared. It appears now that certain implications of stratification (e.g. Lockwood 1981) have been overemphasized and that more strata have been seen in linguistic structure than are actually there. On the other hand, the attempt of this school to treat the structure explicitly as a network of relations still appears to be fruitful. I am willing to accept full responsibility for what I now see as an overemphasis on stratification that was characteristic of that decade.

   In preparing this paper for publication I have endeavoured to correct what I now see as the main infelicities that were present in the 1975 version.
2. This proposal, developed out of that in Lamb 1964 under the influence of Halliday (1961) and Hjelmslev (1961), recognizes OR and AND as elementary relations, with two directions ('downward' or toward expression and 'upward' or toward content or function) and with a distinction between ordered AND (concatenation) and unordered AND (simultaneous components) and a different distinction between 'ordered OR' (involving precedence) and 'unordered OR' (no precedence involved).

   Although it has been increasingly apparent for the last few years that improvements are needed in various details of this proposal, it is the one represented in most of the literature in the field of relational network catalysis and I continue it in this paper, since it will take a separate paper of some length to explain and justify an alternative system of elementary relations.

3. The trend, at least in my thinking, has been from more strata to fewer. The number of strata seen in the linguistic structure depends in large part, of course, on the criteria used to draw boundaries, so that the recognition of fewer strata is concomitant with recognition of greater complexity of structure within the stratal system. We would be lucky if that were the only factor. We also have been misled by some notational devices and methodological principles to see more distinctions than necessary. As pointed out at the outset of this note, however, there has been progress over the years as we have found it possible to account for the observed data with fewer strata. Unfortunately, one of the most often cited works in cognitive-stratificational linguistics (Lamb 1966) represents the worst extreme in recognizing multiple strata, having come up with as many as six (although they were seen as falling into just three pairs). (This extreme view was part of my thinking for only a few months.) Much of the literature recognizes four strata (called phonemic, morphemic, lexemic, and sememic), but it now seems more likely (in keeping with the conclusion of Lamb 1971) that there are three, a view not totally different from that of Lamb 1966 with its three pairs of strata, since in each of the three we may recognize a 'deeper' and more 'surface' layer, mediated by alternation relations within the stratum.
4. There is also another type of microscopic analysis, found to be needed in hypotheses of the passage of activation through the network for the encoding and decoding of utterances. Many of the lines of the networks as discussed in this paper can be analysed into pairs of one-way lines of opposite direction (like divided highways), and the nodes as described in this paper are not atomic but are seen as having internal structures which control the passage of impulses.
5. Note that this situation is impossible to represent in the notation of de Saussure's depiction of the sign as a two-sided object (rather than as a relation).
6. This distinction provided the basis of, for example, the treatment of affixes as resulting from morphological processes applied to stems in Sapir's theory of grammar, formalized as the Item-and-Process Model of Hockett (1954).
7. Actually, these one-way sequencing nections are also found when network structures above the level of phonology are subjected to the kind of microscopic analysis mentioned in Note 4. The sequencing property of the ordered both-and nodes is accounted for by the presence of one-way lines of just the kind found in phonotactics.

BIBLIOGRAPHY

Bennett, D. C. (1975), *Spatial and Temporal Uses of English Prepositions: An Essay in Stratificational Semantics*, London, Longman.

Bloomfield, L. (1933), *Language*, New York, Holt.

Castaneda, C. (1972), *Journey to Ixtlan: The Lessons of Don Juan*, New York, Simon and Schuster.

Conklin, H. (1962), 'Lexicographical treatment of folk taxonomies', in Publication 21: 119–42 of the Indiana University Research Center in Anthropology, Folklore, and Linguistics (supplement to *International Journal of American Linguistics*, 28, No. 2).

Copeland, J. E., and Davis, P. W. (1980), *Papers in Cognitive-Stratificational Linguistics*, Rice University Studies, 66, No. 2.

Copeland, J. E., and Davis, P. W. (eds) (1981), *The Seventh LACUS Forum 1980*, Columbia, The Hornbeam Press.

Garvin, P. (ed.) (1970), *Cognition: A Multiple View*, New York, Spartan (reprinted in Makkai and Lockwood 1973).

Halliday, M. A. K. (1961), 'Categories of the Theory of Grammar', *Word*, 17: 241-92.

Hjelmslev, L. (1961), *Prolegomena to a Theory of Language*, translated by Francis J. Whitfield (original edition published 1943), Madison, University of Wisconsin Press.

Hockett, C. F. (1954), 'Two models of grammatical description', *Word*, 10, 210-34 (reprinted in Martin Joos (ed.), *Readings in Linguistics*, Washington, D.C., American Council of Learned Societies; republished in 1966 as *Readings in Linguistics I*, Chicago, University of Chicago Press).

Hockett, C. F. (1961), 'Linguistic elements and their relations', *Language*, 37; 29-53.

Johannesson, N.-L. (1976), *The English Modal Auxiliaries: A Stratificational Account*, Stockholm Studies in English, No. 36, Stockholm, Almqvist & Wiksell International.

Johannesson, N.-L. (1980), 'On Fictive Sentence Analysis', in Copeland and Davis 1980: 75-99.

Lamb, S. M. (1964), 'The Sememic Approach to Structural Semantics', *American Anthropologist*, 66, No. 3, Part 2, 57-78 (reprinted in Makkai and Lockwood 1973).

Lamb, S. M. (1966), *Outline of Stratificational Grammar*, Washington D.C., Georgetown University Press.

Lamb, S. M. (1970), 'Linguistic and Cognitive Networks', in Garvin (1970: 195-222).

Lamb, S. M. (1971), 'The Crooked Path of Progress in Cognitive Linguistics', *Georgetown Monograph Series on Language and Linguistics*, 24: 99-123 (reprinted in Makkai and Lockwood 1973).

Lamb, S. M. (1980), 'A New Look at Phonotactics', in Copeland and Davis (1980: 1-18).

Lockwood, D. G. (1972), *Introduction to Stratificational Linguistics*, New York, Harcourt, Brace, Jovanovich.

Lockwood, D. G. (1981), 'Total Accountability in a Multistratal Theory of Language', in Copeland and Davis (1981: 165-74).

Makkai, A., and Lockwood, D. G. (1973), *Readings in Stratificational Linguistics*, University, Ala., University of Alabama Press.

Pike, K. L. (1967), *Language in Relation to a Unified Theory of the Structure of Human Behavior* (revised edn.), The Hague, Mouton.

Saussure, F. de (1916), *Cours de Linguistique Générale*, published by Ch. Bally and Alb. Sechehaye, 5th edn, Paris, Payot, 1955.

10 Prolegomena to an understanding of semiotics and culture

Ashok R. Kelkar
CASL at Deccan College, Pune, India

'Only connect!'—E. M. Forster, *Howard's End* (1910)

10.1 SEMIOSIS AND HUMAN SEMIOSIS

Prolegomena are always in the danger of erring on the side of being excessively wide-ranging or excessively confined to the preliminaries or both. While I am aware of this danger, I am also aware of the danger that an enquiry into the semiotics *of* culture may end up as an enquiry into semiotics and an enquiry into culture unless both the entities are rendered penetrable first.

First, I propose to give a step-by-step account of the form of semiosis that will build up to its central problems. If, in doing so, I seem to use a terminology reminiscent of the S-R terminology now discredited (cp. Fodor 1965), let it be understood that what I am using is not so much a 'terminology' with any burden of serious claims or presuppositions as to how things really work inside as a 'nomenclature' for ready identification.

Next, I shall propose a way of looking at culture that is likely to prove more fruitful in relation to semiotics. Briefly, I do not think that the study of society and the study of culture are quite the same thing. I also think that the ethnologist's culture with a small 'c' can be fully understood only after relating it to the culture with a capital 'C' of ordinary parlance.

Finally, I shall gather up the strands, or try to. I shall show how the semiotics of culture and the ethnology of semiosis can be defined severally and then interrelated.

*A considerably revised and enlarged version undertaken when the author held a Senior Fellowship of the Central Institute of Indian Languages, Mysore, India has been published in the form of a book entitled *Prolegomena to an Understanding of Semiosis and Culture* (Mysore: Central Institute of Indian Languages, 1980). The version that is being presented here is a slightly revised version of the paper originally presented at the Symposium. In addition to published sources, the author has benefited from personal discussions with Ashok Gangadean and Ramchandra Gandhi.

Although we are concerned primarily with human semiosis here, it is useful to start with a more general framework and speak in terms of organisms. Somewhere along the line we shall let this generality lapse quietly into a specifically human framework.

10.1.1 A rudimentary cosmology

To begin with, then, there is the universe and the organism within the universe. The organism is an organism to the extent it maintains an internal systemic coherence. This in turn depends at least partly on a harmonious interaction with the rest of the universe—at least, with its immediate space-time neighbourhood. The universe minus the organism—especially in so far as the organism interacts with it—is the environment of that organism. The interaction is harmonious to the extent that the survival of the organism is assured along with the continued reproduction of other organisms homogeneous with it (i.e. with a like internal system). From the side of the organism, this interaction is seen as a series of S-events—impacts, presentations, stimuli. From the side of the environment, this interaction is seen as a series of A-events—overt responses, undertakings, acts. S-events and A-events may be life-promoting, life-harming, or indifferent. Mediating the two, presumably, there is another series of events—let us call them I-events—internal to the organism. S-events and S-elicited I-events collectively constitute the experience of the organism to the extent that these cross the threshold into consciousness. A-events and A-motivating I-events collectively constitute the behaviour of the organism to the extent that these cross the threshold into observability. In addition to the S-I and I-A links there are also I-I links. Are all I-events exhaustively accounted for as either S-elicited or A-motivating or both? Or are there I-events that are both I-elicited and I-motivating? If such is the case, how does an investigator get at them? I do not know the answers to these questions though I am sure others have positions to take on the body-and-mind problem. To recapitulate:

1. The universe = organism + its environment.
2. There is interaction harmonious or otherwise between the organism and its environment:
(a) S-events on the organism-interface of the environment;
(b) A-events on the environment-interface of the organism;
(c) I-events internal to the organism.
3. Experience = (S events + S-elicited I-events) that are self-observable.
4. Behaviour = (A-motivating I-events + A-events) that are other-observable.

5. E-events are events in the universe other than S-, I-, and A-events in respect of the organism. These may be S-causing, A-caused, or neither.

Are causing, eliciting, motivating fundamentally similar or fundamentally different? If the latter is the case, just how are they different? 'Eliciting' and 'motivating' seem to link I with I; 'causing' links E with E, E with S, and A with E. Does 'causing' link E with I and I with E? A putative example will be the thermal, chemical, mechanical, electrical changes in the organism directly affected by the corresponding environmental changes and vice versa as opposed to, say, homeostatic responses in the body to thermal changes in the environment. Either we have to recognize two kinds of I-events—I-events proper related to the environment through S- and A-events and I-events with one foot in the environment, or we have to recognize two kinds of organism. How many kinds do we recognize altogether? I do not know the answers to these questions though I am sure others have positions to take on the physical-world-and-body problem. What may be more immediately useful at this point is to indicate that 'eliciting', 'motivating', and 'causing' can each take one of two forms—'binds/is bound by' and 'release/is released by'.

The continued harmonious interaction depends on the presence of certain regularities and near-regularities that somehow establish themselves either *ab initio* or *de novo* along chains of the following sort: E–S, S–I, E–S–I, I–A, A–E, I–A–E, I–I, S–I–I, I–I–A, and so on. Needs, appetites, sensitivities, drives, motives, capacities, interests are some of the commonly recognized types of such routine-promoting regularities and near-regularities.

The life-history of the organism can be described at three levels: (a) a chronicle of all E, S, I, A events involving the organism (where E events may include S, I, A events in respect of other organisms); (b) a description of the routines and near-routines in terms of the regularities and near-regularities; (c) a narration of the short-term or long-term episodes involving minor or major shifts (losses, weakenings, additions, strengthenings, replacements, rearrangements) in the regularities or near-regularities and consequently in the routines (maturation, senescence, learning, unlearning, shock, injury, disease, degeneration, recuperation are some of the commonly recognized types of shift-promoting episodes). Such episodes may themselves yield new routines. Some of the routines may actually be routine-generating routines. But the primary relevance of the episodes is that they bring about a continual restructuring of the organism. From the side of the organism, however, what is more to the point is that the episodes bring about a continual restructuring of the environment for the organism. A widely accepted hypothesis is that life-promoting routines persist and that episodes promoting such routines recur more often. The opposite is said to be the case with life-harming routines and episodes promoting such routines. Semiotic events have to do primarily with such restructurings. To recapitulate:

6. Experience + behaviour = (typically observable) life-history.
7. Life-history = routine-events + episodic events, i.e. (near-)regularities and (near-)restructurings.
8. (Near-)restructurings: (a) of the organism;
   (b) of its environment.

The structuring and restructuring of the environment has primarily to do with E–S–I regularities. There are two considerations here: first, the recognition of a regularity as life-promoting or life-harming leads to an evaluation of the E-event; secondly, any recognition of regularity is more life-promoting than the absence of any such recognition. The structuring and restructuring of the environment of the organism involves, therefore, the recognition of categories of E-events; some of these categories are evaluative. A category, whether evaluative or not, may be more or less reasoned, i.e. there may be greater or lesser play of cognition. Most of the time, the organism is not aware of any reasons for assigning an E-event to a category, though an observer may succeed in correlating objectively assignable properties of an E-event with the I-event recognized as appropriately elicitable from an E–S event-sequence. (Cp. Slotkin 1950: 51–8.)

The structuring and restructuring of the organism has primarily to do with I–A–E regularities. There are again two considerations here: first, the recognition of an E-event as life-promoting or life-hindering and the recognition of an A-event as promoting or hindering an E-event of a certain category leads to a categorization and evaluation of A-events in relation to their E-sequels; secondly, any categorization of an A-event as appropriate in an E–S–I–I–A sequence or in an I–A–S–S–I sequence is more life-promoting than the absence of any such recognition. The structuring or restructuring of the organism involves, therefore, among other things the recognition of categories of A-events; some of these categories of A-events may be evaluative. An A-event may be recognized as an appropriate sequel to an E–S–I sequence (in human parlance, an appropriate way of dealing with a situation) or an appropriate lead to an E–S–I sequence (in human parlance, an appropriate way of leading up to a situation). Correspondingly, an E-event may be recognized as either a lead to an appropriate S–I–A sequel (in human parlance, a situation calling for a certain kind of dealing) or a sequel to an appropriate S–I–A lead (in human parlance, a situation envisaged in undertaking a certain kind of leading up). An observer may recognize a situation as one that can be dealt with appropriately in either one of two ways. The organism may consistently select, however, just one of them. (This has a bearing later on the rise of conventions—at 31(b), (c).) Like categories of E-events, categories of A-events may be more or less reasoned, i.e., there may be greater or lesser play of intention. A piece of behaviour may be undertaken with a clear hope that a desired situation will be maintained or brought about or with a clear fear that in the absence of such a piece of behaviour an undesired situation will continue or come about. The hope or the fear is the motivating I-event. To recapitulate:

9. An E-event is categorizable as:
(a) to be/not to be negotiated in a certain way;
(b) attainable in a certain way;
(c) avoidable in a certain way;
(d) to be enjoyed/endured so long as present;
(e) to be hoped/feared if expected.
10. An A-event is categorizable as:
(f) appropriate/inappropriate for negotiating an E-event of a certain kind;
(g) appropriate for attaining an E-event of a certain kind;
(h) appropriate for avoiding an E-event of a certain kind;
(i) to be enjoyed/endured so long as undertaken;
(j) to be in readiness for/against if indicated.
11. Either of these categorizations may be more or less reasoned; and more or less evaluative.

10.1.2 The form of a semiotic event

Now we are ready for an understanding of semiotic events. What is a semiotic event? Or rather, what is the *form* of a semiotic event? The organism of whose life-history such an event is a part is the interpreter. The interpreter interacts with a dyad—the signant (signans) and the signate (signatum). The signant is primarily an S-event, secondarily the associated I-event and E-event. So is the case with the signate. Typically, the signant is not identical with the signate. A semiotic episode takes place when the occurrence of the signant-S leads to the occurrence of the signate-I without the prior occurrence of the signate-S. The transfer of signant-I to signate-S presupposes a semiotic capacity. Presumably, not all organisms interpret or interpret similarly. A semiotic episode may establish a semiotic routine. Subsequent semiotic events will then conform to this routine. The presence or absence of signant-I, signate-S, and signate-E in the neighbourhood of the semiotic event is not a part of it, though these certainly provide it with a context. The relationship between the signant-E and the signate-E is a signation. Routinized signations are an aspect of the restructuring of the environment to the interpreter. Such a restructuring of courses involves shifts in the categorizations of E-events and A-events. To recapitulate:

12. A semiotic event has the form:
an organism with semiotic capacity as the interpreter
interacts with the dyad:
the signant I_1- - - -S_1- - - -E_1
the signate I_2- - - -S_2- - - -E_2
The angle S_1 I_2 S_2 represents the semiotic transfer. The line E_1 E_2 represents signation which can be routinized.

A question that one can ask at this point is—what is it that leads to the semiotic transfer and the establishment of the signation in the first place and subsequently ensures its routinization? We have mentioned semiotic capacity earlier. What is this capacity a capacity for? It is a capacity for somehow seizing something about the signant-E and signate-E relationship. There is something about the dyad $E_1 : E_2$ that makes it available as a semiotic dyad ($E_1 \rightarrow E_2$, $E_2 \rightarrow E_1$, or $E_1 \rightleftarrows E_2$). There are three questions that one can usefully ask about such a dyad. What makes a dyad $E_1 E_2$ associable? What determines the direction of the semiotic events involving the dyad? What is the strength of the bond? We can only attempt here a partial answer to the questions with the help of illustrations.

13. Grounds of the associability between signant-E and signate-E:
(a) Space-time contiguity between figure and its ground and between figure and another figure against the same ground:
schoolbell (time 1, space figure) : confused hum (time -1-, space ground)
tail (time 1, space figure) : the whole of the dog (time 1, space ground)
rain (time 1, space x) : wet street (time 1-, space x)
(b) Quality-space contiguity:
pigment (red) : blood (red)
black (neutral 'colour') : white (opposite neutral 'colour')
(c) Mixed:
dog shadow (time 1, space figure, shape x) : dog (time -1-, space neighbourhood, shape x)

heartbeat (time 1-, space x, reassuring rhythm):
mother's bosom (time 1-, space neighbourhood, reassuring warmth)

14. Direction of the semiotic event so grounded:
(a) the signant is more accessible than the signate:
recurrent—nonrecurrent
exposed—inner
foreground—background
present cause—future effect
present effect—past cause
sensible even from a distance—sensible on closer approach
(b) the signate is more interesting than the signant:
recurring attendant circumstances—not so recurring impressive event
smoke—fire
swelling—infection
animal cry or track or scent—animal
face or fingerprint or mannerism—identity of a person
appearance of a mushroom—edible or poisonous
(c) the operative signant is more salient than the other potential signant:
visible/audible, sensible to other senses
more intense (brighter, louder, etc.), less intense
greater contrast with ground, lesser contrast with ground
more persistent, less persistent
more extensive, less extensive

15. The strength of the associative bond:
(a) Signant-S binds Signate-I
Signant-S releases Signate-I
(b) Bond valid for the given interpreter on different occasions
Bond valid for the given occasion for different interpreters
Bond valid for the given occasion and the given interpreter
(c) Bond valid for other Es homogeneous with the given E
Bond valid for the given E as such.

Semiotic events can be in one of two modes—events in which the signant 'alerts' the interpreter to the signate and events in which the signant 'reminds' the interpreter of the signate. In the alerting or signalling mode, the signant in some sense points to the existence of the signate in the space-time stretch of the interpreter's environment: it binds or at least releases the interpreter to attend to and respond appropriately to the signate. This is typically grounded in causal space-time contiguity. In the reminding or signifying mode, the signant does no such pointing: it merely binds or releases the interpreter to entertain the signate and respond to it appropriately, to think of the signate. This is typically grounded in non-causal space-time contiguity or quality-space contiguity. Indeed, in ordinary parlance, 'remind' in one of its senses entails resemblance as its ground. We are using the word 'remind' in the sense in which the ground may or may not be resemblance. To recapitulate:

16. Modes of semiosis:
(a) The signant signals the signate, i.e. the interpreter is alerted to the existence of the signate.
(b) The signant signifies the signate, i.e. the interpreter is led to think of the signate, no existence being implied.
Note: Signalling is the more 'primitive' of the two. A given semiotic event may be both signalling and signifying in character.

The difference between the two modes becomes clearer when we consider the routinized signation. In the context of a routinized signation, the observer (including the interpreter) can and may set out to determine whether the semiotic event is apposite, inapposite, or vacuous (appropriate, inappropriate, or null signate). Further, given two such routinized signations the observer (including the interpreter) can and may set out to determine whether the two semiotic events are related by ambiguity, redundance, or neither; and whether the two underlying signations are such as to yield ambiguity, redundance, or neither. Finally, two semiotic events may be related by fusion (shared signant), fission (shared signate), or neither. To recapitulate:

17. Given that a routinized signation underlies a semiotic event, the signant can be judged as:
(a) apposite, inapposite, vacuous;
(b) ambiguous, redundant, biunique;
(c) fusional, fissional, discrete.
Notes: (1) Judgements under (b), (c) can also be made about signations. (2) All these judgements will have to take note of the mode—signalling or signifying—of the semiotic event.

So far we have thought of the signation as holding between an E : E dyad. The earlier analysis of categorization of E-events and A-events brought out certain relationships involving dyads of certain sorts (cp. under (9), (10)). The directionality of these relationships and that of signation are strikingly similar. The first categorizing member in each of the following illustrative dyads is to the second categorized member what the signant is to the signate. In the formulaic presentation the categorized element is placed in square brackets.

E-[S]	Recurring syndrome of shapes and/or colours and/or sounds and/or smells, etc.: object or state of affairs of a familiar kind; identifying qualities : a piece of one's property; a familiar face : a celebrity.
[E-S] -I	Object with familiar qualities : to be enjoyed/endured; upwards, full, light : desirable; downwards, empty, dark : undesirable, negligible; naked : vulnerable, unendurable, etc.; nude : enjoyable; mother, Lincoln, the navy : no joking matter; sweet : enjoyable; bitter : to be endured; object of a certain kind or identity : reverence/abhorrence, sacred/taboo.
[E-S-I] -I-A	Situation of a familiar kind : to be/not to be negotiated in a certain way; high point : to be climbed up to; tiger : to be fled from; hot surface : blowing on it; miscellaneous set, left-over set : unimportant.
I-A-[E-S-I]	A situation of a familiar kind : attaining/avoiding it in a certain way; a safe place—fleeing to; a dangerous place—rushing from.
E-S-I-[I-A]	Activity appropriate/inappropriate for dealing with a certain situation—that situation; eating raw/cooked—certain foods; activity increased—incentive; act of gratitude/revenge: something done to oneself by another.
I-[A-E-S] -I	Activity with a familiar yield : to be enjoyed/endured; losing : painful; ridding : pleasant anticipation or recall.
[I-A] -E-S-I	Activity : its familiar yield; pounding : powder; wiping : clean surface; smearing : covered surface; heating : something edible.

Obviously many of these relationships are fertile ground for the establishment of routinized signations in the alerting or reminding modes. But perhaps we shall be too hasty in identifying the categorizing relationship with the sign-relationship. To recapitulate:

18. The categorizing or its associate is a potential signant for the categorized and its associate, the latter being the potential signates.

One difficulty about semiotic events of this kind is that they are likely to exemplify a common source of attenuation in semiosis.

19. A semiotic event is an attenuated one if the signant signals or signifies the signate to the interpreter, but the interpreter is not aware of one of the following: the signant, the signate, the signation, the whole semiotic event as such.

Examples: (1) Covert signant reported in: 'There was something about him that told me instantly that he was a crook, but I couldn't say what it was'.
(2) Covert signate: 'I know that his demeanour showed that something was the matter but I couldn't put my finger on it'.
(3) Covert signation: 'My presence reassured him, though I bet he didn't get the connection'.
(4) Covert semiotic event: 'Nature, like a good teacher, teaches a lot without seeming to teach anything at all'.

A covert signate is not to be confused with the null-signate of a vacuous semiotic event introduced earlier. Do the 'hidden persuaders' (Packard 1957) use a covert signant? I believe they do.

10.1.3 The socio-cultural landscape

So far we have chosen to deal with one organism at a time except for a glancing reference to the perpetuation of a population of homogeneous organisms. So, the universe occasionally contains many organisms in the same space-time neighbourhood. Of course, given our definition, the environment is necessarily different for each organism. Environments may overlap; they cannot be identical. Sometimes the environment of one organism includes (or, in the case of a parasite, is included in) another organism. Sometimes organisms with a like internal system occupy the same space-time neighbourhood in the universe—that is, the organism is one of a homogeneous population. Out of this arises the possibility of social experience, social behaviour, and social environment. A social organism has social capacity—i.e. the capacity to experience fellow-organisms and behave towards them in a special way. Typically the fellow organisms in question are homogeneous with the social organism in question. Social behaviour tends to be reciprocal—i.e. to take the form of social interaction. Social interaction tends to be routinized leading to the rise of social roles, relationships, and groups. Given the prolonged infancy, the complexity of the I-system, and the relative absence of determinate regularities in S–I–I–A and I–I–I sequences *ab initio* (whether congenitally or maturationally), the human being, especially the immature human being, depends for its harmonious interaction with the environment on social interaction within a homogeneous population. Social interaction imparts a new meaning to harmonious interaction with the environments: (a) it is a means to the latter; (b) the latter includes harmonious interaction with the social environment; (c) the harmony thus comes to involve the survival not only of the organism and the homogeneous population but also of the socially interacting population.

The routine-promoting regularities and near-regularities of experience and behaviour for a social organism tend to be similar to and/or co-ordinated with those of the other members of the socially interacting population. This similarity and co-ordination is life-promoting and is ensured by the shared genetic inheritance (genes pool) and the experience of spatio-temporarily overlapping environments. The overlapping of environments above all means the presence of a shared social envelope of overlapping social environments. So organisms with a social capacity acquire experience-routines and also behaviour-routines in the course of social interaction. There are respectively social categories of experience and behaviour (cp. Slotkin 1950: 53, 64, 7). Moreover, organisms acquire semiotic routines socially. All of these profoundly restructure the organisms and their environments towards similarity and co-ordinatedness. To recapitulate:

20. An organism with social capacity is involved in social experience of other organisms, social behaviour to other organisms, social interaction with other organisms.
21. These other organisms are typically fellow members of a homogeneous population and therefore also have a social capacity. Social experience and behaviour tend thus to be reciprocal. This creates a shared social envelope of overlapping social environments.
22. Similar and/or co-ordinated experience and behaviour routines are due to:
(a) shared genetic inheritance;
(b) overlapping environments, especially social environments—in the latter leading to the rise of categories and socially routinized semiosis.

10.1.4 The form of a communicative event

Thus, semiotic events are profoundly affected by and profoundly affect social interaction. A socially routinized semiotic event may be judged not simply as apposite, inapposite, or vacuous (see 17(a)) but also as conforming or non-conforming to what is socially categorized as apposite, inapposite, or vacuous. For example, the diagnosis by a physician may be apposite but non-conforming or may be inapposite or vacuous but conforming!

23. When a semiotic event is socially routinized, it can be judged as conforming or non-conforming, according as the situation for the interpreter conforms or does not conform to the socially routinized signation.

Further, semiotic events may be socially induced. An organism with a semiotic and social capacity will induce semiotic events involving other organisms. In other words, organisms act as communicators.

What is the form of a communicative event? A communicative event is a special case of a cybernetic event. Measurement, control, and the transmission, storage, retrieval, and processing of 'information' all involve cybernetic events. We shall not attempt a characterization of cybernetic events; nor shall we try to say whether any or all semiotic events are cybernetic events. Our concern is more limited here: we shall attempt to build a conceptual bridge between semiotic events and communicative events. In so doing we shall have primarily before us man–man communication, though I believe that some of the considerations taken up here also apply in part to communication involving non-human organisms and/or man-made machines in addition to or in lieu of human beings. In building the conceptual bridge, we shall find it useful to talk informally of more 'primitive' and less 'primitive' semiotic events. (Recall note to 16 (p. 108).)

24. Some semiotic events are more primitive than others. In the following pairs the first member is more primitive than the second:

(a) (i) A non-routinized semiotic event.
(ii) A routinized semiotic event, i.e. one grounded in a routinized signation.

(b) (i) A semiotic event in the signalling mode in which the signate-I is wholly appropriate to the signate-E (classical conditioning and operent conditioning yield semiotic routines of this sort).
(ii) A semiotic event in the signalling mode in which this is not the case (i.e. cases in which one is driven to postulate modified appropriate responses or better to accept that this is some wholly new kind of appropriateness, some new kind of 'being in readiness for'). (Cp. Fodor 1965.)

(c) (i) A semiotic event in the signalling mode.

(ii) A semiotic event in the signifying mode.

(d) (i) A semiotic event in which E_1 signals or signifies E_2 to the Interpreter without the Interpreter being aware of the signant or the signate or the signation or of the semiotic event as such.
(ii) A semiotic event in which E_1 signals or signifies E_2 to the Interpreter with the Interpreter being aware of the semiotic event in its fullness.

(e) In some semiotic events, the signant-E may happen to be an A-event of another organism or an E-event caused by an A-event of another organism. Let this other organism be called the Neighbour to be distinguished from the Interpreter; and let the signate-E be called an Emanate of the Neighbour.
(i) The neighbour is not aware of the emanate being a signant to the Interpreter of some signate.
(ii) The neighbour is aware of the emanate being a signant to the Interpreter of some signate.

(f) In some semiotic events of the sort described in (e(ii)) above
(i) the semiotic event does not happen in accordance with the intention of the neighbour (though possibly it may meet with the neighbour's approval);
(ii) the semiotic event happens in accordance with the intention of the neighbour (i.e. the emanate is brought about in order that the semiotic event be brought about).

This brings us close to the communicative event. Some communicative events are more primitive than others. A convenient way of handling this is to propose successively richer definitions of the term 'communicative event'. The more completely communicative the event, the more fully reciprocal the social interaction.

25. (a) A communicative event of the first degree is an event involving two events, namely:
(i) the underlying semiotic event in which the emanate of the communicator is the signant of a signate to the addresses;
(ii) the supervening semiotic event in which the emanate signals the underlying semiotic event to the communicator (i.e. the underlying semiotic event occurs in accordance with the intention of the communicator).
Example: A child (the communicator) shams (the intentional emanate) distress (the signate to the addresses) to the mother (the addressee). The mother may or may not recognize the underlying semiotic event (cp. 24 (d) (ii)). If she does, she may or may not recognize the supervening semiotic event. If she

does she may or may not 'refuse to oblige', i.e. refuse to offer the child a favour. In any case the child has the communicative intent (cp. 24 (f) (ii)).

(b) A communicative event of the second degree is a communicative event of the first degree such that—
(i) the underlying event is a complex of semiotic events in which the addressee is aware of the first-degree underlying event and of the second-degree supervening event;
(ii) the supervening event is a complex of semiotic events in which the emanate signals the second-degree underlying event to the communicator.
Example: A child plays the distress-shamming game with the mother. The mother may or may not 'refuse to play', i.e. to refuse to offer the favour anticipated by the child. Of course the child may or may not have played the game 'in earnest', i.e. may or may not have anticipated any offer of a favour.
Note: Conditions (i) and (ii) have prototypes in Grice (1957) and Strawson's (1964), Lewis's (1969), Gandhi's (1974) refinements thereof.

(c) A communicative event of the third degree is a communicative event of the second degree in which:
(i) there is the second-degree underlying event;
(ii) there is a co-underlying event in which the emanate of the communicator is a signant to the signate also to the communicator;
(iii) there is the supervening event in which the emanate signals not only the second-degree underlying event but also a match between the underlying and the co-underlying events.
Example: A policeman (the communicator) tries to get the motorist (the addressee) to stop the car (the signate) by waving (the emanate). Had he done so by standing in the way or by leaving a large conspicuous boulder or by shooting a bullet into the tyre, we could merely credit him respectively with a communicative event of the second degree, a communicative event of the first degree, a cybernetic event of the control variety.
Note: Condition (ii) and the new elements in (iii) are an attempt to meet certain critiques of Grice (1957), e.g. it is designed to exclude Zipf's counter-example (1967) (the irascible George who says ugh ugh blugh blugh ugh blug blug in reply to what he considers to be the army officer's moronic questions in order to openly offend him) but include Grice's paradigm examples of 'A meant something by *x*' (= *x* non-naturally means something). Zipf's counter-example is also Searle's example of the 'American soldier'

(1965: 229-30, commented on at Lewis 1969: 157) are communicative events of the second degree but not of the third degree.

A communicative event as here considered is, then, a certain configuration of semiotic events amounting to a social interaction. Can there be a communicative event that amounts to a social interaction that does not involve semiotic events? We are not concerned with that here. An organism has to have, in order to act as a communicator or an addressee, not merely the semiotic capacity but also a capacity to behave socially (Gandhi 1974). In order to anticipate the underlying event involving the addressee, the communicator must bring himself to credit the addressee with some semiotic capacity (degrees 1-3) and some social capacity to credit the communicator with communicative intention (degrees 2-3). (The policeman, for example, would not risk his neck by standing in the way of the car if he had a really low opinion of the motorist's intelligence and character. He would rely on the boulder or the bullet instead.) Moreover, communicative intention involves the semiotic virtuosity to select the ground for the underlying event and to gauge the strength of the bond concerned. The addressee in his turn must bring himself to credit the communicator with communicative intention and to gauge the communicator's semiotic virtuosity.

What are the grounds typically supporting underlying (and co-underlying) semiotic events under communicative events? These semiotic events may be in the signalling mode or in the signifying mode. We can only attempt a partial answer to this question with the help of illustrations:

26. The addressee may be brought to be alerted to the signate by selecting a signant that depends on:
(a) simulation of salient associable symptoms (e.g. the so-called expressive gestures);
(b) salient associable space-time contiguity (these are pointers of various kinds as in blazing a trail).
27. The addressee may be brought to be reminded of the signate by selecting a signant that depends on:
(a) simulation of associable resemblance (these are icons of various kinds);
(b) salient conspicuousness against ground (knot on the finger as a reminder; poetic deviations of various kinds; peculiar non-chancy combination).
28. The addressee may be brought to be alerted to or reminded of the signate by selecting a signant that need not depend on associability or salience at all and that depends on:

(a) covenant between the communicator and the addressee
(example: the Paul Revere parable);
(b) convention in which the addressee is inducted previously or specially for the communicative event
(example: traffic signals);
(c) contextualization with which the addressee is already familiar or is specially familiarized in anticipation of the communicative event (the space–time contiguity this time is not between the signant and the signate but between the signant and its semiotic contexts)
(example: most non-technical language).

It will be noticed that in respect of the underlying and co-underlying events in the signifying mode of a communicative event of the third degree, the 'reminding' may not literally be a 're-minding'; the signate may be of a totally novel kind.

It will also be noticed that the constitutive semiotic events in a communicative event need not depend on the association between the signant and the signate (cp. 26(a), (b); 27(a)). Rather it can depend on the association between the signant and the occasions and textual contexts of its previous uses (cp. 28(c)) or on the salience of the signant from its ground (cp. 27(b)) so long as limited, secretive communication is not desired or, finally, on social learning as such (cp. 28(a), (b)). All of these are ultimately grounded in (1) the communicator's communicative intention, (2) the potential resulting by-play (the addressee recognizing the communicator's intention, the communicator recognizing the addressee's recognition, the addressee recognizing the communicator's recognition, and so on indefinitely potentially), and (3) the potential acquiescence of the communicator in the underlying semiotic event. So not only do we have to think of the appositeness, inappositeness, and vacuousness of the original semiotic event (cp. the illustrations at 26, 27, and 28), but also of the supporting events.

29. The communicator may or may not:
(a) succeed in saying what he intended the addressee to understand;
(b) say what he himself would consider to be apposite as an observer;
(c) end up having the addressee understand what he intended the addressee to understand;
(d) recognize it if he has failed under (a), (b), (c).
30. The addressee may or may not:
(a) succeed in understanding what was said;
(b) consider as an observer what he understood as having been said to be apposite, inapposite, or vacuous;

(c) end up understanding the way the communicator intended him to understand;
(d) recognize what the communicator himself would consider apposite;
(e) recognize it if he has failed under (a), (b), (c), (d).

The gap between saying and understanding (30(a)) and between saying and intending to say (29(a)) will arise if there is a gap between conformity and appositeness (cp. 17(a), 23): the addressee and the communicator may commit errors in conforming to the routine. The failures under 29(c) and 30(a) may also be due to channel failure or disturbance. The former's understanding and the latter's intention may or may not jibe if one or both fail to conform or if the two operate on different signations which are not socially normalized. The addressee may understand what is said and intended and yet refuse to agree as an observer. The communicator may play false and the addressee may or may not see through. Finally, the communicator or the addressee or either may not be borne out by the actual state of affairs as seen by the observer.

Communication of the third degree opens the door wide for signates of the underlying (and co-underlying) events that are I-events to the interpreter concerned. Our definition of the semiotic event under 12 thus stands emended. Be it noted, however, that to the extent one is alerted or reminded of one's I-events, they tend to be deemed to be part of one's environment—E-events by courtesy so to say!

The communicator and the addressee may or may not identify each other—this happens in 'broadcast' or 'relayed' communication (e.g. traffic signals, blazing a trail, telephonic communication). There may be interpreters other than the addressee in the communicative event (e.g. the communicator monitoring, the bystanders, the relayers). Finally, the addressee may be no other than the communicator (e.g. the knot on the finger, talking to oneself, using inaccessible 'subvocal speech' as the emanate).

The notion of conformity that is only marginally applicable to non-communicative semiotic events and loosely routinized communicative semiotic events becomes central to formally covenanted or conventionalized communicative events though not to those depending on contextualization. Conformity is the mainstay of these latter, second only to communicative intention. Conformity to a covenant can be regarded as the limiting case of conformity to a convention. What is the form of a convention? (Cp. Lewis 1969.)

31. Given that there are:

(a) a socially interacting population whose members have interlocking interests conducive to and promotable by similar and/or co-ordinated behaviour;
(b) a recurring problematic situation categorized as leading up to n (where $n > 1$) equally feasible ways of negotiating it;
(c) the pressing need to similar and/or co-ordinated ways of negotiating on the part of the members and consequently to the limiting of alternatives;

a convention in favour of m ways of negotiating the recurring problem holds (where m is 1 or some number fairly smaller than n) to the extent that each of the following holds:

(d) every member wants and expects himself to conform if others conform;
(e) every member wants and expects others to conform if he himself conforms;
(f) consequently every member does actually conform;
(g) consequently it is common knowledge that (d, e, f) is the case (that is, every member has reason to believe that (d, e, f) is the case *and* that (g) is the case).

In the present case the pressing need is for the communicator to select a signant efficient for alerting or reminding an addressee in respect of the signate. The need for uniformity or near-uniformity, for absolute or near-absolute conformity, and for the common knowledge of convention is more pressing to the extent that (1) the signant is to be a fully controlled emanate; (2) the signant dispenses with alerting contiguity (deixis) or reminding resemblance (iconism) or context present at the time of the semiosis (contextualization) or salience from its ground (prominence); (3) the population is lacking in close interaction and closely interlocking interests; (4) the semiosis is signifying rather than signalling.

10.1.5 Communicative events as cultural events

To recapitulate, we have seen:

1-11, a general map of events physical, biosomatic, and biopsychic, a rudimentary cosmology so to say;
12-19, a general map of semiosis, its attenuations and accentuations:
20-22, a general map of the biosocial and bioethnic dimension;
23-31, a further account of the attenuations, accentuations, and complications of semiosis in the context of the socioethnic and the cybernetic dimensions—specifically, a general map of the communicative event.

As we home in to the major human modes of semiosis like language, fiduciary matters, logico-mathematics, technical language, ritual-myth-poetry-iconography, ritual-law-power, we have to introduce some more pieces of conceptual machinery. We shall do it in a schematic fashion. A sign is a semiotic network used on a routinized signation.

32. A set of signs constitutes a sign-system to the extent that each of the following holds:
(a) there is an interpreter (or a population of socially interacting interprcters) for whom the signations hold;
(b) the signs are so collated that there is no ambivalence;
(c) the signs are so collated that there is no equivalence;
(d) the set of signates is recognized as a category.

Note: This is the principle of necessity recognized by linguists (cp. Kelkar 1964).

33. Given a sign-system, the following can also hold:
(a) one out of the set of signs may involve a null-signant (i.e. the absence of any other signant itself acts as a signant);
(b) one of the set of signs may involve the overall category: the sign-focus;
(c) there may be another sign-system (subjacent) such that a signant of the latter cannot operate unless a signant of the former (superjacent) operates.

Examples of 32, 33:

(i) Superjacent and subjacent systems

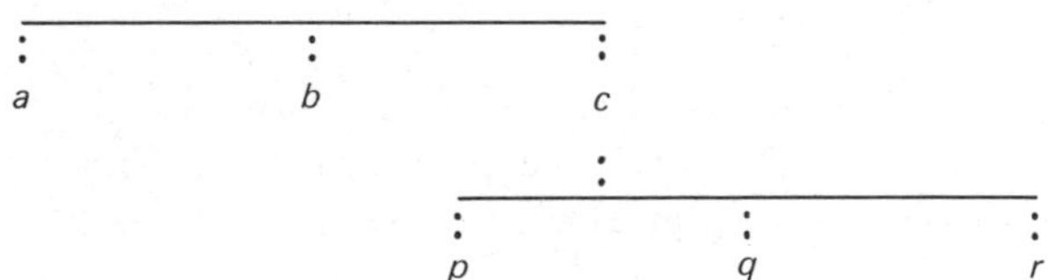

Fig. 10.1 Superjacent and subjacent sign-systems

That is: *a, b, c, cp, cq, cr* can occur, but not *p, q,* or *r* by itself; *c* is the focal signant of *p, q,* and *r.*

(ii) Adjacent systems

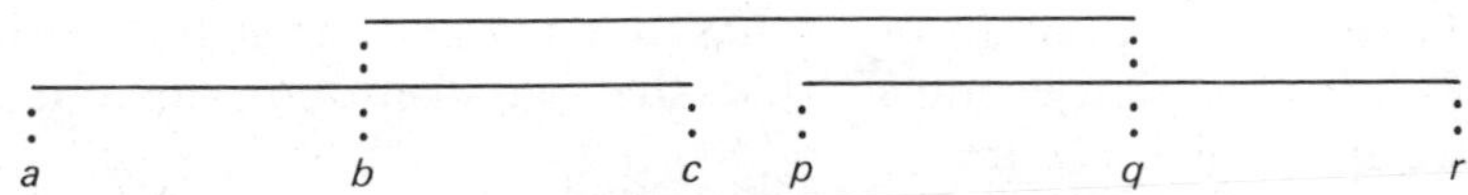

Fig. 10.2 Adjacent sign-systems

That is: *ap, aq, ar, bp, bq, br, cp, cq, cr, a, b, c, p, q, r* can all occur. The homeopath's systems of symptoms are adjacent; the allopath's systems are more apt to be arranged hierarchically as superjacent and subjacent systems. A conventional communicative sign-system (cp. 31(c)) is an attempt to solve the problem of co-ordination (Lewis 1969).

(iii) A sign-system typically offers a bank of alternate messages. To the extent that a semiotic event not merely signals or signifies a given signate but correspondingly signals (or signifies) the exclusion of certain other signates that might as well as have appeared in its place (cp. the notion of measure of information in information theory), all the alternate semiotic relationships constitute such a bank. To say that the wine is not red is to say that it is 'white' (pale yellow); but to say that the flag is not red is to say that it may be white, black, blue, green, or whatever. Again, to say that the wine is not red is to say nothing as to whether it is still or sparkling, sweet or 'dry' (not sweet). Typically a sign-system is a subjacent sign-system where certain alternate messages are 'taken care of' in its superjacent sign-systems. Thus, to say that the wine is red (or not red) takes it for granted that we are not interested in finding an answer there to questions as to whether the wine is a drink, is a kind of beer, is truthful (*in vino veritas*!), is lugubrious, and so forth. The statement that the present King of France is bald is vacuous at the present time, not inapposite, while the statement that France has got a bald king will be inapposite at the present time.

34. A set of semiotic events (especially with underlying routinized signations) constitutes a polarizing semiotic-event complex to the extent that each of the following holds:
(a) there is an interpreter (or a population of socially interacting interpreters) for whom the semiotic-events (and the signations if any) hold;
(b) the semiotic events so concur that there is no fusion;
(c) the semiotic events so concur that there is no fission;
(d) the set of signate is recognized as a complex event.

35. Given a polarizing semiotic-event complex, the following can also hold:
(a) one out of the set of semiotic events may involve a null-signant;
(b) one of the set of semiotic events may involve the signate-complex —the focal sign-event so that the sign-event-complex becomes a complex sign-event;
(c) one out of the set of semiotic events may involve negation or a null-set as a signate;

(d) there may be another complex semiotic event such that a signant of the latter cannot operate unless a signant of the former operates.

36. A set of semiotic events (especially with underlying routinized signations) constitutes a catenated semiotic event to the extent that each of the following holds:

(a) there is an interpreter (or a population of socially interacting interpreters) for whom the semiotic events (and the signations if any) hold;

(b) thc semiotic events are catenated such that the signate of the earlier member is the signant of the next member in the catenation;

(c) there is an initial member of the catenation whose signant is not the signate of any other sign-event and a final member of the catenation whose signate is not the signant of any other sign-event.

Examples:

(i) type—[token= type]—[token= type]—token

(ii) token—[type = token]—[type= token]—type

(iii) use of token—[token= use of a token]—token

(iv) word—literal signate—metaphoric or metonymic signate

(v) sentence—primary signate say, question—displaced signate say, request

(vi) text—conventional signate, say, straightforward signate—stylized signate, say, poem

(vii) vehicle—[message as signate= message as signant]—ultimate signate

(viii) sentence type signifying—sentence token signalling—use of sentence token (Strawson 1950: section II uses the terminology 'a sentence—a use of a sentence—an utterance of a sentence' for this catenation.)

(ix) Common term—diagnostic characteristics—defining characteristics—object referred to
(x) common term—abstract-object-types—object-token token
(xi) text—literal meaning—allegorical meaning—moral insight
(xii) relaying signant—original signant—original signate
(xiii) substitute signant—original signant—original signate

37. Given two sign-systems, one can be the object-sign-system and the other the meta-sign-system to the extent that each of the following holds good:
(a) the meta-sign-system is superjacent to the object-sign-system through the category sign;
(b) several of the meta-sign-signates are the members of the object-sign-system.

Example:

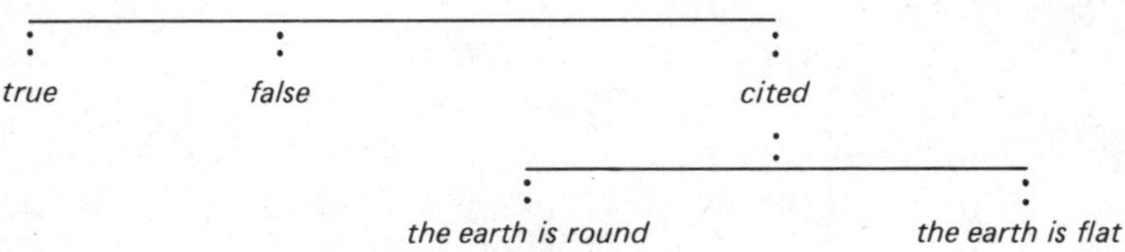

Fig. 10.3 Meta-sign-systems and object-sign-systems

38. Given two sign-systems, one can be the enacting-sign-system and the other the enacted-sign-system to the extent that each of the following holds:
(a) the enacting-sign-system is superjacent to the enacted-sign-system through the category sign;
(b) for several of the enacting-sign-relationships, it is the case that each signals, when combined with the category sign, a token of the enacted-sign-types;
(c) the category signant signifies the enactive intention-type.

Example:

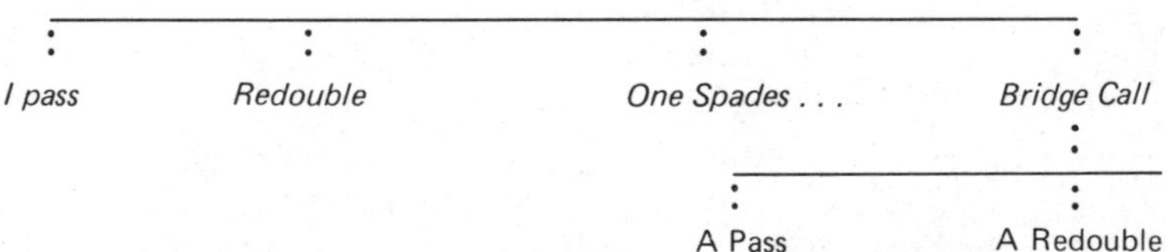

Fig. 10.4 Enacting sign-systems and enacted sign-systems

39. A set of semiotic events (especially with underlying routinized

signations) constitutes a radiating semiotic-event-complex to the extent that each of the following holds:

(a) there is an interpreter for whom all the semiotic events (and the signations) hold or there are a set of interpreters (for example, the addressee, the communicator, and some others in a communicative event) between whom the semiotic events (and the signations) hold;

(b) the set of signants is recognized as a complex object;

(c) the signates are non-identical though there may be an overlap.

40. Given a radiating semiotic-event-complex, the following can also hold:

(a) one of the set of semiotic events may be covert to some of the interpreters in accordance with the intention of the communicator or with the approval of some of the interpreters;

(b) one of the set of semiotic events may involve the signant-complex itself—the focal semiotic-event so that the semiotic-event-complex becomes a complex semiotic event;

(c) each or most of the signates participate in a sign-system (its universe).

Examples of 39, 40:

(i) a pun (different from ambiguity);
(ii) irony, including dramatic irony, Socratic irony, a practical joke, unintended humour;
(iii) a richly complex poem;
(iv) self-announcing and self-effacing ciphers;
(v) a message is very often the focal semiotic event of a radiating semiotic-event-complex, the constitutive semiotic events belong to their universes;

Typically:

message—the occurrence of the emanate over the channel from a universe of admissible emanate occurrences (apposite: intelligible to an interpreter, tenable to a communicator, coherent to both)

message—the subject-matter from a universe of admissible referents (apposite: verifiable to an interpreter, sense-satisfying to the communicator, referring to both; synthetic if universe-sensitive, analytic if universe-neutral; deictic if communicative-context-sensitive, displaceable if communicative-context-neutral)

message—the communicative context from a universe of admissible communicative contexts (apposite: impressive to an interpreter, expressive to the communicator, felicitous to the addressee and the communicator; personal if communicative-context-sensitive, impersonal if communicative-context-neutral) message—the totality of meanings (a polarized complex semiotic event to the observer)

The appositeness-score of the message need not be the same on all counts. In the understanding of this complex, the problem of priorities can be solved by postulating a spiral procedure. If we name the three constitutive semiotic-event-complexes as the message-form, the message-sense, and the message-purport, we begin with form, then spiral through sense, purport, and then continue the round with form, and so on. At each step other than the first, we make use of all that we have learnt up to that point to gain an insight into the particular constituent in hand.

41. Any semiotic event involving a sign-system, a complex sign, a sign catenation, a meta-sign-system, an enacting-sign-system is less primitive than a comparable semiotic event lacking such involvement.
42. A semiotic event (or an underlying routinized signation) is symbolic to the extent that it is less primitive.
43. In semiotic events and signs of certain kinds,
(a) the signant is an abstract object: type-token, null-signant (33(a), 35(a)), categorizing-categorized, enacted semiotic event;
(b) the signate is an abstract object: semiotic event in the signifying mode (e.g. the fact that a true statement is about), token-type, focal sign is a sign-system, a complex semiotic event, meta-sign semiotic event, enacting semiotic event;
(c) both the signant and the signate are abstract objects: constituent semiotic events in a communicative event other than the first degree underlying semiotic event, either the signant or the signate or both in many catenated semiotic events.

What is the ontic status of the abstract objects referred to in 43? Are some of them I-events of a special kind? Are some of them bioethnic E-events of a special kind? Is the distinction between existence and subsistence to be discredited? I do not know. Perhaps abstractness is a matter of degree. In some sense the signate of the signant *William Shakespeare* is also an abstract object though this abstract object has a location in the space–time neighbourhood of the interpreter.

What I have done so far is to offer an account of the form of semiosis in relation to the universe in which it occurs and thus to provide ourselves with a reasonably sophisticated conceptual apparatus to approach even the major human modes of semiosis. In so doing I have managed to refrain from using the overworked term 'symbol'.

What I have not done is to offer a natural history of semiosis in terms of the biosomatic, the biopsychic, the biosocial, and the bioethnic mechanisms underlying semiosis. I have not, for example, tackled the problem alluded to in 24(b)(ii); I have not said whether the progression from primitive to symbolic has a historical significance; I have not taken a position on the question whether the apparatus of categories is individually acquired and socially ratified or socially acquired and individually ratified or both or neither (being largely innate).

Again, what I have not done is to take up positions on the major philosophical questions that arise at various points—the ontology of the various entities, the epistemology of the study of signs, and so forth.

Finally, what I have not done is to apply the apparatus to some of the more interesting details—the form and history of the linguistic sign-system, the problem of the semiotics of quotation, citation, allusion, paraphrase, translation, and the like, the semiotics of poetry, fiction, myth and the like, the semiotics of technical formalisms, the semiotics of style, of perception, of abstractions in thinking, of the sentential moods, and so on.

10.2 A CLOSER LOOK AT HUMAN CULTURE

So far we have looked almost exclusively at one of the major kinds of bioethnic events: namely, semiotic events. In so doing we could not refrain for long getting ourselves involved with other major kinds. The communicative event is built around the communicative intention and the enacted sign-event around the enactive intention. Both of them thus involve an interlacing of semiosis with praxis. (Philosophers have recently been developing theories of action or praxis.) And of course through all semiotic events—especially those in the signalling mode and those based on categorizings—the thread of gnosis runs. (Theories of meaning have always been within hailing distance from theories of knowledge.) In pursuing this line of thinking further, we shall soon face the central bioethnic question: Given that man does not live by bread alone as Jesus reminded Satan (Matthew 4:4 quoting Deuteronomy 8:3), what else does he live by? More pertinently, how else does he live? In what other ways does man maintain his dialogue with the universe?

10.2.1 The forms of life

To offer a schema:

44. The distinctive modes in which the human organism negotiates the universe (the environment and the organism itself included) can be divided into two main groups:
(a) primarily concerned with the interface
   (i) E–S–I sequences:
      gnosis: insight, cognition, memories
      aesthesis: appreciation, evaluation, sentiments
   (ii) I–A–E sequences:
      praxis: play, work, strategies
      gnosis: creation, production, figures
(b) serving and directing the foregoing:
      semiosis: signalling, signifying
      cathexis: love, loyalty
      diopsis: predilection, stance

Note: The choice of the Greek terms is a conscious tribute to the Greeks, the way one uses the terms 'volt' or 'Newton's Law'.

45. Concerning the first four (44(a)), one may point out that with each of these there are two questions:
(a) Gnosis: What is right? What are the grounds?
   Cognition proceeds from the latter to the former.
   Evaluation proceeds from the latter to the former.
(b) Aesthesis: What is right? What are the grounds?
   Appreciation proceeds from the former to the latter.
   Evaluation proceeds from the latter to the former.
(c) Praxis: What is right? What is the payoff?
   Work proceeds from the latter to the former.
   Play proceeds from the former to the latter.
(d) Poesis: What is right? What is the payoff?
   Production proceeds from the latter to the former.
   Creation proceeds from the former to the latter.

Note (i): It should be clear by now, if not earlier, that it is not as if gnosis is to aesthesis what praxis is to poesis. The proportions are on the following lines:
(a) Gnosis (E:S–I) : Aesthesis (E–S:I)
   = Work-Play (I–A:E): Intention-Imagination (I:A–E)
(b) Praxis : Poesis
   = Intake-Output in Gnosis-Aesthesis: Processing in Gnosis-Aesthesis

Note (ii): A seer assimilates cognition to insight, and evaluation to appreciation; a philosopher the opposite. Superstition eliminates cognition; pedantry the opposite. Vulgarity eliminates evaluation; philistinism the opposite. A saint assimilates work to play, production to creation; an artist assimilates play to work, creation to production. Alienation eliminates either work and production (Bohemia) or play and creation (Suburbia). (Many would-be Marxists suffer from Suburbia!)

46. The form of the first four:

(a) Gnosis: Intake: Sensing, Attending to
Primary processing (labelling and storing): Perception, Conception
Secondary processing (computing general possibilities and impossibilities): Intuition, Model-building
Tertiary processing (computing specific probabilities and improbabilities), the output being Judgements, Problem-solutions

(b) Aesthesis: Input: nature, production, creation
Primary processing: Sensibility
Secondary processing: Exploration
Output: Positive/Negative attitude-formation

(c) Praxis: Agent performs Act achieving or failing to achieve Goal overcoming Resistance/Opposition and utilizing Instrumentality/ Assistance as given in the Scene (cp. Burke 1945).

(d) Poesis: Maker transforms Material into Object in a certain Manner in the given Circumstances. The Material may offer Resistance and the Manner may involve Instrumentality.

47. The form of the last three:

(a) Semiosis: Interpreter reads the Signate into the Signant given the Ground.

(b) Cathexis: Object: Person, Object, the Universe of Persons, the Universe of Objects, Value
The Subject gratuitously/routinely shows Love/Hate, Loyalty/ Enmity.
In Love/Loyalty the Subject achieves Intimacy/Involvement.

Note: Charisma (of the Person who stands for the Universe of persons) and Misanthropy are forms of Cathexis. Alienation is the absence of minimal cathexis.

(c) Diopsis: The Subject makes the basic Decisions as to: What is Right? What Grounds/Payoff to look for? What comes first?

48. The Cardinal Dioptic Orientations (in terms of which the other orientations could be located in a Universe of Orientations) are the following:

(a) 'natural' orientations:
 (i) environment;
 (ii) inner urges;
 (iii) residues of previous encounters (mores);

(b) attempts to transcend 'natural' orientations:
    (iv) assimilation of inner urges to environment;
    (v) assimilation of environment to inner urges.

49. Each of the five cardinal dioptic orientations can be characterized in respect of the following:
(a) What is the cardinal principle of Order?
    (Order can release or bind Freedom.)
(b) What is the cardinal principle of Freedom?
    (Freedom can create or destroy Order.)
(c) What is the cardinal social order?
(d) What is the cardinal behaviour prototype?
(e) What are some popular labels available in the modern Western civilization? In the ancient Indian civilization?

50.
(a) (i) environment binds; objectivity principle
    (ii) environment releases; opportunity principle
    (iii) Open Society: Urban: Policies
    (iv) Adult: Ego: Experience
    (v) Realism; Artha; Rājasa
(b) (i) inner urges bind: creativity principle
    (ii) inner urges release: spontaneity principle
    (iii) Open Society: Pastoral: Licences
    (iv) Child: Id: Innocence
    (v) Romanticism; Kāma; Tāmas
(c) (i) mores bind: righteousness principle
    (ii) mores release: security principle
    (iii) Closed Society: Rural: Rituals
    (iv) Parent: Super-Ego: Authority
    (v) Medievalism; Grihastha-Darma; Sāttvika
(d) (i) maturity principle
    (ii) critical detachment principle
    (iii) Closed Society: Urban: Laws
    (iv) Adult-Parent: the Authority after Experience
    (v) Classicism; Nāgara-Dharma; Rājasa
(e) (i) involvement
    (ii) agony and ecstasy
    (iii) circle of love
    (iv) Adult-Child: the Innocence after Experience
    (v) Mysticism: Moksa; Sāttvika

Obviously this sketch (44-50) is the merest beginning. If the first part of this paper is regarded as an expansion of 47(a), one can gauge how much remains to be done in respect of Gnosis, Aesthesis,

Praxis, Poesis, Cathexis, and Diopsis even to offer anything like the prolegomena to the understanding of cultures.

10.2.2 The underlying conceptions of human culture

What I propose to do here instead is to indicate why I consider this way of looking at culture more fruitful. To begin with, I wish to register here certain dissatisfactions:

(1) I am broadly in sympathy with Kroeber's (1949) doctrine of culture as the superorganic and out of sympathy with assimilating the cultural to the social. Towards the end of the first section of this paper I have said that I have not taken a position on the question whether the apparatus of categories is individually acquired and socially ratified or socially acquired and individually ratified or both or neither (being largely innate). I feel that the study of culture should not be cast in a mould that prejudges the issue one way or the other. (A similar prejudging is to be seen in saying social sciences when one means human sciences.)

(2) The approach proposed here will be a better meeting ground for the natural history approach to culture and the humanistic concern for culture shared by historians, philosophers, historians of ideas, literary and art critics, religious and moral ideologues, and the like. The present condition in which psychologists tend to leave the arts alone and sociologists and anthropologists leave love and mysticism alone and in which the humanists have little use for the human scientists' insights is clearly unsatisfactory. The present approach, among other things, is better calculated to let in the penetrating wind of modern philosophical analysis through the study of human sciences.

(3) The study of *a* culture can be endocentric, i.e. in terms of the categories provided by the culture itself, or excentric, i.e. reductive to categories not necessarily ratified by the culture. Both are necessary for a full understanding. What are the possibilities available and the ones actually availed of? Which are the ones sadly missed?

(a) Endocentric:
- (i) in terms of the specific local culture;
- (ii) in terms of the Great Tradition of the inclusive civilization if any.

The only cultures to get the benefit of such study by modern scholars are those in the modern Western civilization. A truly endocentric description should put calligraphy under fine arts if that is where the 'natives' put it; should describe Hindu culture, say, in terms of Dharma, Artha, Kāma, Mokṣa, and the like rather than in terms of the rubrics borrowed from the Modern West.

(b) Excentric:
   (i) in terms of some other culture of civilization;
   (ii) (1) natural history description with minimal interpretation;
   (2) historical chronicle with minimal interpretation;
   (iii) in terms designed to uncover the biotic underpinnings in the broadest sense;
   (iv) in formal universalistic terms.

Out of these the first is reductive in the bad sense unless undertaken in the spirit of clear-sighted comparison. I have already indicated that, while non-Western cultures have had the doubtful benefit of this approach, modern Western culture has never been looked at this way.

The second is of course to be credited with the monuments of ethnography and antiquarian studies coming down from the nineteenth century.

The psychologists, the ethnologists turning their attention to the human animal, and the dialectical materialists have carried out their reductive exercises—chiefly on modern Western Culture—yielding a harvest of penetrating insights into man the unknown and painful distortions of man the known.

Finally, the last approach has made itself felt in modern linguistic analysis, modern economic analysis, the structuralist (inspired by linguistic analysis) and the functionalist studies of portions of various preliterate cultures. Modern analytical philosophers have made notable analyses of modern Western cultural categories—practically unheeded by the human scientists. Psychologists have not learnt much from the economists' analysis of demand.

The sketch presented in this section of the paper is largely an invitation to give the formal approach its due. Having registered my disappointments, let me briefly indicate the possibilities of a full-scale formal approach.

(1) While the separate human sciences have not interpenetrated as much as one would wish in spite of the interdisciplinary seminars and research projects, the formal approach may permit us to speak of the economy of language, the language of the economy, and so forth not as mere decorative verbal flourishes but in more rigorous terms. Certain notions such as style, prophylactic, remedial, palliative, and compensatory praxis, information flow, secrecy, privacy, and esoteric communication recur in various segments of culture and call for an elucidation at the general level.

(2) I have already spoken of the interlacing of semiosis with gnosis and praxis; the study of various such interlacings should serve to throw new light on hitherto poorly defined matters such as myth, art, morality, education, polity, and the like as also on hitherto poorly understood interrelations of the canonical segments of culture.
(3) I have already spoken of the need to offer a natural history of semiosis in terms of the biosomatic, the biopsychic, the biosocial, and the bioethnic underpinnings. Having done that and having done the same for gnosis, aesthesis, praxis, poesis, cathexis, and diopsis one can then come back to the study of society, culture, and human history with greater confidence.
(4) One can do a comparative study of the endocentric categories provided by different local cultures and great civilizations. The present approach suitably developed along the lines indicated just now may yield a revealing metalanguage for such a comparative study.

10.3 THE SEMIOTICS OF CULTURE AND THE ETHNOLOGY OF SEMIOSIS

How do we use phrases of the type X-ology of Y when we use them carefully? We must of course allow for the fact that the names for X and X-ology often happen to be the same—mythology, chemistry, history, grammar, politics, even psychology (as in 'I can't fathom his psychology' which is ambiguous). Some typical examples will be: the chemistry of acids; the zoology of arthropoda; the physics of heavenly bodies; the chemistry of plants. Clearly, before we have a right to speak of the X-ology of Y, either Y must be a species of X or it makes sense of some other sort to say the X of Y. Normally, one would expect, therefore, that the admissibility of the phrase the X-ology of Y will preclude that of the Y-ology of X. If this expectation is correct, how do we account for pairs such as the following?

(a) the art of politics
the politics of art
(b) the psychology of language
the language of the psyche
the language of psychology
the linguistics of psychology (how else does one interpret 'psycholinguistics' when it is not merely a misleading abbreviation of 'the psychology of language'?)
(c) the poetry of grammar
the grammar of poetry

I do not propose to sort out the admissible from the inadmissible in these examples though I may comment in passing that this question has to do with the physical world, body, mind problems. I merely wish to alert the reader that care is necessary in coining such expressions as these:

the semiosis of culture
semiosis in culture
the semiotics of culture
the cultural facts of semiosis
the ethnology of semiosis

I think that it is admissible to speak both of the semiotics of culture (correlatively: semiosis in culture) and the ethnology of semiosis (correlatively: semiosis as a cultural fact). I further think that, for a fruitful exploring of the two, a formal analysis of both semiosis (taken up in sections 10.1.2, 10.1.4, 10.1.5) and culture (on the lines indicated in section 10.2.1) is a prerequisite.

Having done this we can then proceed to divide cultural facts in either of the following manners:

51. Cultural facts:
(a) bioethnic facts proper: the central facts of gnosis, aesthesis, praxis, poesis, semiosis, cathexis, diopsis (section 10.2.1);
(b) their institutionalization, i.e. their biopsychic and biosocial envelope;
(c) their biopsychic, biosocial, biosomatic, physical substratum (consider sections 10.1.1, 10.1.3).

52. Sociocultural facts about semiosis:
(a) semiotic events together with such gnostic, aesthetic, practic, poetic, cathectic, dioptic facts as are subservient to them—all these constituting the semiotic apparatus of a culture;
(b) the deployment of the semiotic apparatus in serving and directing each of the canonical segments of culture such as science, technology of capital and consumer goods, ideology, dogma, myth, ritual, magic, art, craft, games, rapture and conviviality, economy;
(c) the deployment of the semiotic apparatus in each of the canonical segments of the societal fabric such as role and status, modes of social transaction, relationships and groups, social organization, instrumentation, and control (polity, education, morality, manners, crime and deviancy, reinforcement, incentive and disincentive, labour and management).

So, to speak of the semiosis of culture is to speak of 52(b) and to speak of the ethnology of semiosis is to deal with 52(a). The science of language in the large sense will be a branch of the ethnology of semiosis.

The science of language can be studied at any of the three levels indicated under 51:

(a) Linguistics proper where the explanations sought are primarily semiotic explanations (Why is the singular the unmarked member of the category of number?) or explanations of semiotic facts (What are the semiotic consequences of the linearity of the vehicle? Why are negation, proper names, 'I' and 'you' linguistic universals?). This applies equally to the analysis of single languages, and their historical and correlative comparison.

Note: By 'correlative comparison of languages' we understand the kind of comparison that yields language universals and types and not language families and areas.

(b) Institutional linguistics where the explanations sought are primarily cultural explanations (Why does language A borrow from language B but not vice versa?)

(c) Substratum linguistics where the explanations sought are primarily biophysical explanations (Why are vocal sounds the common vehicle? Why do sounds change? Why does language change more slowly and steadily than the rest of culture? How did language originate?)

Finally, semiotic analysis can be a valuable research tool for reconstructing cultural history and for the descriptive analysis of culture. It can streamline methods such as the field interview, the questionnaire, the census, the study of written, inscribed, and mechanically recorded documents. It can render more transparent the covert categories of culture and the societal fabric.

BIBLIOGRAPHY

Auden, W. H. (1941a), 'Criticism in a mass society' in Stauffer, D. A. (ed.), *The Intent of the Critic*, Princeton, N.J., Princeton University Press, 1941, and reprinted in Grigson, Geoffrey, ed., (1948), 1-13.

Auden, W. H. (1941b), *New Year Letter*, London, Faber & Faber.

Black, M. (ed.) (1965), *Philosophy in America*, Ithaca, N.Y., Cornell University Press; London, Allen & Unwin.

Burke, K. (1945), *The Grammar of Motives*, Englewood Cliffs, N.J., Prentice-Hall.

Flew, A. (ed.) (1956), *Essays in Conceptual Analysis*, London, Macmillan.

Fodor, J. A. (1965), 'Could meaning be an r_m?' *Journal of Verbal Learning and Verbal Behaviour*, 4, 73-81 (reproduced in Steinberg and Jakobovits (1971: 558-68)).

Gandhi, R. (1974), *Presuppositions of Human Communication*, Delhi and Oxford, Oxford Univeristy Press.

Grice, H. P. (1957), 'Meaning', *Philosophical Review*, **46**, 377-88.

Grigson, Geoffrey, (ed.) (1948), *The Mint* (an occasional serial), No. 2, London, Routledge & Kegan Paul.

Kelkar, A. R. (1964), 'A reexamination of some of the fundamental properties of language', *Indian Linguistics*, 25, 83-92.

Kelkar, A. R. (1969a), 'The being of a poem', *Foundations of Language*, 5, 17-33.

Kelkar, A. R. (1969b), 'On aesthesis', *Humanist Review*, 2, 211-28.

Kroeber, A. L. (1949), 'The concept of culture in science', *Journal of General Education*, 3, 182-8.

Kroeber, A. L. (1955), 'History of anthropological thought' in Thomas (ed.) (1955).

Lewis, D. K. (1969), *Convention: A Philosophical Study*, Cambridge, Mass., Harvard University Press.

Packard, V. (1957), *The Hidden Persuaders*, New York, David McKay.

Searle, J. R. (1965), 'What is a speech act?' in Black (1965: 221-39), reproduced in Searle (1971: 39-53).

Searle, J. R., ed. (1971), *The Philosophy of Language*, London, Oxford University Press.

Slotkin, J. S. (1950), *Social Anthropology: The Science of Human Society and Culture*, New York, Macmillan. (A classic that never made it in spite of Kroeber's admonition, 1955: 305-8.)

Steinberg, D. D. and Jakobovits, L. A., eds (1971), *Semantics: An Interdisciplinary Reader in Philosophy, Linguistics and Psychology*, Cambridge, Cambridge University Press.

Strawson, P. F. (1950), 'On referring', *Mind*, NS 59, 320-44, reproduced in Flew (1956: 21-52), and Strawson (1971: 1-27).

Strawson, P. F. (1964), 'Intention and convention in speech acts', *The Philosophical Review*, 73, reproduced in Strawson (1971: 149-69).

Strawson, P. F. (1971), *Logico-linguistic Papers*, London, Methuen.

Thomas, W. L. jr. (ed.) (1955), *Current Anthropology*, Chicago, University of Chicago Press.

Zipf, P. (1967), 'On H. P. Grice's account of meaning', *Analysis*, 28, 1-8, reproduced in Steinberg and Jakobovits (1971: 60-5).

11 System networks, codes, and knowledge of the universe

Robin P. Fawcett
The Polytechnic of Wales, Cardiff, UK

11.1 AIM

The title of this book seems to take for granted that there is a relatively close relationship between culture and language.[1] The question to which this paper is addressed is: 'What is this relationship and how close is it?' Or, to express it in terms of what is fast becoming the dominant metaphor for exploring the nature of language and its relationships to other phenomena: 'How, in a computer model of a communicating mind, can we most insightfully model this relationship?' There are a number of possible relationships (and aspects of relationships) to consider, of which the following three are representative. It may be helpful to situate the present proposals in relation to these, and to make it clear from the start that, while in principle a person could assent to all three, I shall not do so.

First, there is the *part-whole* relationship; we may choose to regard our language as a *part* of our culture. One important reason for adopting this perspective is that we learn our language(s), like other aspects of our culture, by virtue of our membership of a particular social group. This is, of course, a fundamental consideration. But are all the different aspects of our culture phenomena of the same order? I answer 'No', because I make a crucial distinction between, on the one hand, a person's *language* or *languages*, together with (a) the other *codes* such as gesture, tone of voice, etc. (see section 11.2.4) and (b) other *programs for behaviour* and, on the other hand, all the other aspects of cultural knowledge. It can be regarded as a distinction between (1) 'knowing how to . . .' (in the sense of 'behaviour potential' rather than knowledge of the *fact* of how to) and (2) 'knowing (or assuming or thinking) that . . .'.

A second possible relationship between language and culture is this: that the models of language that linguists use may be useful in modelling *other* aspects of a culture. Here the healthiest approach is a sceptical one, lest we are misled by equivalences that are merely notational—indicative though these may sometimes be of the need to recognize common ground. To use a grammar of language to describe another class of phenomena involves the same dangers, but on a larger scale, as those familiar dangers that are involved in describing English or Swahili in terms of the grammar of Latin. I suspect that the models provided by linguists can really only be used appropriately—and then only with caution—for modelling other semiotic systems, such as gesture, tone of voice, music, film shots etc. (I have worked or advised on grammars for all these, among others. See further section 11.2.4.) Moreover, where parallels with other phenomena *are* found—and we do of course find some of the same finite set of basic structural relationships at various locations in our total universe—one cannot argue automatically from a notational or even conceptual equivalence in the relationship to an equivalent semiotic function. We shall return to this question in section 11.5.

The notion of 'modelling equivalence' leads on to the third and strongest hypothesis concerning the relation between culture and language. It is a highly attractive (and perhaps too seductively attractive?) hypothesis, and it has clearly been hovering in the background, if no more, both at the symposium that provided the original impetus for this book and in various writings and symposia since then. It is the idea that the culture of a society can be *equated* with the sum total of the semiotic systems used in that society. It is not a totally new idea: La Barre, for example, writing in *Approaches to Semiotics* (Sebeok *et al.* 1964) highlighted the concept (attributed to Bateman) that 'all culture is communication'. Notice, however, that here the sense of the term 'communication' is being stretched beyond that to which the layman, very sensibly, normally limits it. This rests on the theoretically crucial distinction between the unintentional emission and the intentional—if unconscious—transmission of information. It is important to emphasize the word 'unconscious', because for much of the time we are not *consciously* aware of what are in fact our intentional actions: most of these are the result of complex but relatively fixed programmes of behaviour which are quite clearly 'intentional', in the sense that they are designed to 'solve problems' of various sorts, but to which we pay no overt attention. If one watches a young child over a period of time, for example, one may observe how behaviour that is both intentional and consciously attended to becomes behaviour that is intentional but *unconscious*. Abercrombie, borrowing from C. S.

Peirce, has termed the first type of information *indexical.* It is the second type, the intentional transmission of information, which the layman is referring to when he uses the term 'communication'. Thus, we do not normally regard a person with measles as 'communicating' the fact by his red spotted face: if we choose to say that his spots 'tell us' or 'communicate to us' that he has measles, we have a case of metaphor. This distinction between indexical and what we might term *communicational* information is so basic to any adequate models of communication that it must not be lost—even in the coinage of a thought-provoking *bon mot* such as Bateman's.[2]

In this paper, then, the term 'communication' will refer to the intentional (but often unconscious) transmission of information of a wide variety of types. The aim of the paper is to suggest how, *within the frame of a cognitive model of communication*, we may state the relationship between, on the one hand, *language* and the other semiotic systems (especially what I shall term the 'core' codes: see section 11.2.4) and, on the other, the rest of the *culture*, as a part of a person's *knowledge of the universe.* I shall suggest that this relationship can be best understood through the notion of *system networks as a means of modelling options in behaviour*—and specifically communicative behaviour. Hence the title of this chapter.

The approach, then, is from a viewpoint that is more psychologically than sociologically orientated; indeed, it is written with more than half an eye on the problem that will increasingly be preoccupying us in the coming years: that of incorporating such models in computers. Cognitive though the perspective undoubtedly is, this chapter will at the same time be concerned throughout with matters that are usually considered to be the concern of those with a sociological and anthropological orientation.

Section 11.2, which is by far the longest, is concerned with the two concepts of *system networks* and *codes.* It is convenient to illustrate the concept of a system network with reference to the code of *language*, since it was to model language that system networks were first developed. I shall offer as an example a small part of an explicit systemic grammar of English. Then an attempt is made to formulate the distinction between those semiotic systems that we shall term the 'core codes' and some other types of semiotic system. Section 11.2 ends with a proposal that broadens still further the class of phenomena that might appropriately be modelled through the particular notation of system networks. Section 11.3 examines very briefly the notions of culture and knowledge of the universe, while section 11.4 shows how, within a systemic-cognitive model of communication, the fact that the generative base of any code can be modelled as a system network enables one to relate the two concepts of *code* and *knowledge of the universe*, and so of *language* and *culture*. Finally, section 11.5 discusses, highly selectively, the relationship between the proposals set out in this paper and those of a number of other contributors to the symposium.

11.2 SYSTEM NETWORKS AS A MEANS OF MODELLING LANGUAGE AND THE OTHER CODES

11.2.1 The basic concepts

System networks, like the relational networks of stratificational theory of which they are in a sense the parent, have been developed as a means of modelling natural language. But we shall here consider them, as far as possible, simply as a model of certain types of *relationship*, irrespective of the nature of the phenomenon being modelled, except in section 11.2.2. Apart from that section, therefore, I shall use the letters a, b, c, etc., rather than labels for linguistic features.

It was Saussure who, in the early 1900s, set the distinction between syntagmatic and paradigmatic relationships at the heart of linguistics—between 'chain' and 'choice' as Halliday has put it. This is the distinction between, in the two nominal groups such as **this book** and **that book**, the *syntagmatic* relationship of 'determiner plus head', which is common to both, and the *paradigmatic* relationship between **this** and **that**, where only one may be selected. (Paradigmatic relationships are not always simply 'choice' relationships, however, as we shall see in section 11.2.2, nor are syntagmatic relationships simply 'chain' relationships: we must additionally recognize the 'bracketed string' relationships of syntax that tree diagrams are designed to display.) Then, more recently, Firth introduced the word 'system' to denote such 'choice' relationships (1957a/68: 168). But it was Halliday who offered the first full definition of a system (1961: 247), and developed a set of relational concepts which turned it into a major tool for investigating the complex paradigmatic relationships that are found in natural language. Lamb (1966: 9) has further adapted these relationships for other purposes, including the modelling of realizational and syntagmatic relationships, and I shall discuss some aspects of these proposals in section 11.5 of this paper.

Let us begin with some of the central concepts in systemic theory:

1 A *system* is defined as 'a set of features, one and only one of which must be selected if the entry condition to that system is satisfied' (Halliday 1967: 37). Thus, in Figure 11.1, a is the entry

condition to the system '**b** or **c**'. (The fact that **b** is above **c** is not significant.)

2 The first crucial extension of the concept is that a feature in a system may itself be the entry condition to another system, as is also shown in Figure 11.1(a). In this way large networks of systems, each one *dependent* on a feature in another, can be built up. Such a notation sets out economically a set of logical relationships that may in some cases become quite complex.

(a) A dependent system

(Note that this network generates abd, abe, and ac, and rules out adc, acd, ace, ab, bd, etc).

(b) Two simultaneous systems

(Note that this network generates abd, abe, acd, ace, and rules out abc, etc).

Fig. 11.1 Two simple system networks

3 The second crucial extension, which is introduced as a result of the nature of natural language (and which is therefore not necessarily equally appropriate to all the phenomena that might be modelled through system networks), is that two or more systems may be entered *simultaneously*. Figure 11.1(b) illustrates this, and so does the linguistic example in the next section. Notice that this 'and' relationship is not a syntagmatic 'and' (i.e. it does not relate entities in sequential, part-whole or other ordered relationships). This 'and' in fact relates not features but choices between features, i.e. systems. Indeed, the concept of simultaneity is a prerequisite for Halliday's *plurifunctional* model of language: it is what enables us to see that human language can carry several different types of meaning—i.e. serve several different functions—at the same time. This principle applies to all units; while most of Halliday's descriptive work (e.g. 1970a) has been focused on the unit of the English clause, many of the same *functional components* (each consisting of closely interrelated networks) may also be found in the semantics of the nominal group. (See, e.g. Fawcett 1980: 28 and 197 f.) Such a functional model of language, then, involves a major hypothesis about the organization of the semantics. Here, however, we shall not need to pursue this notion further.

4 System networks such as those shown in Figure 11.1 specify a limited number of *selection expressions* (Halliday 1967: 37). These can be thought of as *bundles of features* that are selected on different passes through the network. Note that their sequence is not significant. The network in Figure 11.1(a), for example, specifies three

selection expressions as acceptable but rules out a number of others. It is thus an explicit generative device which makes predictions which are, in principle, testable against data that occur naturally.

5 The fifth crucial concept is that of the *realization rules*. Their work is to state how each of the bundle of features in a selection expression is expressed, or 'realized', at the next level of the code. For an example of such rules we must wait till we consider a model of part of a particular code, in the next section. At this point I shall simply emphasize one fact that is not always made clear in systemic writings: this is that *the realization rules are as integral a part of the total grammar as the system networks*. The reason is that it is only when the realization rules for a network have been written that one can check whether the features distinguished in one's network really are those that are needed. It is relatively easy to draw apparently insightful networks, but it is less easy to ensure that they combine with their corresponding realization rules to generate all and only what *ought* to be generated. (We ignore here the question of delineating what that is.)

11.2.2 System networks and realization rules: a linguistic example

We shall now consider a greatly simplified example of a linguistic network, together with its accompanying set of realization rules. It is taken from my own work on the nominal group, and involves a number of gross simplifications in order to make the example relatively self-contained. It may none the less serve to illustrate the way in which system networks and realization rules handle the classic problem of inter-stratal discrepancy. This mini-grammar is set within the overall framework of Halliday's concept of language as *meaning potential* (e.g. Halliday 1973: 52–4), so that we are modelling the code of language as a program that specifies potential behaviour of a highly complex sort.

We begin with the *system network*. It is intended to be a network of some of the *meanings* that English makes available to its users, and it is therefore a *semantic* network. It is important to emphasize that the meanings in the network are *those that are built into the organization of the language*. For any one language there are always many other meanings that *might* be built into it, but are not. Sometimes these are built into other languages, but there are many possible meanings—concepts, if you like—that are *not* built into the semantic structure of *any* language. (This does not mean that they cannot be communicated, of course: we may always use the meanings that *are* in the language to try to convey them.)

(a) System network

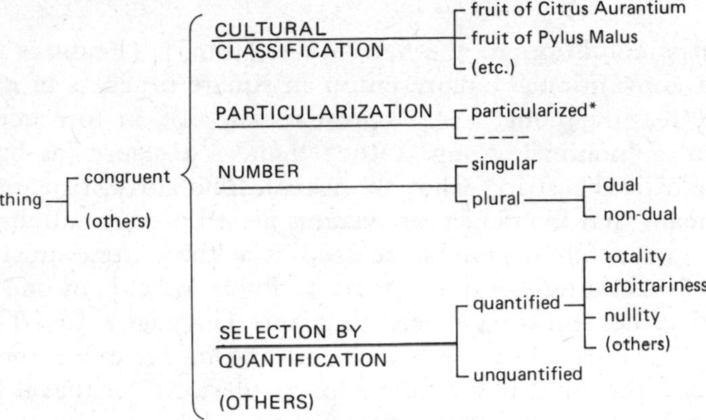

(b) Realization rules

FEATURE	CONDITION	REALIZATION
congruent		ngp
fruit of C.A.		h < orange
fruit of P.M.		h < apple
particularized		d^d < the
plural		h < + s
quantified	particularized	v < of
totality	dual	d^q < both
	NOT [dual]	d^q < all
arbitrariness	dual	d^q < either
	NOT [dual]	d^q < any
nullity	dual	d^q < neither
	NOT [dual]	d^q < none

Key: < = 'is expounded by'

(c) Starting structure

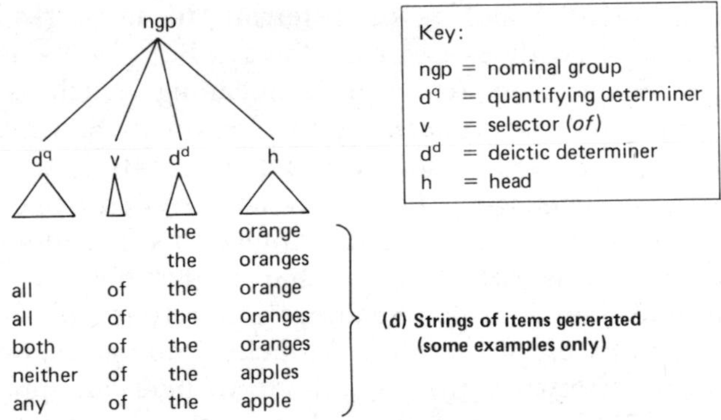

* To keep the model relatively simple we assume that [particularized] is selected in this system, so the extra realization rules that would be needed to handle the discrepancy in the quantifying determiner between for example, **none of the oranges** and **no orange** has been omitted.

Fig. 11.2 A system network and realization rules for a small part of the English nominal group

The entry condition to the network is [thing]. (Features in networks are conventionally represented in square brackets in running text.) The feature [congruent] represents the option to process the referent as a 'nominal group' rather than as a clause (as happens for example in the string **what we want**). The curly, right-opening bracket means that the next four systems are entered simultaneously. Thus, for each referent being processed as a 'thing', one must select [fruit of Citrus Aurantium] or [fruit of Pylus Malus], or one of the myriad of other meaning-labels that our language's CULTURAL CLASSIFICATION of things offers us, and *at the same time* one must select either that it should be 'particularized', or that it should not, and so on for the other two networks.

There are four points to notice so far: first, we have over-simplified the cultural classification to a ridiculous extent, and this skeletal system is only included so that we can generate a couple of simple nouns to expound the *head* of the nominal group. It will be clear that it could easily be extended. Second, the labels [fruit of Citrus Aurantium] and [fruit of Pylus Malus] are used to remind us that we are considering here options in what the user of English can *mean*, and to use instead [orange] and [apple] would fail to make a distinction between a *meaning* and the *item* through which that meaning is 'made real', or realized. (The item **orange**, notice, can mean something other than 'fruit of Citrus Aurantium'; it is also a colour-quality. This neutralization of two meanings in a single item is a typical characteristic of the relationship between these two levels of language.) Third, the *names* of networks are by custom written in capital letters over the line leading into their first systems. They play no part in the network as a generative device, however, and are simply convenient handles for referring to networks when talking about them. Fourth, notice that the symbol [- - - -] is used, in one of the systems, to represent a meaning which is most economically expressed as the *lack* of the feature with which the system is concerned. There is sometimes a temptation to try to model *all* systems in language as (a) binary and (b) consisting of the presence or absence of a feature, but, though this is undoubtedly a frequent pattern, it is *not* the case that all systems are of this type. We shall here only consider meanings where [particularized] is selected. (Realizations of [- - - -] would include **no apples, oranges**, and, from a system network that is not shown here, **an apple, five oranges**, etc.)

Perhaps it would be helpful to spell out how a simple network is to be read. The NUMBER network, for example, says: 'if and only if you have selected [congruent] you must select in the NUMBER network, simultaneously with selecting in the CULTURAL CLASSIFICATION, PARTICULARIZATION and SELECTION BY QUANTIFICATION networks, either [singular] or [plural], and if and only if you select [plural] you must then select either [dual] or [non-dual].' Here there are two more things to notice. First, [plural] is defined in English (though not necessarily in all languages) as 'any number, including fractions, over one'. We therefore say **one and a quarter oranges,** not ***one and a quarter orange.** The point is that each feature in a network represents a precisely defined meaning, part of whose definition is in terms of the knowledge system of the language user, and the label selected to represent it in the network can therefore be no more than a mnemonic. Second, you may wonder why one must choose between [dual] and [non-dual], when there might seem to be no overt realization of the contrast. But there is, in fact, and when we come to the realization rules we shall see why it would be reasonable to suggest that an item such as **both** means both [totality] and [dual].

The last network shows four types of what we shall call here SELECTION BY QUANTIFICATION. Notice that the feature [selected] is not merely the entry condition to the three features of [totality], [arbitrariness], and [nullity]: it also plays a part in the realization rules, because it is only when this class of meaning is chosen that what I have termed the *selector* (always expounded by **of**) is required in the nominal group. This is not the place to discuss the further (inferential) aspect of the peculiarly complex meanings that **all, any** and **none** realize.

The network is used in order to make up a *selection expression.* One does this by moving through the network from left to right, selecting one feature from each system that one encounters, until one cannot go any further. Where a right-opening curly bracket indicates simultaneity, one must follow each of the lines that it initiates. Thus, if we decide to select the top option in each of the systems, we shall collect the following selection expression: [thing], [congruent], [fruit of Citrus Aurantium], [particularized], [singular], [quantified] and [totality].

The selection expression provides the input to the *realization rules.* Here there are three points to make. The first is that most of the features that occur in the system networks occur in one of the first two columns, so that we could have headed both columns with the word FEATURES. The use of the term CONDITION is intended to indicate that the 'conditioning features' often give a less clear specification of an item's meaning than the feature names in the left-hand column. Thus, the feature [dual] (or its explicit exclusion) is a conditioning feature on the realization of the meanings [totality], [arbitrariness] and [nullity]. You may wonder why it is 'NOT [dual]' rather than simply [non-dual]. It is because [non-dual] would not allow us to generate [singular] nominal groups such as **all of the apple**. Realization rules, then, state how a semantic feature is to be realized at the level of form—sometimes by the particular sequence of two elements of structure (particularly at clause rank) or, as in all the cases in the realization rules given here, by stating that an *element of structure* in the unit concerned is to be *expounded* by a given *item*. For example, the first rule states 'The head is expounded by the item **orange**', and the third states 'The deictic determiner is expounded by the item **the**.'

The second point concerns the way in which we ensure that elements of structure such as d^{d} and h occur in the correct sequence. What is needed is a *sequencing rule*, and in most systemic grammars, including those of Halliday (1969/72) and Hudson (1971), rules relating pairs of elements to each other sequentially occur either among or after the realization rules. But, in anything approaching a full model of such syntactically complex units as the clause or the nominal group, there are potentially hundreds of such relationships. In Fawcett 1980, and hence the present grammar, this problem is handled very simply by using the notion of a *starting structure*. This is, in effect, a compound sequencing rule that handles relationships between more than two elements at a time. The highly simplified one in Figure 11.2 therefore states: 'If a quantifying determiner is present, it precedes the selector, if one is present, and both precede the deictic determiner, if one is present, and all three precede the head, if one is present.' We cannot go into the reasons for the alternative approaches here. But it may be of interest to point out that one effect of the present model is to give some degree of autonomy to the purely syntactic relations of language, and so to recognize a separate level of form (cp. Fawcett 1980).

Thirdly, notice that some features seem to have no realization. But in fact they *are* realized: their realization is that there is *no* formal realization, in contrast with other features in which there is. Thus the realization of [singular] in English (but not all languages) is that no suffix should be added to the head, and similarly that the realization of [unquantified] is, as it were, to have *no* realization.

Thus far, the justification of all the features is that they play some part in the realization rules. But how is [thing] to be justified? The answer is that it is needed as a statement of the entry condition to the whole network. It is through this feature that links are made to the parts of the grammar that specify the rest of the structure in which these nominal groups occur. Finally, notice that it is *not* the case that each of the four simultaneously entered sub-networks in Figure 11.2 is necessarily related to a particular element of structure. (If it were, it could be argued that the curly 'and' bracket in fact indicated a syntagmatic relationship.) Rather, the network as a whole and its realization rules specify a number of facts about the meanings that are realizable in a larger unit than the 'word': that of the nominal group. Sometimes the result will be a structure with the meanings dispersed among the various elements, as in the cases we have considered, but often a number of meanings from relatively unrelated sub-networks are realized in a single item. An example would be the item **it**, in which the *informational* option [token classification], which is not shown in this mini-grammar, has been selected in addition to the option [particularized].

This network and its realization rules, therefore, are intended to generate those nominal groups shown, plus others such as **none of the apples, any of the apples**, etc. With minor extensions it could handle **five apples, five of the apples, an apple**, etc. But its ability to be extended is not the crucial point. This is that it *rules out* not only *syntagmatically* unacceptable strings, such as **apples of all the**, but also *realizational* unacceptability, as in **both of the apple** and **neither of the orange**, etc. It is thus an explicit device, and so is liable to falsification—and so it has one of the characteristics that all model-builders must sooner or later incorporate in their models.

There is much more that could be said about this network, but the purpose of introducing this example will have been served if I have demonstrated (a) the types of relationship that system networks are used to handle; (b) the need to formulate realization rules as a complement to the network; and (c) that a systemic grammar is an explicit, and so predictive, model. We shall return to consider the use of this network in the production of a text in section 11.4 (cp. also Fawcett 1973/81 and 1980).

11.2.3 Some extensions of the basic concepts

I want now to introduce quickly some of the other extensions to the concept of the system that Halliday has introduced. Since we wish to focus on the model rather than on the phenomenon being modelled, we shall from now on use letters of the alphabet instead of specific semantic features in our examples.

We have so far considered *right-opening square brackets*, which lead to single *features*, and *right-opening curly brackets*, which lead to *systems*. In Figure 11.3 the *left-opening square bracket* means:

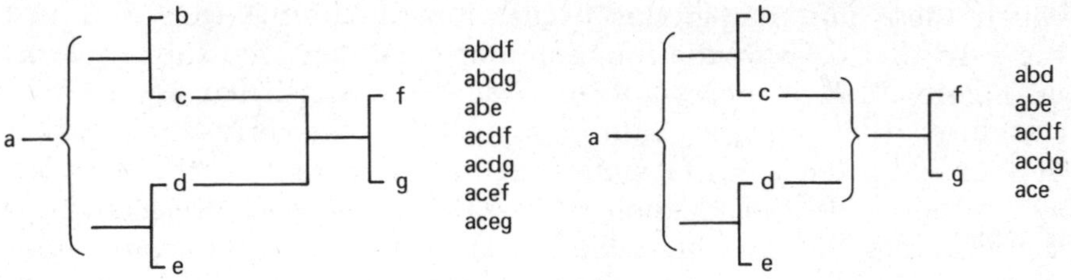

Fig. 11.3 Two system network conventions

'If and only if either or both of c or d are selected, *either* f *or* g must be selected'. Similarly, the *left-opening curly bracket* means: 'If and only if *both* c *and* d are selected, either f or g must be selected'. The selection expressions generated are shown to the right.

This completes the array of relationships presented by Halliday (1967: 38). There is a great deal more that we could say about systemic relationships, but I shall confine myself to two final points. The first is that while most systemic writings assume, very reasonably, that the terminal features which constitute the right-most part of any network (often called the most 'delicate' part) will occur in systems of two or more features, I have occasionally found that I needed to specify a *single* feature. This may be a 'remnant' feature, i.e. one that remains when the other features in a system have been dropped, in the process of language change—but which is still useful for stating the realization rules. Some ways of doing this are shown in Figure 11.4. This point may be especially worth bearing in mind when considering using system networks to model phenomena other than options in linguistic meaning. The second point is that there is an assumption that no feature should appear twice in a network. Here again I have occasionally found

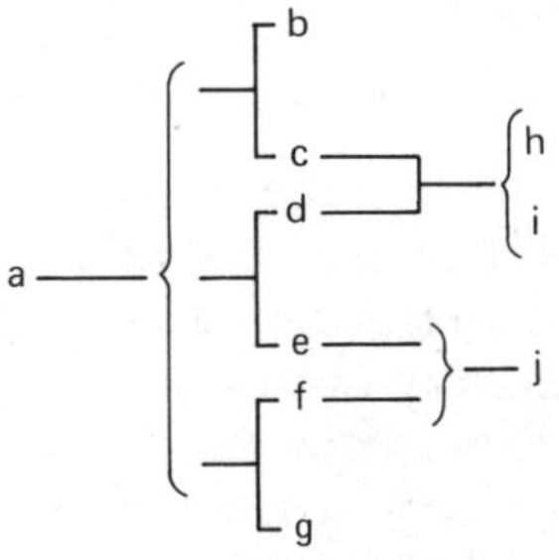

Fig. 11.4 Single features in place of systems

that it is necessary to allow this, especially in modelling the features of phonemes.

11.2.4 Language, codes, and other semiotic systems

We have now considered the system network as a tool for modelling relationships between meanings in language (as well as between abstract features represented by letters of the alphabet). Clearly, the next question is: 'How far can system networks and realization rules provide a means of modelling other semiotic systems?'

To answer this we must recognize that there are a number of different types of *semiotic system*. The first type is what I shall term the *core codes*. The core codes include language and those other codes such as gesture that are used in parallel with language. The messages mediated by such codes can be seen as being 'on offer', as it were, for about the same time-span as spoken linguistic messages. These are the codes such as tone of voice, head movement, eyebrow height, smiling, hand and arm gesture, body posture, eye contact, distance, angle of body, etc.

It is useful to make a prime distinction between such codes and a number of other types of semiotic system. The first are the *self-presentation systems*, to borrow the expression coined by Goffmann (1959). These include choice of house, clothing, ideolect and dialect, car, etc.—that is to say, the **semiotic** aspects of such choices, which may vary between being the whole story of such choices or only a small part. Some self-presentation systems, however, do not send messages about an individual (or a social group with which an individual wishes to be associated), as these typically do, but about a *social group* as a whole. A Victorian town hall, Versailles, and the forms of architecture discussed in this volume by Preziosi are of this type. But the 'form' that realizes the 'meaning' need not have physical shape; the structure adopted by a social group such as a school or a nation-state (or a family, as Bernstein has shown) presents a meaning to itself and to outsiders.

Second, we need to acknowledge the fact that all *other artefacts*, whether or not they are easily identifiable as part of a self-presentation system, have some semiotic value. But this will vary from the minimal semiotic function of an object such as a gasket in a car engine to the predominantly semiotic function of an artefact such as a short story, in which the events that are recounted or the images that are present 'stand for' some more generalized 'meaning'. O'Toole's paper in this volume examines an example of this type of innovatory semiotic, and folk tales, pop songs, and symphonies may well be phenomena of the same order.

Within the core codes such as language, gesture, etc. we distinguish the primary codes (the codes themselves) and *re-interpretation codes.* These take the output of a primary code (often language) as their input. Those that re-encode language are 'codes' in the layman's sense: backslang and rhyming slang are of this type, and so (in principle) is the writing system. Watt's paper in this volume discusses some central issues in semiotics in relation to the latter. Clearly, there is much more that could be said about such a taxonomy, and Figure 11.5 takes these ideas a little further. (It includes some distinctions in re-interpretation codes that I discuss in Fawcett 1983, section 2.6 'An exceptional class of code: codes with no semantics'.) Note that the systemic notation has not been used; this taxonomy is *not* offered as a model of the choices facing a communicator, so I have adopted this alternative notation (cp. the next section).

Here our purpose is to define a primary core code. As a first approximation, I suggest that it is a *phenomenon whose explanation must be in terms of a network of options in meanings and their realization at some other level (or levels), such that this explanation gives a sense of completeness with no major aspect of the phenomenon left unaccounted for.* (Note that although this definition appears to be formulated in systemic terms, it is in fact broad enough to include other models of language, such as stratificational and even transformational grammars. The term 'realization' is itself taken from Lamb's stratificational grammar (Halliday 1966: 59), and transformations, after all, are simply one possible approach to the problem of modelling realization.)

Let us now reconsider the 'core codes' in the light of this definition. We have seen in section 11.2.2 a little of how system networks may be used to model relationships among the semantic features of language. Will they serve equally well for the other codes? In other words, how like language are these other codes? The simplest route to an answer is to consider the components that would have to be built into a model of each, and then to look for equivalences.

Language can be regarded as a *tri-stratal* code, consisting of the three levels of semantics, form (syntax and items), and phonology. (This is in fact an oversimplified model (see Fawcett 1975, 1980, and 1983), but it will do for our present purposes.) However, those codes which are used in parallel with language (such as gesture, facial expression, tone of voice, etc.) seem to be essentially *two-level* codes consisting of, as it were, a semantics and a phonology

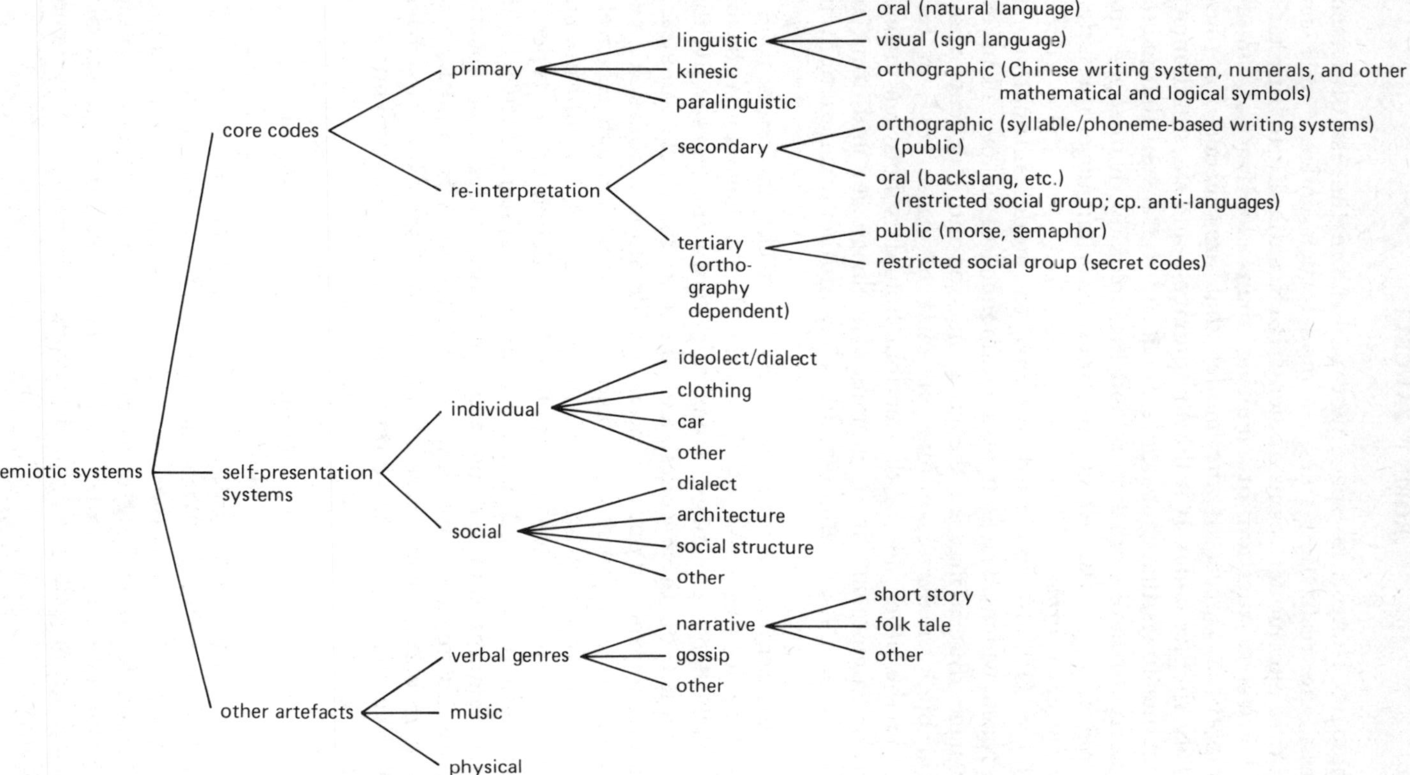

Fig. 11.5 Sketch towards a taxonomy of semiotic systems

or kinology. There is no space here to explore the use of system networks and realization rules to model such codes, but I can vouch that the model seems to lend itself naturally to this task. It is far less a question of adapting than adopting: of simply selecting those aspects of the model that are needed for these essentially simpler codes. It is the complexity—and the simultaneity—of the meanings that language is organized to transmit that makes it necessary to have both *syntax* and the break-down of *items* into phonological *segments*, which together give language the intermediate level of *form*.

Halliday (1970b) has used systems to model intonation, in an approach which regards it as a component of an overall model of language. But it may be the case that the more delicate variations in pitch, realizing options in what he calls 'key', in fact belong on the other side of the tenuous boundary between intonation as a component in a grammar of language, and tone of voice. This is an area that would repay further examination, in my view.

Thus, the term 'codes' in the title of this chapter refers to the core codes, in the sense of the term that I have been trying to establish here. Language, from this viewpoint, is simply the most complex of these codes, and the one to which we attach the most importance in our conscious consideration of codes.

However, it may be that we can go further. Though relatively little work of this sort has been attempted as yet, I would predict that we shall find that we can insightfully model *all* of the types of semiotic system described above by drawing system networks of semantic features and writing the realization rules that specify how these are realized (cp. Fawcett 1983). But it is important to realize that, except in the case of the core codes, such an approach would leave some principal characteristic of the phenomenon concerned unaccounted for. Thus a full account of a self-presentation system such as clothing will involve non-semiotic factors. Many artefacts are designed to serve functions that are non-semiotic, and in the re-interpretation codes the features between which one chooses are not meanings, but abstract entities that are themselves the realizations of meanings. With the proviso, then, that we must not imagine that we have *necessarily* provided a full account of a semiotic phenomenon by modelling it as a bi- or tri-stratal code, I would recommend system networks and realization rules as a promising means of modelling all of the types of semiotic system considered here.

11.2.5 What system networks can model and what they should model

I have suggested that system networks can appropriately be used to model the semantics of language and other semiotic systems. But they are often described as a *classificatory* device—which they certainly are. The implication of this is that they may be used to classify phenomena of a large variety of types. Lamb, in his paper in this volume, makes essentially this proposal, among others, though in stratificational rather than systemic terms. And there is no doubt that this is a very inviting position to take. System networks (or their stratificational equivalents) can be used to model relationships between any set of taxonomically related phenomena, as, for example, in the taxonomy of British Leyland vehicles for use in rugged terrain shown in Figure 11.6.

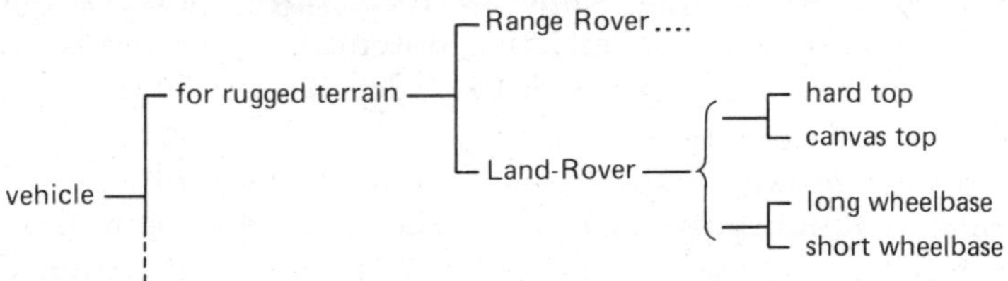

Fig. 11.6 A system network as a classificatory device

But, I want to suggest, it is not in modelling relationships between classes of *objects* that they should be used, but in modelling *options in behaviour.* So far they have been used, almost exclusively, for modelling options in *linguistic* behaviour. Some related applications (which I shall refer to in section 11.5) are in essence sets of options related to communicative behaviour *in general*, and my proposal is that system networks should be considered as an aid to modelling *any kind of behaviour.*

Winograd, whose work constitutes a pioneering breakthrough at the point where linguistics and artificial intelligence meet, makes a similar point in different terms. He has constructed a computer model of an interacting mentality that understands natural language, and he ascribes his impressive achievement in part to the fact that the grammar with which he equipped his complex program was a systemic grammar. The advantage that it had over other models was that, in it, 'knowledge [about language] is expressed as procedures' (Winograd 1972: 2). It is this characteristic of the grammar that enabled him to mesh it so relatively economically with a (then) new type of problem-solving language developed by Hewitt called PLANNER, which is a 'goal-oriented procedural language'. What Winograd's program knows about English is how it can *behave* through English.

We have in fact been anticipating this point throughout the chapter so far. In referring to networks we could simply have talked of them as classificatory devices which set out the relationships to each other of 'objects' (and in such a view the class of objects would include chunks of language), in terms of the features which they did and did not have. Instead we have talked of *selecting* features, and selecting is very clearly a behavioural action. Thus, when referring to natural language, our approach has implied a *performer-orientated* model, in which the relationship of what a language user 'knows' (or 'knows he can do') to what he 'does' is that of *potential* to *actual*. Moreover, even when the same problem is that of *understanding* language, as in Winograd's work, the same performer-orientated grammar is required, because it is the meaning potential of the *performer* that natural languages are organized to reflect. (This idea is taken up again at the end of section 11.4.6.)

System networks, then, provide a neat method of modelling taxonomic relationships, including relationships of complex types. My proposal is that we should limit their use to the modelling of *behaviour*, in order to draw a clear line between phenomena that are options in behaviour and phenomena that are not. In this view, system networks may appropriately be used to model the paradigmatic relations in language and the other codes, and, as we shall see in section 11.5, a number of other types of option that are open to a behaving organism.

Before we leave this topic, some mention should be made of another well-known notation for modelling behaviour; the *flow chart*. The precise nature of the relationship between system networks and flow charts has not so far received much attention: for present purposes it must be sufficient to point out that while a flow chart is defined as 'the diagrammatic representation of a *sequence* of events' [my emphasis] (Chandor *et al.* 1970: 163), a system network represents *paradigmatic* relationships. However, flow charts also contain points where choices have to be made and these may be regarded as simple systems. The corollary, which is that flow charts have a part to play in systemic grammars, is a topic that requires more attention than it has received so far. System networks may perhaps usefully be regarded as a means of modelling options in behaviour that occur at certain points that are related syntagmatically in an overall flow chart. In such a model the main interest would still be in the system networks, because it is here that the decisions are made (cp. Fawcett 1980: 198-200).

11.2.6 Summary

In section 11.2 we have laid the foundation for establishing the relationship between culture and language with which this chapter is concerned. We have illustrated the fundamental tenet of systemic linguistics, which is that paradigmatic relations between meanings—that is, *systems*—lie at the heart of language, and we have shown the similarities between language and the other semiotic systems: they are all to be modelled in terms of a mode of organization that reflects the purpose of communicating meanings.

In section 11.3 we turn, rather more briefly, to the question of the culture, and then in section 11.4 we shall attempt to relate the two.

11.3 THE PLACE OF CULTURE IN KNOWLEDGE OF THE UNIVERSE

11.3.1 Why 'knowledge of the universe'?

What is to be understood by the term *culture*? To answer this question we shall begin with the concept of *knowledge of the universe*, and then go on to locate the particular type of knowledge that we refer to as 'culture' within it.

There is an important implication here. We are adopting a standpoint which implies that a culture is not something that some outsider can observe about the social group that he is studying; rather, it is *what a member of that social group knows*—whether or not he is conscious of the knowledge, of course—*that is also known by the other members of the social group*. We shall examine some of the sub-categories of such knowledge in due course.

One characteristic of cultural knowledge is that no single individual, in the typical case, knows it all. We shall not be denying this, nor the interesting questions that centre around the question of how culture is learnt, if we postulate an idealized 'culture-knower', as it were. Even though no individual may know his culture in its entirety, every typical individual knows something of all the various types of knowledge that are involved. Indeed, a model such as this may be useful in charting the stages by which a child acquires a knowledge of the universe: we cannot hope to list all the individual pieces of knowledge that he acquires, but we can hope to list all the *types* of knowledge—and perhaps to indicate something of the *quantity* of the knowledge.

Let us now examine what is meant by 'knowledge of the universe'. It is not knowledge in any sure or settled sense: it is a tangle of assumptions, frequently emotionally coloured, and it is constantly changing. It is a person's 'subjective reality', to use the term of Berger and Luckman (1966/71: 173). Thus, in the expression 'knowledge of the universe', 'knowledge of' could reasonably be replaced by 'assumptions about'. The individual, however, perceives most of his assumptions as facts that he 'knows'; indeed it is essential for him to regard them in this light if he is to be able to make decisions in a sufficiently brief time for everyday life to continue. It is because he perceives his assumptions as knowledge that we may term the sum of them his 'knowledge of the universe'.

Perhaps the term 'universe' also requires comment. It is intended to convey the all-embracing nature of the knowledge: it is everything that a person knows, however broad or trivial it may appear.

We shall now look at some of the dimensions that must be taken into account in locating, within an overall model of a knowledge of the universe, a number of types of knowledge—of which one is cultural knowledge.

11.3.2 Two dimensions of contrast within knowledge of the universe

There are a number of dimensions of contrast that can be used to sub-categorize the vast domain of 'knowledge of the universe', but we shall confine oursεves to the two most relevant to defining culture. These are the distinctions between short-term and long-term knowledge, and cultural and idiosyncratic knowledge.

Let us accept that, whatever the current state of play in psychology over the nature of memory, there is something in the traditional distinction between *long-term* and *short-term* memory. The psychologists' 'memory' is our 'knowledge'. Thus some of our knowledge is very short term indeed, lasting no more than a few seconds, and is never transferred to the permanent record. It may none the less be a significant influence on how an interactant in an encounter behaves, including behaviour that is mediated through the code of language. We might think of short-term memory as rather like a jotter pad on which everything that is said in a meeting is recorded in shorthand by a secretary. Shortly afterwards a decision is taken as to what bits of the notes should be transferred to the permanent record of the minutes of the meeting, perhaps in summary form, and the original is torn up. It is the official minutes—the long-term knowledge of what happened—that will be used on future occasions. Cultural knowledge is almost always long-term knowledge, and it too is stored for use on future occasions.

We now turn to the second dimension of variation. We shall consider it in relation to long-term knowledge, though it may in principle be relevant to short-term knowledge too. We must draw an initial distinction between the *cultural* knowledge that is held in common with the other members of a social group, which we might represent in our analogy as printed books, and a person's *idiosyncratic* knowledge, which might be thought of as handwritten records in exercise books. (The word 'idiosyncratic' is preferred to 'individual' to emphasize the arbitrary nature of the knowledge that each of us, as individuals, acquires.) As Figure 11.7 suggests, much idiosyncratic knowledge is short term.

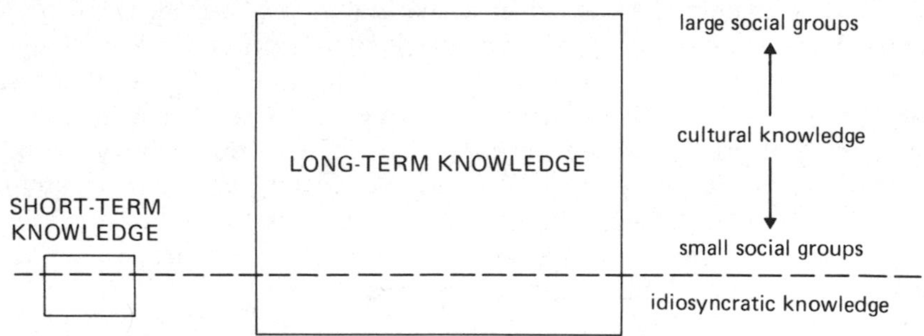

Fig. 11.7 Two dimensions of variation in a knowledge of the universe

There is, however, one additional complexity that we should note. This is the fact that most individuals are members of several different social groups, some separate from each other, some overlapping with each other, and others contained within larger ones. And each has its own culture. So we need a complex model in which each of us has many *different cultural knowledges*. Thus Figure 11.7, which illustrates the two dimensions of contrast with which we are concerned here, allows for the concept that a person will be a member of a number of small social groups as well as a member of several larger ones.

Culture, then, is socially shared knowledge, and it is typically long-term knowledge (though one can think of cases of short-term socially shared knowledge, particularly where the social group is small, as Figure 11.7 suggests. But the important thing about it is that it is knowledge that is there for a purpose: it is useful, and this will be the theme of section 11.4. A very similar perspective was suggested by Keith Basso in the course of the symposium from which this book has emerged, and it illustrates the idea that the anthropological and sociological approaches to culture may usefully be set within the sort of framework that we are proposing here. He said: 'A culture consists, at least in part, of a body of knowledge, much of it tacit, which a member of a society uses to assign meaning to actions and events in the culture [or, to avoid the appearance of circularity, we might say 'in the society'] and to guide their own behaviour.' It seems to me to be important that sociologists and anthropologists should make explicit that a culture resides in the brains of the members of the social group in this way, because hypotheses about the culture can only be tested through the individual members of that social group. Either directly or indirectly, it is the cultural knowledge of individual members that is tested. But not all knowledge, as we have emphasized, is cultural: we all have a large and important stock of idiosyncratic knowledge, and it may sometimes be hard to draw the line between this and the quasi-idiosyncratic cultural knowledge of a small social group, such as that of a married couple or the Communist Party of the Scilly Isles (which may for all I know be no larger). Such problems do not, of course, mean that the distinction is not worth making, and it is one that we *must* make if we are to relate, as we are attempting to do in this chapter, culture and language.

11.3.3 The location of culture summarized

We are suggesting here that the notion of 'culture' is for our purposes —and, I suggest, for many others—best understood in the framework of a cognitive model. Thus, a person's *culture* is that part of his knowledge that is shared with the other members of the various social groups, large and small, to which he belongs. A person therefore typically has several cultures, some overlapping with each other, some included in others, some quite distinct. For all practical purposes, cultural knowledge is also long-term knowledge.

Yet we have also brought short-term knowledge into the picture, in order to avoid distorting it unduly. Indeed, section 11.4 will illustrate the fact that very many of the decisions that a performer in an encounter makes are based on short-term knowledge: on short-term, perceptually-acquired knowledge of the addressee's affective state, for example, or of whether some relevant object is or is not in the immediate environment. This is clearly *not* cultural knowledge, in itself. Yet cultural knowledge does come into the picture, because such knowledge would make no sense to the performer if he were unable to relate it to his long-term knowledge: specifically, to his long-term 'typic' knowledge—as opposed to his 'particular' knowledge (to introduce a third dimension of variation that is not relevant to our present concern to define cultural knowledge).

Finally, note that while we have *located* culture, we have said nothing about *how it is stored*. We leave open here the question of whether it is stored in propositional form or procedural form (to mention one debate in artificial intelligence circles) or perhaps in some form that transcends this distinction, as might be claimed for the notation suggested in the chapter by Lamb in this volume.

11.3.4 Discourse grammar

As a tailpiece to section 11.3, I should make it clear that the particular types of knowledge that a person has of the behavioural options that are open in discourse (whether spoken or written) at various points are not part of the knowledge of the universe but constitute a separate 'grammar' from the sentence grammar, which we might term a *discourse grammar*. The papers by Halliday and Regan in these volumes illustrate, from rather different perspectives, some of the issues at stake here. For a preliminary account of some of the many aspects of discourse to be included in such a grammar, see Fawcett 1980: Chapter 5 (where, however, syntagmatic relations are not discussed).

In section 11.2 we established some of the characteristics of a model of language, extendable to both the other 'core' codes and to other types of semiotic system, in which the notion of the system network is central. Here we have examined the notion of culture, setting it within the framework of a person's knowledge of the universe. In section 11.4 we shall attempt to show how the two can be related in the notion of the structure of communication.

11.4 SYSTEM NETWORKS AND THE PROCESS OF COMMUNICATION

11.4.1 Some possible approaches

If we want to relate the concepts of 'language' and 'culture', we shall need a model in which to do it. Where is one to be found? We shall naturally look first at the ideas of those whose work lies in the intersection of these two areas of interest: the *sociolinguists*. If we do this we shall find that the larger issues of 'macro-sociolinguistics' are increasingly being seen as needing to be studied as the sum of many 'micro-sociolinguistic' studies: that is, studies of the types of texts that are likely to be produced in given 'contexts of situation', to use Firth's term (1950/57: 182). There is, for example, the work done in Britain in the 'register' tradition, which derives from Firth and is found in the work of Ellis, Gregory, Halliday, Leech and Ure, among others (cp. Ellis's chapter in this volume). Rather similar work, though with a stronger methodological base in sociology, was developed soon after in the United States and the names of Gumperz, Hymes, Labov, Cedergren, and Sankoff might be taken as representative. Such work adopts a 'componential' approach to the structure of an encounter: the components being the text itself, the performer, the addressee, the relationships between them, the code, the channel, the subject matter, the setting, and, at least in some approaches such as that of Hymes (1972), many more. Thus, a great deal of work has been done in the last three decades that seeks to establish correlations between variations in the various components of encounters and the texts produced in these encounters.[3]

A broader and more promising perspective—but one that is still largely programmatic—can be found in Halliday's *Language as Social Semiotic* (1978), and, since culture and ideology are not unconnected, we might also mention the related *Language as Ideology* (1979) by Kress and Hodge. As a matter of historical record, however, my own starting point was not, as might be expected, in Firth's 'context of situation'—which I found too 'linguocentric' for a semiotic as opposed to a linguistic enquiry—but in Goffman's notion of the **encounter**. He writes (1964/72: 64):

> It is possible for two or more persons in a social situation to jointly ratify one another as authorized co-sustainers of a single, albeit moving, focus of visual and cognitive attention. These ventures in joint orientation may be called *encounters* or face engagements [his emphasis].

Goffman's definition of an encounter implies that communication, in the sense that is advocated at the start of this chapter, is occurring: it is not enough that indexical information, such as the fact that one participant is tired, should be perceived—unless it is the performer's intention, in a sense that includes as always subconscious intention to communicate this subject matter.

One would logically expect the *social psychologists* to provide models of communication: they are, after all, concerned with 'minds in interaction'. But the experimental tradition still seems to rule: I have looked in vain for creative model building. I have learnt instead from the *psychiatrist* Berne (1964/68), and from the *philosopher* Austin (1962) and the follow-up work by Searle (1969). But it is probably the *cognitive psychologists* and those working in *artificial intelligence* such as Winograd (1972) that have been the biggest influence on the way in which my own model has developed.

11.4.2 An introductory outline of the structure of communication

Here we shall develop an outline model of communication, within which we shall then be able to locate and relate the two concepts of language and culture. In doing so we shall be going a long way beyond the simple view of communication as the transference of some 'concept' from one mentality to another, such as is described by Saussure (1916/74: 11-12). The approach taken here owes a good deal, indirectly, to the pioneering work of Miller, Galanter and Pribram, whose *Plans and the Structure of Behaviour* (1960) opened a new era in cognitive psychology. In outline, we shall need to take account of the following:

1 the potential performer's *needs* (physical and psychic);
2 his *problem solver*, which identifies the effect which he must procure in himself in order to meet each of those needs that is selected to be satisfied;
3 the *overall plan* which the problem solver puts together as a means of achieving that goal;
4 in cases where communication, and so an intermediate goal, are involved, the *socio-psychological purpose(s)* (which correspond to the purposive role(s), or 'function(s)', that the message serves);
5 the *plan for a communicational action*, using one or more *semiotic systems*, by which he hopes to achieve this intermediate goal (the plan for the 'message', or *text*, that he aims to produce);
6 the process of *implementing* this plan, which leads to the production of
7 the *communicational action*, or *text*, itself;
8 the psychological *effect* that he hopes to procure in the addressee;
9 the *action* to which he hopes this will lead (where applicable).

Within a cognitive model of this sort we can accommodate such Austinian notions as 'perlocutionary force' ((4) above) and 'illocutionary force' (one aspect of (5) above), and 'perlocutionary object'. The model outlined above and in the following sections is the same as that introduced first in Fawcett 1973/81 and described more fully in Fawcett 1980. But here I have chosen to bring out a number of different aspects of it. This outline will serve as a general framework within which we may locate precisely the link between knowledge of the universe and codes—and thus between culture and language—with which this chapter is concerned. It is here that the notion of system networks re-enters the picture.

At the end of section 11.2 we suggested that system networks are an appropriate notation for modelling behaviour potential. In what follows we shall not consider *all* of the choices that face a potential communicator before he or she speaks, but it may be helpful to illustrate the general principle in relation to the first choice to be made. Then, in section 11.4.6, we shall see how similar principles apply in relation to language itself.

11.4.3 Needs as problems to be solved

We begin with the concept of *needs*. Needs may originate *inside* an organism or *outside* it. Internal needs may be classified as *physical* (eating, defecating, etc.) or *psychic* (stimulus-hunger, recognition-hunger, and structure-hunger, in one approach: see, for example, Berne 1964/8). External effects on an organism, such as being struck by a blast of cold air, may cause needs too, and one type of external effect to which we attach great importance, naturally enough, is a communicational action by a fellow member of our species. Not all outside effects trigger off needs, of course, but when one does, that need may in turn stimulate *other* needs, thus complicating the model from the very start. (If we here take as an illustration a simple case, it should not be inferred from this that the principles involved cannot be extended to modelling more complex cases: it is simply a necessary strategy in explaining any complex phenomenon.)[4]

We shall here take the view that a person perceives a need as a problem, and that the action which he takes to try to meet that need is an attempt to solve a particular problem. In such a model we envisage that a part of the mind named the *problem solver* (which may in fact be a generalized process rather than a locatable entity) is more or less continuously occupied in devising and evaluating plans for possible future behaviour—rejecting some, revising some and finally approving some—in an effort to attain (or retain) a state of relative physical and psychic equilibrium. (This is the homeostasis principle: 'nirvana' and 'heaven' are perhaps religious expressions for some ultimate desired state, while 'peace of mind' and 'a state of grace' are simply labels for a slightly more attainable equivalent.) We might therefore summarize a person's problem as:

I want (state of affairs),

where the desired state of affairs may be, for example, to return the level of liquid in his system to the norm.

11.4.4 The first system

The first system provides the entry condition to any act of communication (and so, ultimately, to any linguistic act). The choice facing our performer's problem solver is this: to try to solve his problem on his own, or to try to get someone else to help him. If he selects the latter, he is automatically setting up a *sub-goal* (i.e. one which is intermediate to the achievement of his *main goal*): that of getting the addressee to understand that he wants him to do something (cp. Searle 1969: 60). We might represent this as follows:

I want (you know (I want (you cause (state of affairs))))

where everything inside the brackets is the subsidiary desired state of affairs. The proposal is that the 'referent-situation' that is the point of origin to the options in behaviour that we shall consider here—and ultimately to the semantics of the code of language in those cases where the action of the addressee is mediated linguistically—can be represented in some such forms as this. The crucial part of the predication in distinguishing communicative from non-communicative behaviour is:

I want (you know . . .).

The difference between the various types of purposive role (or 'function') that communicative actions may serve can be expressed as variations in the part of the formulation that follows 'you know'.

But since we are modelling *behaviour potential* rather than the registration of desired states, we must first turn 'I want . . .' into 'I cause . . .', so that the performer selects between the following types of behaviour:

I cause (state of affairs), and
I cause (you know . . .).

While such formulations are needed when we attempt to specify precisely the meanings of options in behaviour, they are too long to be included in a network. In practice, the labels on networks are mnemonics for meanings which must ultimately be defined with all the precision that we can muster. The system might be represented like this:[5]

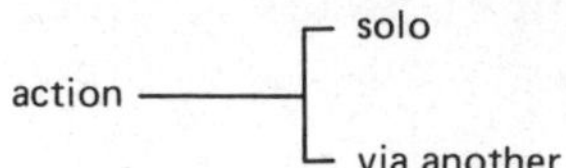

Fig. 11.8 The entry condition for communication

In principle, behaviour may be of two types. It may either consist of programs that are already prepared, or it may take the form of a program specially constructed to deal with a particular problem. When humans use language they are in principle constructing programs of this second type: this is the aspect of the 'creativity' of language that Chomsky likes to emphasize. But in practice even this type of program will be built up from bits of previously known programs that are already in the repertoire. Anyone who has watched a young child discover and practise how to solve problems that adults are usually not even aware of (such as how to grasp an object or to turn to face a different direction) will appreciate the need to postulate such a model as this if we are to account for the difference between the child's behaviour and our own. Creativity therefore consists not in the construction of totally new programs, but in juxtaposing old programs, and bits of old programs, in new relationships. The question asked by an adult's problem solver is therefore not 'What plan shall I invent?' but 'Which plans and bits of plans shall I select?'

11.4.5 Knowledge of the universe and system networks

Our model, up to this point, has these three components:

1 a means of registering needs;
2 a problem solver;
3 a store of possible programs of behaviour (where the choices are modelled in system networks).

There is one more crucial component. We have seen that the problem solver must choose between alternative options in behaviour—between systemically related choices. The question is: 'How does it choose?'

The answer is that it chooses *in the light of the relevant knowledge of the universe*. In other words, a system network only models *potential* behaviour, but if we want to understand *why* an organism behaves in a certain way in an *actual* instance (or indeed in a full model of the *potential* behaviour of an organism) we must recognize that the problem solver selects between the available options in behaviour after matching various components of the present situation with more long-term aspects of its knowledge of the universe. We therefore add a fourth component to the model:

4 knowledge of the universe.

The relationship between the four is shown in Figure 11.9.

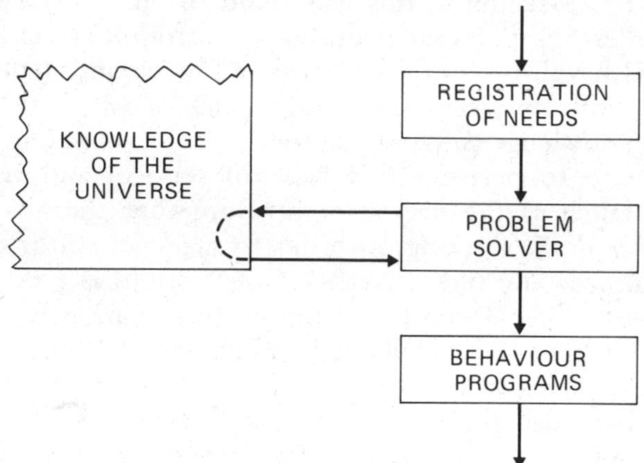

Fig. 11.9 Some of the components in a model of a mind

Let us consider an example. A man is thirsty: he has therefore perceived a simple physical need. His problem solver is faced with the choice, in principle, between solving his problem on his own or enlisting the help of someone else: between [solo] and [via another].

These options are, of course, only *options in principle*, and the perceived facts of any particular situation may effectively preclude one of them: if there is no one in earshot who can help the performer to achieve the goal of relieving his thirst, the chances of achieving it [via another] would be negligible. It is precisely here that knowledge of the universe comes in. If we consider this case carefully, we shall see that any of the subcategories of knowledge that we distinguished in section 11.3 might have a part to play. For example, even in a situation where a potential helper can be communicated with, the performer draws on a number of aspects of his knowledge of the universe before deciding to select [via another]. One factor that he will take account of is his perceptually acquired *short-term* knowledge of the physical environment, such as the relative distances between himself and the addressee (his wife, let us say) and between each of them and the source of the refreshment (a jug of iced water in the fridge). But he will also draw on his *long-term* knowledge of the social role relationship between himself and the addressee, and of the current affective relationship that may modify it. Similarly, he must examine his knowledge of the addressee's probable future movements (which are in turn derived from her own goals and plans), so that if he knows that she is likely to be coming in his direction in any case, it is likely to be more acceptable to ask her to assist him in this way. And so on . . . the list is long, but *not endless*. Notice that it draws on both *short-term* knowledge, most of which will be forgotten within a few seconds (such as where his wife is) and *long-term* knowledge (such as where the fridge is); on *cultural* knowledge (such as whether or not one may appropriately ask one's wife to perform this type of service) and *idiosyncratic* knowledge (such as the degree of pressure that there is on him to remain at his desk, working, in order to meet an editor's deadline). To 'explain' how any one utterance comes about is a complex task, as anyone who has attempted it knows (e.g., variously, Bloomfield 1935: 22f; Hudson 1973; Halliday 1977; Fawcett 1980). But it is not impossible, it seems to me, to relate an utterance to all the different *types* of knowledge that are seen as significant, and it might even be possible, ultimately, to build computer models of minds that have a knowledge of the universe that resembles that of a human being rather more closely than is the case in models such as that of Winograd (1972), impressive as that is, by following principles such as those suggested here.

To summarize: we have seen here the place of knowledge of the universe in relation to this first system: it is what enables the problem solver to choose between options.

11.4.6 Culture and language: a model

There are large numbers of options in behaviour that should be included in a full model of the decisions that must be made prior to those that are the semantics of the code of language itself. One such decision is the choice as to which code or codes to use. Another —which is in fact a set of simultaneous choices—is that between alternative *registers* (or 'styles') of language. Yet another is the choice that leads to *metaphor*. All of these can be seen as aspects of a broad and inclusive discourse grammar, as already suggested, and as outlined in Fawcett 1980. But for the sake of brevity we shall ignore these here, and assume that we have reached the point in the process of communication where semantic options are to be selected, in a vast and complex network of which Figure 11.2 models only a tiny part. Since we have now reached language, we have arrived at the point where we can make explicit the relationship between language and culture with which this chapter is centrally concerned.

The principle will by now be clear. Just as a person selects between the option to try to solve his problem on his own and the option to enlist the help of someone else in the light of his knowledge of the universe, so also *he selects between the semantic options of his language in the light of his knowledge of the universe.*

However, the title of this book prompts this question: how important is *cultural knowledge* in this decision-making? The answer is clear: since cultural knowledge is knowledge of all types that is not idiosyncratic knowledge, it will play a very important role. However, it is by no means the sole criterion in deciding between options, and precisely the sort of factors that we took account of in discussing how our subject decided between getting his glass of iced water for himself or asking his wife to do so will be relevant to the decisions that he makes between one option in the semantics and another. And here too *idiosyncratic knowledge* has a part to play—sometimes a very large part.

In a similar way, the *affective state* that the performer is currently in may affect his semantic choices. Sometimes the attitude that a word such as **nice** or **great** or **terrible** expresses is part of a *continuing* emotional reaction to some object or person or situation, but at others it simply reflects a *temporary* delight or annoyance. Thus, there are long-term and short-term affective states, just as there are long-term and short-term memories for 'facts'. There are too, in a similarly parallel way, both *cultural* and *idiosyncratic* affective states, or attitudes. Finally, we might note that sometimes emotional reactions to a general situation are expressed, quite unreasonably, by attaching an expression of emotion to some object that is not causally related to the affective state.

The idiosyncratic knowledge and the affective state of the performer, then, are as relevant to his semantic choices as is his cultural knowledge. All this implies an important warning, in the light of the possibilities discussed right at the start of this chapter, against asserting too close a link between culture, in the sense in which we have defined it, and language. The next section provides an example to illustrate this.

The relationship that this chapter suggests between *language* (and the other codes) and *culture* (and those aspects of knowledge of the universe that are not cultural, together with the affective state) is set out in Figure 11.10.

The problem solver—if we let ourselves think of it for a moment

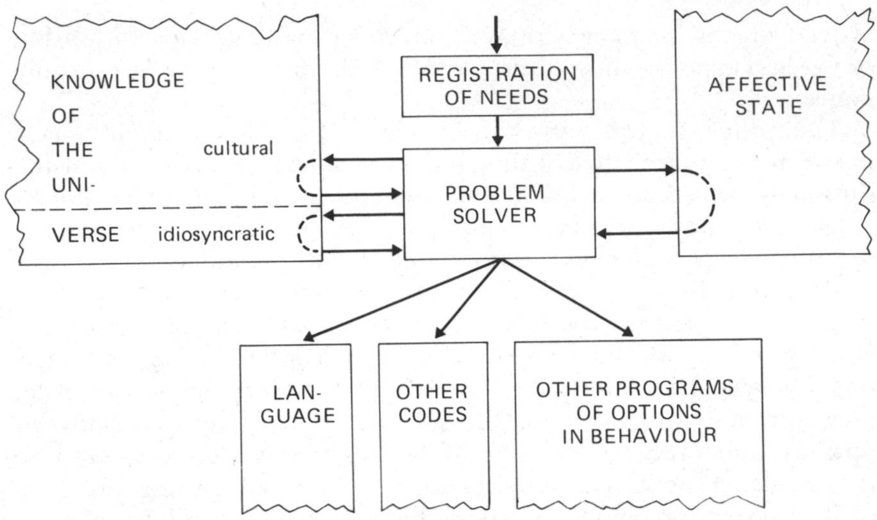

Fig. 11.10 The relationship of culture and language

as an entity rather than an activity—is at the centre of all decisions. Thus, it does not simply produce a referent situation for transmission to the addressee and feed it into the semantics: it supervises each decision between alternative meanings, making judgements in the light of the various aspects of the accumulated knowledge of the universe.

The semantics is thus a **procedural** semantics as well as a systemic semantics; that is, before it is selected each feature is tested against the relevant aspect of the knowledge of the universe using what I term **procedural felicity conditions** (cp. Fawcett 1983: section 3.2). These seem to be very similar to the concept of 'inquiries', as developed independently in the computing mode by Mann and Matthiessen (1983).

The choices between options in the semantics, we must emphasize, are choices *in principle*. In practice many sets of options may on particular occasions be selected automatically, the choices having been facilitated through repeated use in similar situations. My suggestion at the end of section 11.4.4 that 'creativity consists . . . in juxtaposing old programmes, and bits of programmes, in new relationships' holds for language as much as for other types of options in behaviour.

Finally, I should make it clear that, although we have been looking at the relationship in the framework of a model of a *performer*, the same essential relationships would hold in an *addressee*-orientated model. In other words, we would envisage that the addressee, in interpreting an incoming message, would be continually consulting his knowledge of the universe as he attempts to decode the significant variations in air pressure, the items and syntax, and the semantic features, and to extract the 'referent situation' from them. The same principle applies to messages mediated through codes other than language, and indeed to all incoming data, including indexical information emitted by other persons. It is in this way that 'a member of society uses [his culture] to assign meaning to actions and events' as well as 'to guide their own behaviour' (to repeat Basso's definition of a culture from section 11.3.1).[6]

11.4.7 Culture and language: an example

To illustrate the language-culture relationship in specific terms, we shall consider a case which makes use of the system network that we examined in section 11.2. (Figure 11.2)

Our performer is, let us say, the mother of a family, and she is instructing one of her children to give something to another. Her referent is a type of fruit about the size of a tennis ball—and more specifically two of several such in a bowl—and she has already formulated, let us say, **Pass Jonny. . .**

Let us begin, in the network shown in Figure 11.2, *not* with the options realized in the lexical items **orange** and **apple** but with the second system where the choice is between [particularized] and [- - - -] (the second term meaning 'absence of particularization'). What part of her knowledge of the universe does the performer draw upon in selection between these two? Her problem is to decide whether the referent is to be regarded as 'identified' (in a sense that really needs further explanation) by (a) herself and (b) the addressee. Only if she thinks that the object is adequately 'identified' by *both* of them may she appropriately select the meaning [particularized]. She must therefore first inspect the current and ever-changing list of things that are 'identified' for her (typically, but not necessarily) in her *short-term*, idiosyncratic knowledge. (This could be because it is either exophoric or anaphoric reference, in the terms of Halliday and Hasan 1976 and Hasan's chapter in Volume I of this work; cataphoric reference is a somewhat different matter in a cognitive approach.) Note, however, that our performer must at the same time tackle the far harder task of estimating whether the object concerned is in the addressee's similarly ever-changing list of 'identified' things. This knowledge too will, for the brief moment of time when it is available in the performer's mind, be a part of her *short-term, idiosyncratic* knowledge. If the performer decides that the object is only 'identified' for herself, or that it is not 'identified' for either of them, the other option is to be chosen, and nominal groups such as **apples, any apples,** and **an apple** will result. In our case, however, the speaker decides that her referent—or, more accurately, the set of referents from which she in fact 'selects' two—*is* sufficiently identified for all concerned. She therefore chooses [particularized]. The components of Figure 11.9 that are involved, then, are the problem solver, the semantics of the language, and certain aspects of the knowledge of the universe. But so far, as it happens, *cultural* knowledge is not involved.

But supposing the same performer had been discussing the William Tell story with another person familiar with it. In such a case [particularized] would naturally be selected in an initial reference to the apple concerned (as I have just done). This time, however, the knowledge that is drawn on would be *long term* and shared by a large social group, and so is clearly *cultural.*

The same sort of consideration applies in the NUMBER system network. In our example the selection of [singular] or [plural] depends on an inspection of the referent, and so it will typically draw on short-term, idiosyncratic knowledge. (In the example involving the William Tell story, however, we know that there was one apple, and not two, from our *cultural* knowledge.) Here then our speaker chooses first [plural] and then [dual], [plural] being realized in the suffix on the *head* of the *nominal group* and [dual] in the *quantifying determiner.*

Let us turn to the options in the top system in Fig. 11.2. As I emphasized in section 11.2.2, it is a ludicrously simplified representation of the whole network of options in classifying 'things' in terms of the culture by which we live. But it will serve to illustrate the question that I want to raise, namely, 'Is there a distinction between the range of *concepts* (i.e. long-term cultural knowledge of *types* of things) and the range of *meanings* that are built into the semantic organization of the language?' That is to say, 'Are there, in the knowledge of the universe of the speaker of a given language, concepts that are not matched by selection expressions of features in that language?' In principle there clearly could be, and in a society subject to rapid technological and social change one might well predict that there would be. Such concepts would of course normally be *describable* in terms of the language, and so ultimately in terms of the semantic features already available in the language. But this is a very different matter from a systemic semantic specification. Such concepts would be stored in a separate part of the mind. However, if this were the case, one might go on to claim that for *all* of the lexical items in a language there should be not only a specification at the level of semantics (i.e. within the code of language) but also a separate specification in the knowledge of the universe.

If this was how things were, how would the model in Figure 11.10 work? Very simply: the performer, in selecting between alternative options in the cultural classification network, would classify his actual referent in terms of his set of cultural concepts, and select the semantic option that corresponded most closely.

The alternative possibility is that when a person selects between the relevant meanings of his semantics he is *in doing so* selecting between the equivalent concepts that his culture makes available to him. The fact that I have termed the parts of the semantics that specify nouns and verbs CULTURAL CLASSIFICATION networks (Fawcett 1980) gives away the fact that for practical, everyday purposes it is the second position that seems to me to come closer to psychological reality—at least in relation to lexical items. In fact I know of no evidence for the former position. (An apparent exception is what Quirk has called 'nonce-formations'—words invented 'for the nonce'. But if they are understood by someone else they have, of course, been introduced to a micro-culture.)

It therefore seems to me that for practical purposes we should assume an identity between those parts of the cultural knowledge of the universe concerned with *things* and that part of the semantics that handles features of our cultural classification of things.

To return to our example: before one can classify a referent as [fruit of Citrus Aurantium] or [fruit of Pylus Malus], one must decide whether it has more of the features of an orange or of an apple. These 'features' will be tested by what will in some cases be fairly complex procedural felicity conditions, such as 'Does it grow naturally in a climate such as Britain's?' or some such. If, for example, we envisage a performer who does not know what a pomegranate is, but who is in the position of wishing to refer to one, he may draw on what he knows about the appearance, texture, taste, etc. of apples and oranges in order to decide whether to use **apple** or **orange** (perhaps preceded by **sort of**). These 'facts' about them are a part of his knowledge of the universe. Thus, precisely the same three components are involved here as were used in the options considered earlier: the problem solver, the semantics, and the knowledge of the universe. The fact that the part of the knowledge of the universe related to 'types of thing' (and other sorts of concept) coincides with a part of the language's semantics does not alter the basic three-component relationship.

In the case of our speaker, she chooses [fruit of Pylus Malus], since the referents are in fact exemplars of the category of entity we call **apple**. And let us say that she also chooses [totality] in the SELECTION BY QUANTIFICATION network—choosing the meaning [totality] because she anticipates that the quantification will be a little beyond the expectation of her addressee. When the realization rules are applied we find that she has produced (and the grammar has generated) **both of the apples**—which occurs, you will recall, as a Complement to **Pass Jonny** . . .

Too often, in the past, those who have attempted to relate language and concepts have limited themselves to lexical items such as nouns. In such cases it was possible to convince oneself that an adequate explanation could be provided in some such framework as the famous Ogden-Richards triangle (which relates, it will be recalled, the referent and the lexical item via the concept). Distinctive feature analysis, as propounded by Katz and Fodor (1963) and many others writing in the sixties and early seventies, is simply a more complex version of the same model. But when the model of language is extended to handle meanings such as [particularized] in the nominal group or [directive] in the clause, it becomes clearer that the meanings that are available in the semantic organization of any particular language are selected in the light of certain complex *conditions*, such as those exemplified informally earlier in this section. Hence the development of the notion of felicity conditions by Austin and others, and the development of the field of 'pragmatics' (which for many includes 'definiteness').

But when one returns from examining such areas of the semantics to reconsider the problem of nouns and their related concepts, one finds that here too it is not in most cases primitive semantic features that are required, as Katz and Fodor had proposed, but semantic features backed up by, and indeed explicated by, procedural felicity conditions of the type that we have been illustrating informally here. (See also Labov 1973, and the insightful critique and extension of these concepts in Leech 1976.) Once one sets one's model of language in the wider framework of a model of a communicating mind, as it is ultimately necessary to do, it becomes clear that such conditions are to be modelled in terms that include aspects of the performer's knowledge of the universe, rather than as some further extension of the code itself.

This concludes the presentation of the model which—for me at least—is necessary in order to state the relationship between culture and language. Although we have examined it chiefly from the viewpoint of the performer, it is equally valid for the viewpoint of the addressee—or, for that matter, for the viewpoint of the ethnographic observer, trying to make sense of what he sees and hears.

In each case the text that is being produced or received or studied is to be explained in the light of the fact that the options in the semantics of the language(s) and/or other codes being used are selected by the problem solver after consulting the knowledge of the universe—which includes, along with other types of knowledge, cultural knowledge.

11.5 CONCLUDING DISCUSSION

It might be useful to finish with a brief discussion of the relationships, as I see them, between what I have suggested here and the proposals that are made in some of the other papers in this volume—particularly those that suggest an overall framework of one type or another. Although we shall here only refer to those of Kelkar, Watt, Lamb, and Halliday, links might also have been made with most of the other papers, and some of these have already been indicated.

11.5.1 Kelkar and Watt

It is particularly hard to make a detailed comparison with Ashok Kelkar's immensely comprehensive 'Prolegomena', precisely because it *is* so comprehensive. It is as if we were being invited to view the cosmos through a telescope whose magnification is steadily increased as we home in on what he terms the 'communicative event' (section 10.1.4). Here, for a few brief pages, we are focusing on roughly the same phenomena that I am concerned with—interacting mentalities—but interpreted in terms of the very general categories that Kelkar has already established. His description of the properties of a 'sign system' (section 10.1.5) has parallels in some of the relationships between features that system networks make available for modelling language and other codes, as described in sections 11.2.1 to 11.2.3 of this chapter, perhaps most notably the simultaneity of systems. But, because of the vast scope of his paper, Kelkar cannot indicate in more than very general terms what he takes the nature of language to be, and he moves on to the rest of his impressive overview of the human condition. This chapter, focusing as it does on the problem of modelling (a) the nature of the codes that humans use to send messages to each other and (b) how they choose between the options in meaning that these codes make available to them, occupies only a corner of Kelkar's cosmology. His Chapter 10 combines in a fascinating way the objectivity of the space traveller who chances upon the new phenomenon of individual and interacting organisms, and the spiritual values (which in some ways are more familiar) of the philosophical and even the mystical traditions. My chapter, on the other hand, remains earthbound, but it does make the step, which Kelkar's early paragraphs show him to be reluctant to make, of attempting to construct a model of what happens inside the human mind.

Watt's chapter, in contrast, emphasizes the need to try to do just this (Chapter 6). He sets out with admirable clarity the set of principles that should govern the investigation of language and other semiotic systems. They are principles that I subscribe to so that, although I have perhaps risked rather broader proposals in this chapter than he does in his, it must be emphasized that I am doing so in the awareness that what I am proposing is no more than an outline model. It is one that is built on some of the types of evidence that Watt commends, but it is not yet adequately tested, and is undoubtedly very much liable to modification in the light of future evidence.

11.5.2 Lamb

Watt's chapter, however, does not discuss the relationship between, on the one hand, language and the means of modelling it and, on the other, culture and the means of modelling it. For this we must turn to Sydney Lamb (Chapter 9). The relationship between Lamb's chapter and this one is clearly very close: both set out explicitly to relate culture and language; both are concerned to build explicitly cognitive models; and there is a fairly close relationship between stratificational and systemic models of language, in that both emphasize, as did Saussure, relationships rather than entities. The degree of magnification of the telescope is therefore about the same in both cases, and it is focused on the same subject—with the important exception that this paper is concerned with modelling the relationship of language to culture in the framework of an explicitly *communicating* mind.

Let us consider the central proposals concerning the language-culture relationship in Lamb's chapter in two stages. We shall first interpret his suggestions about the relationship as follows: that the same basic logical relationships of 'and' and 'or' that we are familiar with from stratificational and systemic models of language are applicable to the relationships between entities in a culture too. But while most linguists keep paradigmatic and syntagmatic relationships carefully separated, Lamb uses essentially the same notation for both in the 'tactic' portions of his model. In fact, the same notation is drawn on in a stratificational grammar of a language to represent *three* distinguishable types of relationship:

1 *systemic* (or 'subcategorial') relationships (see sections 11.2.1 to 11.2.3);
2 *realizational* relationships between the different strata of a language (see section 11.2.2);
3 *syntactic* relationships (handled here in section 11.2.2, as in most models, as tree diagrams).

Then, in his chapter in this volume (and elsewhere) Lamb proposes extending the notation's application even further, so that it will be used to model various aspects of the *culture*: some paradigmatic, some syntagmatic and some 'realizational' (in a greatly broadened sense of the term). All this leads to an important question: when Lamb constructs such models, is he capturing a central generalization about the types of relationship that exist between phenomena of many (all?) different sorts? Or does he, in highlighting this similarity of pattern, at the same time run the risk of *obscuring* important distinctions between these various kinds of relationships?

It will be clear that I incline to the second view. I take this perhaps unadventurous position because although I note, and accept, the similarities, I do not find that the model which such a notation presupposes leaves me with that satisfying sense of *explanation* that a good model gives. Let me try to be more specific: a satisfactory model should bring out the differences as well as the similarities, and so should its associated notation. Networks drawn on paper are, after all, a code: an iconic code. The ideal code will have one *signifiant* for each *signifié*, and there seems to be no reason why this principle should be breached where the problem is that of representing these relationships in language. One possible solution might be along these lines: the systemic notation might be used for the *paradigmatic* relations of choice, as at present in systemic theory; the stratificational notation for *realizational* relationships (alongside the column notation that is at present the most frequent in systemic theory, such that the latter would be regarded as derived from the former: cp. Lamb 1966: 8); and tree diagrams might represent the *syntagmatic* relations of constituency, as in most current theories. In this way we would preserve the notion that each type of 'relational network' represents a different type of relationship between phenomena.

The essence of Lamb's proposal is (a) that these same types of relationship occur in the culture, and (b) the fact that they do is to be taken as evidence that the culture is a phenomenon of the same type: that is, a semiotic system. In fact, however, his proposal is even stronger: he does not merely suggest that the same 'ands' and 'ors' that occur in language are needed in culture too, as we have been interpreting him so far, but that the 'nections' (corresponding to Saussurian signs) in a stratificational-relational model of language also occur in a model of a culture. The line of argument in the chapter turns upon our acceptance of formal relationships as criterial. Lamb's argument is that, since 'nections' also occur in the relations between the entities in cultural taxonomies, activities, social groups, roles, etc., *these are therefore semiotic systems.*

It may now be clear why I have felt the need to discuss Lamb's use of one notation for three distinct types of linguistic relationship. I am happy to recognize that phenomena other than semiotic systems (e.g. vehicles for rugged terrain) display language-like paradigmatic relationships (including simultaneity) in their taxonomies, and even language-like syntagmatic relationships (e.g. the structure of a meal, as discussed by Halliday in 1961 in 'Categories of the theory of grammar' and here by Lamb). But it seems to me that the relationship of *realization* is one that is peculiar to semiotic systems. I suggest, therefore, that the impression that there are sign-like relationships of realization in, let us say, a taxonomy of plants such as that presented by Lamb in his chapter may result from the fact that stratificationalists use the same notation for those general types of relationship that I have distinguished. So far as I can see, therefore, the case that language and the cultural patterns that Lamb has indicated are essentially the same type of phenomenon remains to be made.

I should like to make it clear, however, that although I have here been unable to accept some aspects of Lamb's proposals, the originality of his thinking has forced me, as often before, to re-examine my own ideas, and so to refine them. Lamb is here attempting an enormous task. In Section 11.3 I sketched in a couple of the distinctions between types of knowledge of the universe which I have found it useful to recognize, in attempting to think clearly about various sorts of knowledge that are related to language. But Lamb has begun on the task of exploring the nature of the relationships between specific entities in knowledge of the universe. I have no proposals for this area, except to acknowledge Lamb's work as a promising beginning (with the caveats that I have already expressed).

11.5.3 Halliday

Finally, a brief comment about the relationship between Michael Halliday's chapter and this. Halliday is the principal architect of systemic theory, and the debt that my systemic model of language owes to his work is enormous, as any reader familiar with his writings will readily recognize. But he has always emphasized the sociolinguistic rather than the psycholinguistic dimension of the relationships that inevitably exist between language and other phenomena, just as Firth did. Much of the stimulus to the development of the cognitive model presented here has come from an effort to provide a framework that is large enough and sound enough to include all those aspects of language with which Halliday is concerned within a cognitive model of a communicating mind. It seems to me that ultimately, as I tried to show in section 11.3, the culture of the society in which the anthropologist or sociologist interests himself must be seen as residing in the heads of the members of that society. Thus a cognitive model with at least the components recognized here—and perhaps more—is what is required, and in it we can locate the various phenomena that Halliday discusses in this chapter. (It may be helpful to point out that the options in Halliday's 'semantic' or 'speech function' network seem to correspond fairly closely to the 'moves' that I would recognize in a discourse grammar. The choices in his MOOD network would for me be semantic—and indeed Halliday himself at times also describes them as semantic.)

11.5.4 Conclusion

In closing, let me cite again the definition of culture offered during the Wenner-Gren symposium by Keith Basso. He suggests that a culture is a body of knowledge that a person uses to guide his own behaviour and to interpret the behaviour of others. In the model presented here, for which the diagram offered in Figure 11.10 can stand as a summary, possible behavioural programs are separated out as a special type of 'knowledge'. Thus, the distinction upon which this chapter is based is that between:

1 knowledge of potential behaviour—i.e. knowledge of programs, including codes, which in turn include *language*;
2 knowledge of the universe, including knowledge of the *culture* of each of the social groups to which the performer (or, in modelling reception, the addressee) belongs.

What makes it possible for us to make the connection between the two? It is the fact that the model of language that we are using is one where the generative base consists essentially of *semantic system networks*, i.e. complex sets of options in meanings. In a model which does not emphasize relationships of choice in this way, the crucial question of *how* a performer selects between the various options does not stand out so clearly. And it is in answering this question that the connection is made: a performer selects between the semantic features of his language in the light of the many types of knowledge of the universe that we have discussed here—including his cultural knowledge.

NOTES

1. I am deeply grateful to all those who attended the Wenner-Gren symposium on the semiotics of culture and language, for pointing out weaknesses in the very different original version of this chapter and for encouraging me in one aspect or another of the model presented here.
2. An interesting complication arises when a person utilizes, for communicational purposes, what is normally regarded as indexical information (as when he shifts his accent towards that of the social group of an interlocutor in order to communicate a meaning such as 'I'm not as socially remote as you might think'). But such cases do not invalidate or even blur the distinction. Rather, they reinforce it, because it is only when we have made the distinction between the passive emission of indexical information and the active communication of messages that we can provide an adequate explanation of such cases.
3. In the correlational approach to sociolinguistics, where linguistic variation is related to variation in the components of the encounter in which a text is produced, there is, it often seems, the implication that the question of why a text turns out to be as it is can be answered quite adequately in terms of such correlational statements. I would question this assumption. I am not, of course, denying the value of such studies, since if this is the correlation that the investigator is interested in, his study will be valid in those terms. What I *am* suggesting is that other factors contribute significantly and systematically to the determination of texts. In the light of what has been said in section 11.3, I suggest that: (1) the effect of the components of an encounter on texts produced in that encounter is an *indirect* effect, that must first become a part, however temporarily, of the performer's *knowledge of the universe*, and that *most variation studies do not recognize this* (however much their authors may actually do so informally); (2) that *other* aspects of the performer's knowledge of the universe also influence the texts produced; (3) that there are influences outside his 'knowledge', such as his *affective state* at the time.
4. The preceding discussion of needs has in fact implied a simple taxonomy. We might ask: would it be appropriate to model these needs in a system network? The answer is that it would not, if we accept the criterion that I proposed in section 11.2.4. This is because, although needs may be the *result* of behaviour, and although they may in turn *lead to* behaviour, they are not in themselves ways of behaving.

5. As Basso has pointed out (1970/72: 69), a culture sometimes imposes on a member an obligation *not* to communicate, as is indicated by a remark to a child such as 'Don't you know when to keep quiet?' One might therefore be tempted to reflect this by placing before this network another, where the choice is between [action] and [no action]. But this would be wrong, because in a case such as that just cited, 'no action' in fact requires an act of will on behalf of the child, as is demonstrated by the fact that we may say, without anomaly, 'What you must do is to keep quiet' (where the verb **do** implies 'action').
6. Many linguists favour a 'directionally neutral' model of language. The model presented here, it will be seen, is unashamedly performer-orientated (while being usable, as we have just emphasized, in decoding as well as encoding). The reason is that it is the *performer's* meanings that the codes are organized to reflect. The code of language makes this very clear: the notion of deixis, for example, cannot be understood unless this assumption is accepted, and there are other aspects of the semantics, such as theme, that demand an explanation in such terms.

BIBLIOGRAPHY

Abercrombie, D. (1967), *Elements of General Phonetics*, Edinburgh, Edinburgh University Press.

Austin, J. L. (1962), *How To Do Things with Words*, London, Oxford University Press.

Bailey, C-J. N. and Shuy, R. W. (eds) (1973), *New Ways of Analysing Variation in English*, Washington D.C., Georgetown University Press.

Basso, K. H. (1972), ' "To give up on words": silence in western Apache culture', in Giglioli (1972: 67–86).

Berger, P. L. and Luckmann, T. (1966/71), *The Social Construction of Reality*, Harmondsworth, Penguin.

Bloomfield, L. (1935), *Language*, London, Allen and Unwin.

Candlin, C. N. (ed.) (1977), *The Communicative Teaching of English* (conference pre-prints for AILA/BAAL seminar), Lancaster, Lancaster University.

Chandor, A. *et al.*, (1970), *A Dictionary of Computers*, Harmondsworth, Penguin.

Fawcett, R. P. (1973/81), 'Generating a sentence in systemic functional grammar', University College London (mimeo) and in Halliday and Martin (1981: 146–83).

Fawcett, R. P. (1975), 'Summary of "Some issues concerning levels in systemic models of language" (paper read to the Nottingham Linguistic Circle, December 1973)', *Nottingham Linguistic Circular*, 4: 24–37.

Fawcett, R. P. (1977), 'Two concepts of function in a cognitive model of communication', in Candlin (1977: 1–60).

Fawcett, R. P. (1980), *Cognitive Linguistics and Social Interaction: Towards an Integrated Model of a Systemic Functional Grammar and the Other Components of a Communicating Mind*, Heidelberg, Julius Groos and Exeter University.

Fawcett, R. P. (1983), 'Language as a semiological system: a re-interpretation of Saussure', in Morreall (1983).

Firth, J. R. (1950/57), 'Personality and language in society', in Firth (1957b: 177–89).

Firth, J. R. (1957a/68), 'A synopsis of linguistic theory', in *Studies in Linguistic Analysis*, Oxford, Blackwell and in Palmer (1968: 168-205).

Firth, J. R. (1957b), *Papers in Linguistics 1934-1951*, London, Oxford University Press.

Giglioli, P. P. (ed.) (1972), *Language and Social Context*, Harmondsworth, Penguin.

Goffman, E. (1956), *The Presentation of Self in Everyday Life*, Edinburgh, Edinburgh University Press.

Goffman, E. (1964/72), 'The neglected situation' in Giglioli (1972: 61-6).

Gumperz, J. J. and Hymes, D. (1972), *Directions in sociolinguistics: the Ethnography of Communication*, New York, Holt, Rinehart and Winston.

Halliday M. A. K. (1961), Categories of the theory of grammar', *Word*, 17, 241-92.

Halliday, M. A. K. (1966), 'Some notes on "deep" grammar', *Journal of Linguistics*, 2, 57-67.

Halliday, M. A. K. (1967), 'Notes on transitivity and theme in English, Part I', *Journal of Linguistics*, 3, 37-81.

Halliday, M. A. K. (1969/72), 'Options and functions in the English clause', in *Brno Studies in English* 8 and in Householder (1972: 81-8) and Halliday and Martin (1981: 138-45).

Halliday, M. A. K. (1970a), 'Language structure and language function' in Lyons (1970: 140-65).

Halliday, M. A. K. (1970b), *A Course in Spoken English: Intonation*, London, Oxford University Press.

Halliday, M. A. K. (1977), 'Text as semantic choice in social situations', in van Dijk and Petöfi (1977: 176-225).

Halliday, M. A. K., (1978), *Language as Social Semiotic*, London, E. Arnold.

Halliday, M. A. K., and Hasan, R., (1976), *Cohesion in English*, London, Longman.

Halliday, M. A. K., and Martin, J. R. (eds) (1981), *Readings in Systemic Linguistics*, London, Batsford.

Halliday, M. A. K., McIntosh, A., and Strevens, P. (1964), *The Linguistic Sciences and Language Teaching*, London, Longman.

Householder, F. W. (ed.) (1972), *Syntactic Theory 1: Structuralist*, Harmondsworth, Penguin.

Hudson, R. A. (1971), *English Complex Sentences—an Introduction to System Grammar*, Amsterdam, North Holland.

Hudson, R. A. (1973), 'An exercise in linguistic description', in Thornton, Birk and Hudson (1973: 57-101).

Hymes, Dell (1972), 'Models of the interaction of language and social life', in Gumperz and Hymes (1972).

Katz, J. and Fodor, J., (1963), 'The structure of a semantic theory', *Language*, 39.

Kress, G., and Hodge, R. (1979), *Language as Ideology*, London, Routledge & Kegan Paul.

La Barre, W. (1964), 'Paralinguistics, kinesics and cultural anthropology', in Sebeok *et al.* (1964: 191-220).

Labov, W. (1973), 'The boundaries of words and their meanings', in Bailey and Shuy (1973).

Lamb, S. M. (1966), *Outline of Stratificational Grammar*, Washington, Georgetown University Press.

Leech, G. N. (1976), 'Being precise about lexical vagueness', *York Papers in Linguistics*, **6**.

Lyons, J. (1970), *New Horizons in Linguistics*, Harmondsworth, Penguin.

Mann, W., and Matthiessen, C. (1983), *Nigel: A Systemic Grammar for Text Generation*, Marina del Rey, Calif: ISI, University of Southern California.

Miller, G. A., Galanter, E., and Pribram, K. H. (1960), *Plans and the Structure of Behaviour*, New York, Holt, Rinehart and Winston.

Morreal, J. (ed.) (1983), *The ninth LACUS forum 1982*, Columbia, Hornbeam Press.

Palmer, F. R. (ed.) (1968), *Selected Papers of J. R. Firth 1952–59*, London, Longman.

Saussurc, F. de (1916/74), *Course in General Linguistics*, trans. W. Baskin (1959), London, Fontana.

Searle, J. R. (1969), *Speech Acts: An Essay in the Philosophy of Language*, Cambridge, Cambridge University Press.

Sebeok, T. (ed.) (1960), *Style in Language*, New York, Wiley.

Sebeok, Thomas A., Hayes, A. S., and Bates, M. C., eds (1964), *Approaches to Semiotics*, The Hague, Mouton.

Thornton, G., Birk, D., and Hudson, R. A. (1973), *Language at Work*, London, Longman.

van Dijk, Teun, A., and Petöfi, J. S. (eds) (1977), *Grammars and descriptions*, Berlin, de Gruyter.

Winograd, Terry (1972), *Understanding Natural Language*, Edinburgh, Edinburgh University Press.

Index